THIS BOOK BELONGS TO

SELF
Portrait

5 Steps to Turn
Your Life
Into a Masterpiece

Annette H. Evans

 authorHOUSE®

AuthorHouse™ LLC
1663 Liberty Drive
Bloomington, IN 47403
www.authorhouse.com
Phone: 1-800-839-8640

Published by AuthorHouse 01/09/2014

ISBN: 978-1-4918-3459-6 (sc)
ISBN: 978-1-4918-3616-3 (e)

Library of Congress Control Number: 2013920530

This book is printed on acid-free paper.

To my mother
Jeanie Lawyer Hackney
for instilling in me the belief that creating
things is a worthwhile use of my time.

To my daughters
Camille Alexandra Evans
&
Isabella Rose Evans
for the colorful memories of the past 20 years
and for being lovely young women inside and out.
This book is my gift to you.

CONTENTS

LETTER TO AN ARTIST

Getting the Most From This Book

Every human is an artist.
The dream of your life is to make beautiful art.
Don Miguel Ruiz

During my time as a fine arts major in college, I carried everywhere with me an "ArtBin," the artist's version of a tackle box. Inside this special case, artists keep all of the materials we need to create our art. This book you are holding now is an "ArtBin" too, for life. Inside it, you will find materials we can all use to create increasingly beautiful, meaningful, happy lives.

As you explore the Steps of this book, you will discover answers to some of our common life questions:

COMMON LIFE QUESTIONS

"How can I be happy more often?"
"When will I get the appreciation I deserve for all I do?"
"I put everyone else first. When is it my turn to come first?"
"My big dreams haven't come true. Is it too late for me?"
And the mother of all questions…
"Does my life even matter?"

Portrait of the Artist at His Easel (Self-Portrait), by: Rembrandt

Learning the answers to these questions will bring you a feeling of peace and a sense of purpose that you may never have experienced before. And you *can* learn them. You can answer all of these questions positively and proudly.

Build the Foundation for Your Life

Self-portraits are a popular genre in fine arts, historically and today. Artists who use themselves as models for their art learn to sit still and see themselves carefully. The Seventeenth Century Dutch artist Rembrandt, considered by many people to be the most important artist in Dutch history, painted eighty-six self-portraits during his lifetime. We see this kind of focus and self-analysis again in the thirty-seven self-portraits painted a century later by French painter Elisabeth Vigée-Lebrun, also known as Madame Lebrun. Madame Lebrun is recognized as the most important female painter of the Eighteenth Century. Each of the self-portraits of these painters reveals a rich palette of their experience to us, in part because of all the time they spent looking in a mirror!

What Rembrandt and Madame Lebrun did in their work, we do everyday in our lives without realizing it. Perhaps you too are an artist, like a painter, a sculptor or an illustrator. Or, perhaps you are one of the many people who say, "I'm not creative at all," or "I can't even draw a stick figure!" The reality is, brushes and paint on canvas are not required to be creative. Every moment you are alive, you are creating. Your thoughts and actions create the self-portrait of your life. You are the artist! You have the choice to create something you are proud of!

To create a masterpiece, artists first develop solid drawing skills. These skills give them a strong foundation upon which they build a successful painting they are proud to show. To create a masterpiece with your life also requires a clearly drawn foundation. You will build that foundation by applying the 5 Steps laid out in this book.

Self-Portrait, by: Elisabeth Vigée-Lebrun

To help you create your masterpiece, I have written this introduction "Letter to an Artist" for you, and Chapter 1, "My Self-Portrait," to share with you what prompted me to write this book. The 5 Steps follow. Each contains short sections, created with care, to illustrate the foundations and actions of each Step. After the Steps, I offer concluding thoughts and a simple "Framework" of the 5 Steps you can copy to keep with you as a reminder of how to create your life masterpiece every day. The outline of the Steps reminds me of the memory rhyme from childhood, "30 days has September, April, June, and November..." By reading *only one chapter a day*, you will comfortably finish the book in one short month. That's all it takes! Just 30 days to build the foundation for your life to create your life masterpiece.

Travel Through the Book

Reading this book for the first time, it's best to follow the chapter order because each Step builds upon the previous one. After you have read through the book in this way, go back and skip around the pages. Examine things up close, in any way you like best, just like you would as you look at a painting, or anything you find interesting in your life. Foundation and then expression – that's the key!

As you read, I will ask you many questions. Take the time to answer them honestly. This book is about your inner truths being drawn out in creative, fun, safe ways to help you develop your life masterpiece. You will be surprised what your answers reveal, and what positive transformations take place in your life because of them.

You will be guided through these 5 life-changing Steps:

Step #1: Feel Good

> By learning how to feel good a majority of the time with where you are now, right now, all aspects of your life will improve.

Step #2: Believe You are Deserving

> By truly believing you deserve love, happiness, and abundance, your thoughts and actions will have full power, and you will live without limits.

Step #3: Envision Your Future

> By learning how to see in your mind the life you want, you will easily move towards it.

Step #4: Take Divine Action

> Learning to listen to that soft, quiet voice within, and *then* taking action, will get you to your goals quickly.

Step #5: Allow the Masterpiece

> By allowing yourself to live your most joyous self-portrait, you will turn your life into a masterpiece.

Now, I know many of us grew up hearing our parents or teachers say, "Don't write in your books!" Let go of that rule with this one. I hereby give you permission, and I request sincerely, that you mark up this book. Highlight! Circle! Make notes! Doodle! Underline sentences that speak to you! Make this book uniquely your own.

I too, remember days of resistance to interacting with books. I used to get upset if I accidently wrinkled a page, or dripped coffee on a favorite book. Not anymore! Wrinkled pages, stains, all such things remind me of moments of life lived. The page that is wrinkled is the page my dog smooshed when he jumped on my lap while I was reading, so he could be part of a quiet moment in my life. Someday he'll be gone, and I'll miss those moments we share now. So, the wrinkled page becomes the symbol of a time of affection which I appreciate fully, now, in the moment. The coffee stain reminds me of being at my local coffee house, enjoying a frothy cappuccino and another rare moment of solitude, and allowing myself to be messy, dripping onto the pages. Here is another moment I have lived, and know to appreciate openly when it happens again. This is what a wrinkled, marked-up book can mean: the wrinkles, stains and marginalia are notes *you* make about appreciating the now. So! This book is allowed to be heavily marked up and even develop a cracked binding. That way, it will become a part of you and your life, and remind you to love all that you are, now. (Note: eReaders, make all the notes you want to. I suggest, however, to avoid the coffee spills – LOL!)

Finally, throughout the book I refer to a higher power as God, the Creator, and sometimes the Universe. Maybe you use the nouns Source, Higher Being, Infinite Intelligence, or Supreme Mind. Use whatever concept is comfortable for you.

Be Joyous in Your Spectacularness

I grew up going to church, and in my experience, most sermons could be titled, "How to be Content in Your Mediocrity." Often preachers tell us that we can only be content when we are happy with what we have and don't want for more. That is *not* my message. My message is "How to Be Joyous in Your Spectacularness!" I believe God wants us to be content with what we have, but also to definitely create more, and more, and more!

When we read, or hear someone speaking a truth, we don't just logically know it's true, we *feel* it's true. While reading this book, don't blindly take my word for it. Notice how the ideas presented feel to you. If it makes you feel good and brings more joy into your life, then it

> *We know truth, not only by reason, but also by the heart.*
> Blaise Pascal

is true for you. Everything in this book is about feeling positive and developing your self-expression; it just has to feel right to you to work.

My prayer for you, fellow artist, is that by reading this book your life will be filled with more abundance, more purpose, and more joy than you even know is possible. For your life, I envision a masterpiece. Let's get started!

~ Annette

DRAWING
ON MEMORIES

When you stand and share your story in
an empowering way, your story will heal
you and your story will heal somebody else.
Iyanla Vanzant

My Self-Portrait

A happy life is just a string of happy moments.
But most people don't allow the happy moment,
because they are so busy trying to get a happy life.
Abraham-Hicks

As I stood in my picturesque backyard, watering the herb garden, the afternoon sun sparkled off the running water. I was wearing a blue-and-white-striped French T-shirt with khaki shorts; the scene could have been a photo in Martha Stewart's *Gardening: Month by Month* book. I was even sporting yellow rubber gardening clogs á la Martha. At 32, I had manifested most of the things I thought would bring me happiness. I had been married for ten years to a loving husband whose good-paying job allowed me to be a stay-at-home mom. We were the proud parents of two healthy, beautiful daughters—three-year-old Camille, and two-month-old Isabella. We owned a two-story home, with two nice cars in the garage, all on a half–acre lot. Plus, I was building a successful portrait-painting business.

I inhaled deeply, and then exhaled. *Ahhh,* I thought, *People tell me this is the best time of my life. As good as it gets.* But my next thought rose up and bobbed on the surface before I had a chance to submerge it. *If this is the best time of my life…as good as it gets… then LIFE IS NOT ALL THAT SATISFYING!*

I let that thought float in my mind and tears came to my eyes. I felt exhausted, scared, and depressed. Was it postpartum depression?

Maybe. Maybe partially. But it was more than that. I had been so busy trying to get a "happy" life, and had gone about it in a way I believed the world had taught me. Yet honestly, I still wasn't happy. What went wrong?

IN 2 CA

"IN 2 CA" is my mom's personalized license plate. It means Indiana to California, as in, we lived in Indiana and then moved to California. Our hometown is Orleans, and the population was 2,142 at the 2010 census. Orleans is known as the "Dogwood Capital of Indiana." Hundreds of beautiful flowering Dogwood trees are planted in yards, along roads, and in the town square. They burst into bloom in late April, the perfect backdrop for the annual Dogwood Festival, which includes live entertainment, a parade, and a carnival in the town square.

You might think a resident of Indiana would be called an Indianan, or an Indianian, but the regional nickname for a person living in Indiana is a "Hoosier." The origins of this nickname are varied. But, it is widely known that Hoosiers love their basketball! In the fall on Friday nights, it seemed our entire town went to Orleans High School to cheer on our team. This love for the sport even inspired the 1986 movie *Hoosiers,* which is based on a true story of a small town underdog basketball team in Indiana who wins the state championship.

As a child in the late '60s and early '70s, I didn't have to work at being happy. Most of the time, I just was. I come from a fairly large family of five kids. In order from oldest to youngest they are Teri, Sandy, Ronny Dale, me, and Dennis. Believe me, we had some fights that were real doozies, but overall we had fun together. On a typical summer day, Mommy would take us to the public pool, one town over, and us kids swam and then would see who among us was brave enough to jump off of the high dive. In the late afternoon, we might walk to our grandparents' house, first stopping to pick an apple off of our neighbor's tree, then inspecting it for wormholes before taking that first bite. At dusk, we played hide-and-go-seek, and competed to see who could catch the most fireflies to put in our clear glass jars.

Our parents weren't overly physically or verbally affectionate, but they hadn't been brought up that way either. Caring friends, relatives, and a church family supplemented the affection we received, and that made us a pretty happy "Hackney Bunch" overall.

I had one more source of love, the love of my life: art! I loved art so much that my pinky on my right hand, my drawing hand, is one-quarter inch shorter than the one on my left. My pinky has never been broken; its growth was stunted from being bent and squished against paper as I clutched pencils, crayons, and markers, to enthusiastically create art from my earliest years.

So, with few exceptions, I typically remember my childhood as a string of happy moments. But then, in 1976, America's Bicentennial of the adoption of *The Declaration of Independence*, and the year I turned twelve…we moved.

To California.

Now I was a "Californian."

To Los Angeles County.

I was a "Los Angeleno," or an "Angeleno."

To Canoga Park, in the San Fernando Valley.

I was a "Valley Girl," fer sure, fer sure.

I skidded into my new stomping grounds in January 1976, during the middle of sixth grade. It feels like there should be fewer people to love you in a small town, with a total area of 1.6 square miles, and more people to love you in a town nearly three-times that size. The opposite was true.

IN: In Indiana, it seemed I was related to half of the town's population. Daddy owned Hackney Auto Repair, where I spent hours playing and watching him work on cars. His cousin owned Hackney's Market, where my siblings and I regularly walked, usually barefoot, or rode our bikes. My best math lessons were figuring out how much candy I could buy with 25 cents! I took for granted that contained within one square block on East Monroe Street, up from the library and across the railroad tracks, lived Grandma and Grandpa Hackney, a great aunt and uncle, two other great aunts, two second cousins and two third cousins!

CA: In California, my closest relatives, one aunt and a cousin, lived a whole city away.

IN: In Indiana, my older sisters and brother were popular with their classmates, so by association, I was popular too. Not to mention I could draw, do an ever-gymnastically-impressive back-walkover, and I had long blonde hair like Marsha and Jan Brady on the TV show *The Brady Bunch*.

CA: In California, I wasn't popular. I was the girl with the funny accent. One day in the lunch line a girl asked me to recite the alphabet, and gave a snarky laugh when I got to H. I pronounced it with a drawl, "a-i-c-h." She enjoyed the sound so much, I was requested, to my great chagrin, to repeat it again and again for the entertainment of everyone at the lunch tables.

IN: In Indiana, my siblings were good students, so every fall my new teacher liked me right away simply because of my surname. I also got good grades and followed rules. And yes, I was usually teacher's pet.

CA: In California, it was impossible to wiggle my way into teacher's pet status because of all the competition. I got lost in the crowd of kids and it felt like my teachers didn't care if I succeeded or failed.

IN: In Indiana, we were members of the First Baptist Church of Orleans. I was involved in all the usual church activities: Sunday school, children's choir, vacation Bible school, Christmas programs, and the occasional local contests for a talent or for genuine dedication to a cause. For instance, I once won a five-foot-long candy bar for bringing the most friends to church within four weeks. As you can see from the photo on the opposite page, which appeared in Orleans' newspaper *The Progress Examiner*, the candy bar was taller than I was!

Baptist young people were honored recently for their efforts in bringing new youth to the church during a four week period. Recipient of a five foot peanut butter fudge candy bar, was Annette Hackney, pictured, receiving the prize...she is the daughter of Mr. and Mrs. Ronnie Hackney. Orleans.

CA: In California, I didn't "feel the love" at church. What church? We no longer went to church. Values from my Midwestern upbringing clashed with popular values on the West Coast. It seemed everyone around me belonged to the "Church of Materialism." The Baptist Church taught God loves me. The Church of Materialism taught people love me...*if* I had the right stuff.

IN: In Indiana, family told me I inherited my artistic ability from my mom's mom, Grandma Frances. When I visited her, the first thing I would do was look to see if she had started a new painting and what her progress was on it. I can still hear her say, "Now don't stand too close, it'll just look messy. Stand back a little bit and it looks better." I liked the attention I got for being like Grandma, and enjoyed drawing pictures for relatives, friends, and teachers.

Grandma Frances, by: Annette Hackney Evans

CA: In California, I still had my art. Even though I missed our large extended family, missed my friends and popularity, missed my teacher's pet status, and missed my church family and activities, I did, thank you God, still have my art. So sadly, most of my early life in California I felt abnormal and self-conscious, and the song "I Wish They all Could be California Girls" by the Beach Boys wasn't comforting. I couldn't relate to anything, and I cried myself to sleep many nights. And, as bleak as my middle school years were…fasten your seat belt…high school was even worse.

MY BLUE PERIOD

Most people go through an emotionally blue period sometime in their life, but artist Pablo Picasso took it one step further. During his Blue Period, 1901-1904, he chose to only paint within the hues of the color blue. His inspiration? Loss. Depression. And distress about his friend Casagema's suicide. Picasso wrote, "I started painting in blue when I learned of Casagema's death." The images he painted were in essentially monochromatic shades of blue and blue-green, and the subjects were always somber and melancholy.

Although I didn't limit my artist's palette to blue, I did have an emotional blue period that began in 1980. I was sixteen, and my friend Laura was braiding my long blonde hair. She asked, "Annette, did you get in an accident…um…or something, when you were younger?"

I couldn't imagine why she was asking this and replied, "No. Why?"

Laura hesitated, and then said, "Well, you have some bald spots on the back of your head."

"What?!" I asked.

I held up a hand mirror and turned my back to the full-length mirror on my bedroom door. Sure enough, if I lifted my hair, I could see three, nickel-size, smooth bald spots. I was shocked. But there had to be a simple explanation. An easy cure.

Unfortunately, neither of those hopes was true.

"You have alopecia," said the doctor who examined me three days later. "It's an auto-immune disease."

"Will the spots grow back?" I asked. I had never heard of this disease. Worse, in the poorly lit office, with only the reticent doctor in front of me, I had to do all the questioning. My mom and dad were at work, and my sister Sandy, like a good, disinterested chauffeur, was waiting in the car.

"They might," he said. "But they might also get bigger. In fact, all of your hair could fall out and never grow back."

All of my hair could fall out and never grow back? My heart dropped to the cold linoleum. How could this be happening to me? My thick, long blonde hair was my trademark, a characteristic that set me apart from the hundreds of other girls in my high school. "Is there medicine I can take to keep it from falling out?" I managed to ask, trying to be brave, alone.

"There's really nothing that works," he said without compassion. "I'll give you some shampoo. It probably won't help, but you can try it."

I left the doctor's office carrying my bottle of worthless shampoo in hand, dragging my broken heart behind me. Pushing open the glass doors, I squinted into the bright Los Angeles sun. I found our car and wearily got in. *L.A. traffic is dangerous*, I thought. *Hopefully on the way home we can get in a fatal car accident. Of course, I want my sister to live, but with any luck I'll die, and exit this nightmare.*

Obviously, and thankfully, that didn't happen.

The dictionary defines my condition as:

al·o·pe·cia Pronunciation: /ˌal-ə-ˈpē-sh(ē-)ə/
Function: *n* : loss of hair, wool, or feathers : BALDNESS

I've had allergies and asthma since birth, and now I learned that alopecia was a new way for my immune system to turn against me. I experienced no physical discomfort from my loss of hair (or my wool loss, or my feather loss, if you will; it all certainly felt like the loss of my pelt or plumage) but my emotional discomfort was genuinely almost unbearable.

Throughout the remainder of tenth grade, and my 16th year of life, the year many people believe should be charmed with luck, beauty and love, I spent my time camouflaging my increasing baldness with very tricky hair-dos. By the summer, I had lost too much hair to do that, so during eleventh grade, I attended every day wearing a hat. No longer able to slip under the fairly "normal" radar, I endured immature teenagers (a.k.a. stereotypical teenage jerks), continually taunting me with cruel comments.

"I'll pay someone a dollar to go pull her hat off!" yelled Chris, a good-looking twelfth grader, in the crowded lunchroom. Ah, the lunchroom—a center for public humiliation in so many schools. Another boy routinely threw his arm around my shoulder as he mockingly asked, "Hey baby, will you be my girlfriend?" Pre-alopecia, I had after a while established myself confidently enough in school that not one, but *two* boys had asked me to the Winter Dance. I even had a boyfriend at the time I was diagnosed, Frank, who was very kind. Yet, within the first year my alopecia developed, I had became the easy target of extremely painful jokes, and all of my hard-won confidence fell apart daily, until it seemed like it would never come back.

During my blue period, I created a somber and melancholy self-portrait with my life. I broke up with Frank, likely because I felt I needed to reject him before he rejected me. I know I thought, *What guy wants a bald girlfriend?* I daydreamed of being someone else, of being an actor, maybe. For a while, every Friday after school, I rode a public bus to North Hollywood to take acting classes. What I discovered was that actors like people to look at them, and the last thing I wanted at that moment in life was "all eyes on me." So, I quit. I had a job at Kentucky Fried Chicken and I quit that too, because it also became about me in public, being noticed. I would have quit going to school if it hadn't been mandatory to attend. The more hair I lost, the more I stayed indoors to avoid the pain of strangers staring, or worse, voicing their repulsion by hurling names at me.

The summer before twelfth grade, I finally lost hope that my hair would grow back. Senior portraits were fast approaching and as much as I *loved* fashion (and still do!), I didn't want to be the trendsetter of wearing a hat in my Utopian '82 yearbook photo. I surrendered to alopecia and bought a wig. I wore it to school my senior year.

The wig was brown, darker than my natural color, and the hairstyle short. I purchased it at a small wig shop on Ventura Boulevard. Because I was ashamed of my condition, I parked my car in the back lot, off of the boulevard, hoping no one would see me entering or exiting the store.

When I got home I went to my room, took off my hat and put on the wig, and then nervously walked into our family room for my parents to see the new me. Daddy looked up at me and said, "We're going to have to start beating the boys away with a stick!" That was his way of saying I looked pretty. I smiled, turned around, slowly walked back to my room, closed the door, and quietly sobbed. His words were intended to make me feel good, but they had the opposite effect. The message I received was that as long as I hid my condition, and fooled boys into thinking I was "normal," they would be lined up out the door for a date with me. But what I wanted, what I believe we all want, is to be loved, just the way we are. Flaws and all.

When school started, many classmates, both girls and boys, approached me and said how happy they were that my hair grew back. I just said, "Thanks," and then would try to immediately change the subject. Inside, I was anxious and sad, wishing it were true, and hoping they wouldn't find out the truth.

There was no doubt about it, Daddy was right, I did receive more male attention with a wig on my head. But that created more anxiety for me. If I thought of a guy as a friend, I could easily carry on a conversation with him and be myself. If I thought of a guy as a potential boyfriend, my personality was cold and abrasive. I was fearful of liking a guy, having him like me, and then him finding out I was a bald phony, rejecting me, and me ending up feeling worse than I already did. I carefully guarded my feelings to protect myself from further pain.

I was jealous of the cheerleaders, who could jump up and down cheering, and do tumbling tricks, not worrying about their hair shifting positions. I was jealous of the swimmers, who could jump in the pool and not mind getting their hair wet. I was even jealous of two of my best friends, Keri and Kim, who both showed up one day with their hair in pony tails, something I couldn't do.

I invited Keri's older brother to the prom. Declan and I had been friends for several years, and he was the perfect gentleman. He brought me a dozen yellow roses that matched my yellow prom gown, and was nearly the same yellow color of my hair. Throughout the school year, I learned that wigs made of human hair fade. What had started out as brown in the fall had turned to auburn in the winter, and now a pale yellow in the spring. Many people thought I was just into punk music and expressing myself through my hairstyle. I was an unintentional rebel without a cause.

Thanks to a lot of friends, some of whom I am still in contact with today, I made it through school. Prom even turned out okay! Yet, overall, middle school and high school life pretty much sucked. Big time. I'm told this is a common experience, and perhaps your middle and high school years weren't so great either. I did have one un-sucky thing, though, that was always there for me…art.

In the beginning of middle school, I was doing pencil drawings, composed only of lines. Pretty soon, I began experimenting with shading, which is drawing an object with shadows to create the illusion of a three-dimensional (3D) object on a two-dimensional (2D) surface. By high school, I had graduated to painting, which combines drawing and shading, but now in color. I'm "drawn" to surrealism and the subject of much of my art had a magical element to it. One drawing I particularly like from this time is of young girls sitting on the edge of picture frames hanging on a wall. Another painting from then I still enjoy is of a young girl looking out her bedroom window at Planet Earth hanging in the sky, implying that she perhaps lives on the moon. By creating these pieces, and countless others, art saved me and protected me within myself. During these years, my greatest pleasure, and source of self-esteem, was creating art, in solitude.

11

Like many teenagers graduating high school, I decided that my adult life was going to be different. Better. I had no control over whether my hair would grow back, but I did have control over the only other thing I thought would bring me happiness. As a new disciple of the Church of Materialism, I was convinced all I needed was lots and lots of money. Money was going to put things right.

I went to college with this focus in mind. At first, though, I focused on what I loved, thinking maybe I could make money from art. I attended CSUN, California State University Northridge, as an art major. I lived with my parents and commuted to school. Yet, after one year in college fine art classes, I thought, *Even after I graduate in three years, I won't make much money as a fine artist. I'll never be able to move out of Mommy and Daddy's house!*

I had heard that being a fashion designer was a more lucrative profession than that of fine artist, so I transferred to FIDM, the Fashion Institute of Design and Merchandising. In 1985, the year Madonna's "Material Girl" hit No. 2 on the *Billboard* charts, I graduated FIDM with a Fashion Design degree, holding firmly onto the plan to make a lot of money to achieve happiness. Madonna and I were two peas in a pod. Two Material Girls, living in a material world.

The percentage of boys who had attended FIDM with me had been small. And the percentage of *straight* boys who attended FIDM had been smaller still. Fate stepped in though, and a boy from my hometown of Orleans moved to the big city of Los Angeles. Because he was a good friend of my older brother Ronny Dale, we would hang out as a group, and soon began dating. Because he was a family friend, he knew about my alopecia, and it didn't seem to bother him a bit. After a short courtship, we were married one year later.

Things were falling into place. College...check! Marriage...check! There was nothing to stop me on my trajectory of making money, and for six years I worked, and worked, and worked some more as a fashion designer. I was earning what most would consider a lot of money, and was even sent on business trips to Hawaii, Tokyo, and Hong Kong! And then something happened that changes so many women's lives. The thing that will slow you down, and make you grow up, like nothing you've ever known before. We had a baby.

Before Camille was born (I refer to that time of my life as "B.C.") I was undecided if I would continue my career or be a stay-at-home mom. After she was born, I felt that mothering her was the top priority in this season of my life. My husband and I chose to make sacrifices and live off of his income. We moved back to Indiana where the cost of living is more doable on one income, and 3 years later gave Camille a baby sister, Isabella.

BACK HOME AGAIN, IN INDIANA

So, here I was, watering the herb garden, back home again in Indiana. Family. Money. Security. *People tell me this is the best time of my life. As good as it gets. But it's NOT ALL THAT SATISFYING! Why don't I feel good? What more do I have to do to be happy?*

The truth was, I was exhausted. I was exhausted being a loving wife, attentive mother, house cleaner, laundress, interior decorator, landscape designer and yard girl, family grocery shopper and cook. I also exercised to maintain my pre-baby weight so that I didn't need to buy a new wardrobe, and in what little spare time I had left, ha ha, I was growing a small business as a portrait painter. Because all this work left me drained, I attempted to stay motivated by reading self-help books and listening to audiotapes by motivational speakers. This was my drug of choice. I craved to learn how to cram more "doing" into my schedule and keep my energy level up. Thus, here I was, working hard to get a happiness that wasn't appearing like it was supposed to. *Why was I still not happy?* The question plagued me daily, and only added to the struggle.

That question, and its answer, are the inspirations for this book. I still don't have hair. I'm still not rich. Yet, I *have* discovered how to be happy. And how to be happy is what I share with you here.

If I could go back in time, I would wait on the sidewalk for my sixteen-year-old self to exit the doctor's office building that day I learned I had alopecia. When that younger me walked through those doors, carrying that useless bottle of shampoo, I would throw my arms around her and say, "Be sad, cry, get angry, but I want you to know, not only will you get through this pain, one day at a time, but you will *thrive in your happiness.* Alopecia may steal your hair but it cannot steal your happiness. You will be surrounded by people you love, and who love you. You will be loved for your inner *and* outer beauty. You will be an example of a woman who loves herself in spite of physical imperfections. And, the day will come when you will share your story with others, hoping to help transform their lives from the inside out."

So, read this story, explore the 5 Steps, and discover for yourself how to feel good now. Believe you are deserving. Envision the future you want, take Divine action, and allow blessings into your life. You will find your happiness, and invite in more happiness, too. I am happy now, busy, living in the now. I'm living my life masterpiece every day. I absolutely pray the same for you because I know it's possible.

STEP #1

FEEL
GOOD

You feel good
not because your world is right,
but your world is right
because you feel good.
Dr. Wayne W. Dyer

Think Good Thoughts

*You feel the way you do right now because of
the thoughts you are thinking at this moment.*
David D. Burns, M.D.

S tep #1 is all about learning clearly how to change your daily experience on both an emotional and a material level so that you genuinely, persistently, feel good about yourself.

We begin with a story about my 17th birthday and my hope for feeling good that day. For my 17th birthday, I wanted a birthstone ring. Since our home was always stocked with the latest Service Merchandise catalog, a renowned retailer of jewelry, home goods and electronics, I enjoyed thumbing through the jewelry section to find the perfect ring. Occasionally, I would go with my mom to the catalog showroom and while she looked at crystal candy dishes, vinyl suitcases, or hot air popcorn makers, I perused the glass cases of sparkling jewelry. It was on an excursion like this one that I spotted *the* ring. It was 10 Karat gold and had seven small semi-precious garnets perched together in a circular cluster. When I tried it on, it fit! That was the one!

Even though this perfect ring was among the least expensive rings, it was still more than the limit my mom had set for my birthday gift. When finally, the day came—my birthday!—I used the gift money from my parents, matched the amount with money from my part-time job, and had enough to buy the ring. I sat in my school classroom with such anticipation, waiting for the bell so I could be off to buy my own gift. I was going to feel so good wearing it! It looked expensive, so I thought I would feel expensive with it on my hand. Tomorrow at school, I would be a new person.

Suddenly, there was the "*Brrring!*" I quickly gathered my things and headed for the makeshift school parking lot across Vanowen Street, at Topanga Plaza. I jumped into *The Tomato*, the nickname of my faded red Ford Pinto (you know, that car with the unfortunate tendency to explode if rear-ended) and drove to Service Merchandise.

Bounding up to the jewelry case, I was giddy with the anticipation of feeling good. *Really* good. Pointing out the ring to the sales lady, she took it out, and I was able to slip it right on my finger. Happy birthday to ME! I paid cash, looked down at my hand in admiration, and twirled around towards the exit.

I am wildly unhappy. I'm trying to buy it (happiness), and it's not working. Jacob, from the movie *Crazy, Stupid, Love*

The day of buying that ring was like the start of a Ferris Wheel ride. It felt special from the moment I woke up that morning and got dressed. In that moment, I took an imaginary seat at the bottom of that Ferris Wheel, ready for the fun and exciting ride up! With each passing hour, my anticipation of getting the ring brought me higher and higher on the ride. With the ring now securely on my finger, I was "on the top of the world, lookin' down on creation!"

But the wheel kept turning, and there was nowhere to go but down.

With each step towards the door and each step across the parking lot, the Wheel turned down. I was wearing the ring, but I wasn't actually any happier than I had been before I bought it. I had a moment of elation, only. It wasn't lasting. I was still wearing knock-off jeans, driving around in an exploding *Tomato*, and had a hat on my head to cover up my ever-present baldness. The only thing that changed was now I had a birthstone ring.

In that moment I learned a valuable lesson, one of the most

valuable, though it took a long time to understand it. A small material thing in my external world will not keep me at the top of the Ferris Wheel of happiness for long. You might be thinking, "Of course a simple, little plain old ring can't bring you lasting happiness! Only a seventeen-year-old would think that." But, have you ever thought you could gain abiding happiness from a house, a job, or a relationship? It seems it all comes down to the same experience I had with that ring. Over a long time, and a long struggle we all have shared in many ways, I came to learn what does bring long-term happiness, and it originates with our thoughts, not our materials.

Thinking on Autopilot

Most of us leave our thinking on autopilot. We observe and interact with our surroundings regularly with our five senses. We see, hear, taste, smell and feel things in our "external world" and this information is sent to our brain. This external world consists of the material things and events happening outside of our body. Yet, because we normalize these experiences, we are easily apt to believe that our surroundings *determine* our thoughts and moods. Thus, we tend to conclude that if our surroundings are good, meaning they are comfortable and full of nice things, we will think good thoughts, and our mood will be good. With good surroundings, we will be happy.

Our "internal world" is everything taking place inside our body. Our senses give our brain a constant briefing of our surroundings. This triggers our thoughts, which psychologists call our "internal dialogue." If we are awake, we are in this dialogue with ourselves, and often talking about our experience with our surroundings. Whether this conversation is positive, neutral, or negative determines if we feel good, neutral, or bad.

The following diagram illustrates how our observance of our external world starts the chattering of our internal dialogue, which then helps to create our mood.

THINKING ON AUTOPILOT	
EXTERNAL WORLD	INTERNAL WORLD
Surroundings Material things and events happening outside of you that are good, neutral and bad.	**Thoughts** You interpret your external world with continuous thoughts called your "internal dialogue." **Mood** Your thoughts interpret your surroundings to be good, neutral or bad. These thoughts create an emotional response and you are in a good, neutral or bad mood.

If we are normally in a bad mood, we often think that if we had better material things and more exciting events happening in our external world, then we would be in a better mood. **Everything we want in our external world is because we think it will make us feel good in our internal world.**

A simple way to illustrate this is to look at why we buy the things we do. A manufacturing company hires a slick marketing firm to advertise its product. The marketing firm is savvy in knowing how to place the product in surroundings to best grab our attention. We see this material thing being advertised in our external world via print media, radio, television, the Internet, etc. There is no escaping it. Even gas stations show commercials while we pump gas! If the advertising is convincing, we believe in some way this product will make us feel better...*happier.* The advertisement travels to our brain and our internal dialogue says, "Yes, I want to buy a month's supply of Breast Enhancement Capsules for $26. The ad says I'm sure to turn some heads when I walk in a room. That will feel fantastic!" Or maybe, "I would feel great about saving so much time if I owned that blender/ food processor. I will be able to do any job in 10 seconds...or less! It truly is a countertop magician!"

These thoughts so many times work to trick us into thinking that if we purchase what's being advertised we will feel good, and *voila!*—we willingly give the seller our money. You've heard of buyer's remorse? That's when we regret what we buy after the fact. How many times do we buy a product whose advertising promised us perfection and, sometimes, even if it works, we don't feel any better than before we owned it? Our breasts didn't improve; we didn't turn heads because of them. Our vegetables didn't chop themselves and we didn't become better cooks because of that food-processing machine. We bought these things with hope, and the things failed us, and we are no happier than before.

Step #1 to turn your life into a Masterpiece is about taking your thoughts *off* autopilot. To do this, we simply no longer let advertisers, or even family and friends, tell us what we need to buy to feel good about ourselves. Materials are not the answer. Instead, we take a moment, self-reflect, and determine for ourselves whether our thoughts are good, neutral, or bad, regardless of what we own. And, we can *choose* to think good thoughts to make ourselves happy.

Proactive Thinking

How do you feel right now? If you feel good, your thoughts might be, "Wow, I'm enjoying this book. I am excited to read more about this idea!" If you feel bad, you might be thinking, "OMG, this self-help silliness is not making sense to me. I can't be happy just by thinking myself happy." If the latter describes you, put this book down, take a deep breath, and go do something you know you enjoy! Anything simple will do. The way you feel is created by the thoughts you are thinking. Doing something you enjoy creates better thoughts. This will work —just try it to see.

It works because, though we all continually have thoughts that are good, neutral, and bad, whichever thoughts are predominant determine whether our mood is good, neutral, or bad. Simple, huh? **Thinking positive thoughts, a majority of the time, is the only way to feel good a majority of the time.**

If the majority of our thoughts are bad, it doesn't matter what we do in our external world, we won't be happy—we won't feel good. That good feeling that comes after acquiring a material thing *will often just not last.* How many people do we know who buy expensive shoes that are painful, but they believe showing them off will make them happy? Every time they wear the shoes, they pretend they are elated, as they grimace through the pain in that pretense. It's just like buying a 10 Karat gold semi-precious garnet ring at seventeen, though a lot more dramatic. We thought, "If I have this, which the world tells me I should have if I'm successful, beautiful, and happy…then I *will* be happy!" We rarely ask ourselves what would really make us happy—we let other people tell us instead. Now we're in pain, or we've spent too much money, and we become stressed, thinking bad thoughts about it all. It just didn't work to our benefit, as much as we wanted it to.

Our internal state determines our experience of our lives; our experiences do not determine our internal state.

Marianne Williamson

If you want to feel good, and if you're reading this book you do, then you can no longer let your external world determine your thoughts about what is enjoyment for you.

The following diagram illustrates how, when we consciously direct our thoughts and mood to the positive, we will attract all the material things and positive events into our external world that really do create good, stable, solid feelings of happiness within our internal dialogue.

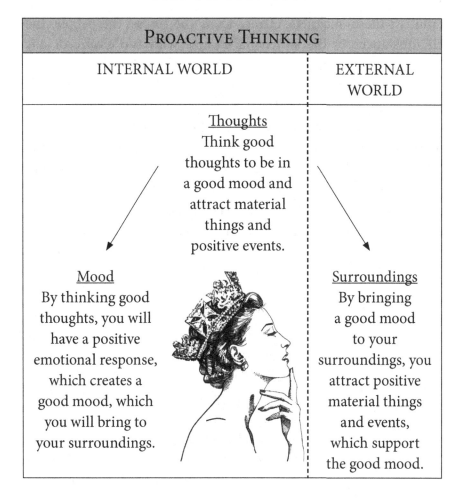

PROACTIVE THINKING	
INTERNAL WORLD	EXTERNAL WORLD
Thoughts Think good thoughts to be in a good mood and attract material things and positive events.	
Mood By thinking good thoughts, you will have a positive emotional response, which creates a good mood, which you will bring to your surroundings.	**Surroundings** By bringing a good mood to your surroundings, you attract positive material things and events, which support the good mood.

ALL THOUGHTS ARE PRAYERS

prayer / noun: a solemn request for help or expression of thanks addressed to God, an object of worship, or an external force.

I believe that all our thoughts are prayers. The law of attraction simply says that you attract into your life whatever you think about. That means, whatever we are thinking about, we are asking for more of! Napoleon Hill wrote in his book *Think and Grow Rich*, way back in 1937, "…our brains become magnetized with the dominating thoughts which we hold in our minds, and by means with which no man is familiar, these 'magnets' attract to us the forces, the people, the circumstances of life which harmonize with the nature of our dominating thoughts."

Please, do me a favor, and re-read Napoleon Hill's words above. I repeat them often to myself.

Think about it in this way: do you know people who seem to be unlucky, and bad things are always happening them? God didn't decide to punish them. They are unlucky, and bad things happen to them because they have *predominantly negative thoughts!*

"Now wait a minute!" you might be saying. "I know someone with cancer. You're telling me it's her fault?!" No. We are all born with a predisposition to some illnesses over others. We are born with genetics we can't control. But what we can control is our diet, exercise, and our attitude. Negative thoughts create stress in our bodies, which negatively affects our health. A major way to undermine, prevent and even cure disease is to reduce stress. We reduce stress by having a good attitude—that's thinking good thoughts!

Let a man radically alter his thoughts, and he will be astonished at the rapid transformation it will effect in the material conditions of his life.
James Allen

Similarly, God didn't single out as special, people who seem to be lucky, with good things happening to them all the time. Their luck and happiness comes from their positive attitude, about themselves and their lives. And what's more, they generate those thoughts on their own. They don't require the external world to make happiness for them. Good things happen to them because they have *predominately good thoughts!*

Of course, life isn't black and white, and we all have some good, some neutral, and some bad thoughts. What you have to ask yourself now is, "Do I want to start feeling better, feel how I normally do, or start feeling worse?"

The answer is simple. If you want to start feeling better, consciously make the dominant amount of your thoughts good. If you want to feel like you normally do, just keep letting your internal dialogue chatter away about your external world. If you want to feel worse, make the dominant amount of your thoughts negative. It genuinely is that simple.

You feel the way you do right now because of the thoughts you are thinking at this moment. It is those thoughts that are creating your mood, as well as drawing material things and events into your life. Monitoring your thoughts, and making sure the majority of them are good, may seem like a daunting task, but feeling good is worth it. To simplify the process, let's learn about The Art of Happiness and how to achieve it by using THE ART OF HAPPINESS SCALE...

The Art of Happiness

What everyone wants from life is
continuous and genuine happiness.
Baruch Spinoza

Controlling our moods is *quite* a challenge; it takes thought and practice. I know that well. I can recall specifically a time, over twenty years ago "B.C." when I was clearly unable to control my mood, despite my desire to get myself together. My husband and I took a road trip up the California coast. I was relieved to have a week off from my stressful job as a fashion designer and excited to visit the attractions between Los Angeles and Napa Valley. We planned to spend our first night in a quaint hotel in Cambria, a small seaside town, one hundred and eighty miles north of L.A.

Within just a few miles of the hotel, my husband said something that deeply annoyed me. It was *so* irritating, so *pain*ful, that I went straight into a shockingly bad mood, and our vacation had just barely begun! I sat in the passenger seat, stewing in angry silence until we arrived at our hotel.

While he went inside to check in, I slumped down on a chaise lounge outside by the pool and stared into the water. *How sad*, I thought, *Here we are on this long awaited vacation and I'm spending the first night angry.* I was sure the rest of the day was shot, and maybe even the next day. All I knew how to do was wait for the bad mood to fade and hope another arbitrary event didn't bring me down again.

Thankfully, by morning my bad mood had lifted, just like the hot air balloon we rode in later over the vineyards of Napa Valley.

Since then, I have learned how to better control my moods, instead of having my moods control me. That moment was triggered by an external event, yes. But at the end of the day, it was my choice how to feel about it, and what to do about it as well.

THOUGHTS AND THE LAW OF ATTRACTION

Thoughts which are mixed with any of the feelings of emotions constitute a "magnetic" force which attracts other similar or related thoughts.
Napoleon Hill

My husband's job took our family to scenic Buck's County, Pennsylvania, and we moved in the summer of 1998. Camille would begin kindergarten in the fall, and Isabella was just entering her "terrific 2s." The area is rich in history and culture, and we took many trips to the Philadelphia Museum of Art. Entering the Great Stair Hall, I would pick up a floor plan of the museum and observe how related works of art were logically grouped together. If I wanted to view Monet's landscapes, they could be found to my right, in the European Art 1850-1900 hall. The museum assumed if I like Monet, I may also enjoy related French Impressionist's work such as Manet and Renoir. The majority of their paintings have visible brush strokes, show a common, everyday scene, and create an impression of that scene, not a literal depiction. This order of paintings made by the curators was a logical decision, which in a way also emulates what we learn as children when we group like things together, and set aside other things that don't relate in shape, color, size, etc.

The way a museum groups related artists is also the way God groups related thoughts. First we have a thought, then an emotional response to the thought, and then a "magnetic" force attracts other similar or related thoughts. If we are having loving thoughts, God assumes we will also enjoy other positive thoughts such as joy and gratitude. In this way, we attract more and more positive thoughts and our mood is good. Likewise, if we are having negative, fearful thoughts, God assumes we will "enjoy" other similar negative thoughts such as worry or anger. We then attract more and more negative thoughts, and our mood is bad. What this means, in the bigger picture, is that if we are attracting towards us negative thoughts, it is impossible to feel good.

When we consistently think positive thoughts, we attract *more* positive thoughts and positive circumstances into our lives. We also enjoy better health, improved relationships and draw like-minded positive people into our lives. In addition, when we feel good, our goals are easier to attain. It's an upward spiral!

Thinking back to the Impressionists again, before artists pick up a brush, they ask themselves, "What mood do I want this painting to convey? When viewers observe my art, do I want them to feel content, happy, joyous?" To produce any emotional response in a viewer, artists make choices regarding subject matter, composition, and color.

The moment you have a certain thought and believe it, you will experience an immediate emotional response. Your thought actually creates the emotion.
David D. Burns, M.D.

As the artists of our lives, we also choose the composition of the mood we want to be in, and just like artists, what we present creates a symbiotic response from the world. This is so empowering! We can actually create ourselves as the masterpiece of our lives! And, our world—our surroundings, loved ones, and co-workers—will respond to the mood we create. To do this, we only need to take our thinking off of autopilot and use *proactive* thinking.

What mood do you want to be in right now? Tomorrow? What about for the rest of your life? Choose it on THE ART OF HAPPINESS SCALE:

THE ART OF HAPPINESS
Assess, Request, and be Thankful

Good Mood	10	happy, loving, grateful, joyous, empowering
	9	enthusiastic, eager, passionate
	8	positive expectation, believing
	7	optimistic, hopeful
	6	content
Neutral	5	bored
	4	pessimistic, impatient, overwhelmed, frustrated, irritated
	3	disappointed, doubtful, worried, blaming, discouraging
	2	angry, vengeful, jealous, hateful
Bad Mood	1	depressed, powerless, unworthy, insecure, guilty, fearful, grief

The first column visually illustrates that when we are feeling our worst, our mood is dark, or black, and we are at the bottom of the SCALE. When we are feeling our best, our mood is light, or white, and we are at the top of the SCALE. (To view a color version of THE ART OF HAPPINESS SCALE, just go to my website: www. annettehevans.com)

The second column shows our bad moods at the bottom of the SCALE, neutral moods in the middle, and good moods at the top.

The third column numerically illustrates that when we are feeling our worst our mood is a 1 and we are at the bottom of the SCALE, and when we are feeling our best we are a 10, and we are at the top of the SCALE.

The fourth column defines the thoughts we have when we are thinking in dark moods—the depressed, guilty, fearful thoughts we feel at our worst, when we are at the bottom of the SCALE. When we are thinking happy, loving, grateful thoughts, we are feeling our best and we are at the top of the SCALE.

How to Use the Art of Happiness Scale

To move up THE ART OF HAPPINESS SCALE, just remember the acronym ART. A stands for Assess, R stands for Request, and T reminds us to be Thankful.

'A' stands for 'Assess'

Before we can make any changes in our lives, we first have to **assess** where we are. This is all about patient, thoughtful, open self-reflection. What mood are you in at this moment? Good, neutral, or bad? If you are in a good mood, the words at the top of the SCALE, in the 7-10 range, will feel right to you. Words like: optimistic, enthusiastic, joyous, will fit your mood. If you are in a neutral mood, your thoughts will be in the 5-6 range: bored or content. If you are in a bad mood, your thoughts will be in the 1-4 range: overwhelmed, jealous, depressed. Take a long moment to truly reflect on which ones feel right to describe your mood right now—not what you think you *should* be feeling, but what you actually *do* feel.

Before taking action to lift your mood, allow yourself to feel what you are feeling now. Really feel it. Sit with it. Many of us will do whatever we can to avoid feeling our negative emotions. Who wants to feel powerless or unworthy? Not me. When I am overwhelmed, my favorite diversion is grazing in my pantry. Yet, I find that as good as chocolate tastes, it is not enough to lift my mood permanently—it lasts only as long as it takes for chocolate to melt. What do you do to avoid feeling negative emotions, to "numb"? Do you overeat, drink, or maybe stay really, really busy? What we resist does indeed persist, so recognizing what you feel is the deeply important first step to feeling better.

If you do find yourself at the bottom of the SCALE, assess if the reason is because of a habit of negative thinking, or a legitimate reason such as a loss. If you assess you are angry because a salesperson was rude to you, you can quickly improve your mood. If, however, you assess you are grieving because of a loss of your health, job, or a relationship, you will need to acknowledge and accept it, to move through it. In this case, improving your mood will take time to allow you to get through the grief.

'R' stands for 'Request'

Nothing is as important as feeling good, so **request** to think better thoughts. Request it of God, request it of the Universe, and request it of yourself! Knowing and stating to yourself what you want is the only way to get what you want.

If we assess that we are having No. 2 "angry" thoughts because of the rude salesperson, we can request to have improved thoughts. Letting go of the anger and replacing it with a No. 7 "optimistic" thought is fairly easy. We might think, "Maybe the salesperson is going through a difficult time in her or his life right now. I'm glad that overall things are going well for me, and I'm enjoying this free time I have shopping today."

Sometimes it is more difficult to let go of negative thoughts. We might have a No. 2 "angry, vengeful, jealous" thought such as, "I am so angry at him for leaving me to be with her. I hope they both live miserably ever after!" One reason we keep our jealous thoughts is because we worry that if we let go of the hurt, then the happy couple will *win*. The reality is, whether you let go of the hurt or not, their experience is not effected. Explore the hurt you feel from the loss of something you wanted, or believed in. Appreciate that your pain is a response, a feeling, like any other. Recognize then, that you can *request to let pain go* from the space in your heart that it filled. Where the pain sits is space that can be filled beautifully with good thoughts about yourself and *your* experience. You only need to request the exchange, and it happens. Again, it's that simple.

If you assess you are having a No. 1 thought of "grief," take the time you need to weep and mourn. Grief is a healthy response to loss. Simply request the strength to move through this season of your life, and to someday come out the other side with an ability to experience joy.

'T' stands for 'Thankful'

Be **thankful**. Gratitude is the quickest way to move up the SCALE to happiness and joy. Be thankful for the food you have to eat. Be thankful for the people who care for you in your life. Be thankful for the material possessions you have, even if you may desire more. Even be thankful for the mood you are in. Especially if you are in a No. 1 – No. 4 bad mood—this is a great starting place to know what you *don't* want, and to clarify what you *do* want! That information is definitely something to be thankful for. When you are thankful for what you *already have*, you learn that appreciation is fundamental to feeling joy.

Moving Up the Scale

While moving up the ART OF HAPPINESS SCALE, keep in mind that we can only flow up 1 or 2 levels at a time. A leap from No. 2 to No. 10 isn't really possible, as I discovered one rainy summer day, because the process needs time in self-awareness to keep you confident at the top. Without contemplation time, you can bounce uncomfortably all over the chart.

It's really important that you feel good, because this feeling good is what goes out as a signal into the Universe and starts to attract more of itself to you. So the more you can feel good, the more you will attract the things that help you feel good, and are able to keep bringing you up higher and higher.

Dr. Joe Vitale

Summer 2005 was when my husband, daughters and I relocated from Pennsylvania back to Indiana. We bought a house but we didn't move in right away. The original owners were in the process of building a new house, which wasn't yet completed, so we struck a deal: They could live in the house and pay us rent for three months, and our family would move into an apartment. This, ahem, turned out to be a bad idea.

Living on the third floor of an apartment building was not for me. First, at our old house I was used to letting our dog, Fritz, out the back door and into the yard. Now I was walking him up and down three flights of stairs to go out, five times a day. Second, my girls had always had their own bedrooms, but in our temporary setting, they shared a small room, which created good ole' sisterly fighting that drove me to distraction. To try to make it better, I let them watch more television than I previously had. That resulted in an overplay of young people's shows such that, to this day, I want to scream when I hear anything even related to one show in particular. All the main character seemed to do was complain and there I was, just trying *not* to complain and keep everyone together! Lastly, and this was the hardest bit, I had an art show coming up and it was difficult to paint in the cramped quarters. Yet, all of this I could do, I could hold it together and live like this for three months, because I knew the *exact* date I would be moving into my beautiful, spacious home, less than a mile away.

Then, two days before it was time for us to move in, the previous owners informed us they *weren't* leaving yet! The building of their house was delayed, and they said if we had a problem with that, to contact their attorney! Well, we surely did contact their attorney, and we also ended up hiring one of our own. By the time this mess was over, I had been living at the bottom of THE ART OF HAPPINESS SCALE for much more than the three months I could barely handle. I felt impatient, powerless, and really, really angry!

So, it came down to this. A few days after moving in, *finally*, to our new home, I was tired of being indoors unpacking, and decided to get outside and trim the front hedges. The previous owners had let the landscaping go since they were just "renters" from us at the point they sold. My electric trimmer was somewhere in a storage unit, so I found the local home improvement store and bought a new 24" hedge trimmer. Let me tell you, I am good at trimming hedges and topiaries. I got home and started her up! But, in my rashness and angst, I immediately almost cut the top third of my right middle finger right off! Blood was everywhere. I just missed the bone, but cut through nerves. And there you have it. A summary result: a perfect, painful example of how anger can attract a very bad experience.

The next day, while I was running errands in the rain (bad to worse!) my friend Barb, who works as a therapist, called and asked how things were going. "Terrible...awful!" I told her. "Apartment life was a nightmare, and then the people wouldn't move out and we had to hire an attorney to get into *our* house. Yesterday, I severely cut my finger, *and then* my friend Sue called and told me her father died. Nothing good has happened since we moved here!"

When I was done with my rant, Barb said, "You have a lot to be grateful for, Annette. Have you been watching the news?"

"No," I said. "I've just been unpacking and injuring myself."

"Well, a massive hurricane hit the gulf coast and the news is showing videos of bodies floating down streets in New Orleans," she said. "Tell me, right now, some things you have to be thankful for."

I had heard briefly about Hurricane Katrina on the radio, but I hadn't turned on a television in days. I immediately felt awful for everyone who suffered in that disaster. And yet, as my mind scanned my life, I'm embarrassed to say, at that moment I couldn't come up with anything I was thankful for. Nothing. And although I knew her intentions were good, and I was logically aware that other people were truly traumatized in the world, I was really just annoyed with Barb for asking!

Looking back on that moment, I've since learned that when you're feeling a No. 1 depressed, and you try to immediately feel a No. 10, grateful, the leap is too great. Barb's news could have been "you've won the lottery!" and it would not have mattered. I likely would have thought, "I don't want a camera crew showing up at my house right now. It's a mess!" Stepping up THE ART OF HAPPINESS SCALE requires much more patience and thought. If we look closely at several elements of the SCALE, we can see how much I would have had to accomplish mentally to get from No. 1 to No. 10 in the space of a ten-minute phone call. You can see, it's like becoming enlightened in 600 seconds, and that's not how enlightenment works.

#1 depressed – This was my starting point. It was exactly my mental and emotional location when Barb called.

#3 blaming – Blaming is higher up on the SCALE because it's active. To get to gratefulness, we do need to go through the blame game because it helps us articulate what we see happening to us in the external world. I blamed the previous owners of my house for all of my current problems. I blamed them for undermining my plans, confusing my routine, delaying my family's happiness, and ultimately causing all the unhappiness that occurred.

#4 overwhelmed, irritated – Overwhelmed and irritated are also not good feelings, but they are an improvement from blaming others. Many of us can move past blame to realize we need to take control, but that demand can leave us *overwhelmed* and super-irritated. I was, for sure, with taking care of my daughters, the dog, finding everyone new doctors and dentists, and then dealing with the lawyers. The house had a million tasks waiting to be accomplished, tasks we all know—everything from washer and dryer hook ups, to room scrubbing, wall painting, landscaping, plus just general living with lunches and dinners to be made. Boxes were stacked to eye-level in many rooms, and when I unpacked, the pain from my cut finger was unbearable. It felt like a total catastrophe every single moment.

#7 optimistic – From a place of being overwhelmed, however, we can move to thinking more optimistic thoughts. We can organize, we can achieve small goals: One room down! Washer is working! Dinner came out well tonight in the new kitchen! We can think, *You know, I will eventually get all of this work done. It won't happen today, or this week, but it will get done.* And then, things seem to move positively more quickly, because we see progress.

#8 positive expectation, believing – With these new, improved thoughts, the dark rain clouds start to part, and the longer-term future looks brighter as a reality. Our vision of the external world expands more proactively, naturally: The neighbors are very friendly. I think my family is going to like living in this neighborhood, in this house. I believe we might be as happy here as we were in Pennsylvania.

#10 grateful – At this top point on the SCALE, we can be thankful for what we have because we are able to see what is truly valuable to us: I am so blessed and grateful my family and I are all healthy, and we have moved successfully, finally, into this beautiful home.

And at that point, I could have said to Barb, "You are right. We have it great. I feel awful for all those people experiencing the devastation of Hurricane Katrina." That was where Barb wanted me to end up. She is always listening, always guiding others to feel better. My problem was, I just couldn't get there over a ten-minute phone call. I was just too low, at No. 1, to move that quickly through the different moods all the way to No. 10. And I didn't even know there was a SCALE of thoughtfulness and emotion I had to move through to get there.

Your success and happiness lies in you. Resolve to keep happy, and your joy and you shall form an invincible host against difficulties.

Helen Keller

Helen Keller, by: Casey Childs

Does it take effort, and proactive thinking, to move up the SCALE from a No. 1 to a No. 10? Yes! Of course it does! Is it worth the effort? Yes! Of course it is! The good news is this process becomes quicker and habitual the more you are aware of it and the more you use it. As you have observed, nothing in my external world had to dramatically change in order for me to feel happy. The only change required was a shift in my thinking. I needed to recognize I was in a funk, and that I was not prioritizing, or even seeing, the good that was clearly around me.

RESOLVE TO KEEP HAPPY

It's important to understand that when you use the SCALE to consider how to improve your mood, you'll need to consciously "keep" the good feelings you rise to. Become aware of the dramatic demand for us to envy what we don't currently have—this envy is encouraged by television and advertising. Don't let these common outside sources bring you down. Also, become aware of wasting your energy trying to lift a negative person higher on the SCALE with you. Down people who stay down don't use their energy for the positive; otherwise they'd work to find the means to lift themselves up too. Imagine you are up on a stage, feeling great, and a negative person is standing at floor level. If you bent down and took his hand, who would have more leverage, you to pull him up, or him to pull you down? Consider physics, and consider this: If you keep yourself strong, if you protect your mood, you can pull away from that downward tug, which can pull you down emotionally as easily as it could physically. Put all of your energy into your own happiness, and let it naturally spill over onto the people around you. Let that inspire them to come up to joy on their own path.

10 WAYS TO STAY AT THE TOP OF THE SCALE

THE ART OF HAPPINESS SCALE is the calculable process of getting to the No. 10, happy, loving, grateful, joyous, empowering, place in your mood. Once you are there, you'll want to keep it going. There are a variety of methods to consciously stay at No. 10. Here are 10 of them! Add some of your own, too!

1 Be Consciously Thankful
   Write down on an index card 10 things that you have to be grateful for. Read it every morning and every night. It will keep you consistently aware of the good in your life. Add to the list and change it, too. Life is ever changing!

2 Move That Body
   Fluid thoughts = fluid motion. Our bodies are meant to be in motion as much as at rest. Get up and move! Interact and explore your world inside your home and out. You'll see more, and find more to value, when you move about more.

3 Get Outdoors
   It is scientifically proven that those who spend at least an hour a day outside are happier. We aren't meant to be indoors all day. We need fresh air. Go for a walk, a bike ride, or even something you might rarely do, like roller-skating.

4 Play
   Children know how to have spontaneous activity, and so should you! Engage in fun activities meant only to amuse yourself.

5 Associate with Positive People
   Positive people influence each other positively. Their attitude will rub off on you.

6 LOL!
   Laughing raises endorphin hormones while lowering production of stress hormones. Watch movies that are comedies, socialize with funny people, find the humor in all situations.

7   Consider Owning a Pet
    Pet owners literally "feel the love" because pets love
    unconditionally. Owning a pet lowers blood pressure, lessens
    anxiety and boosts our immune system. If you have the space
    and time for a pet, become a pet owner.

8   Listen to Music
    Listen to positive music that makes you happy to improve, not
    confirm, a down feeling. Listening to upbeat music increases the
    level of dopamine in your brain, which produces happiness.

9   Read Inspirational Books
    Read the Bible. Read inspiring biographies. Read motivating self-
    help books. If you don't have time to read, listen to the audio
    versions. Fill your mind with positive messages.

10 Get Enough Sleep
    If you have trouble sleeping, or you find yourself sleeping so much
    that you wake up exhausted, don't delay in getting professional
    help to get a good night's rest. Getting the right amount of sleep
    for you reduces stress, bolsters memory, reduces inflammation in
    the body, keeps us emotionally stable, spurs creativity, improves
    physical performance, assists in maintaining a healthy weight,
    and helps us live a longer and better life.

When I get right down to it, it wasn't moving into the house that
could give me joy, it was me, and my perception of myself and my
circumstances that controlled my mood. Choosing good thoughts
creates happiness, in a true, real, conscious way. We *do* have control
over our moods. We *can* move up the SCALE, and be predominantly
in a good mood, to acquire *a grateful mind*.

A Grateful Mind

*A grateful mind is a great mind which
eventually attracts to it great things.*
Plato

On a vacation to San Francisco in 2000, I learned a simple question I can ask myself to help me identify what I have to be grateful for. My first stop on that trip was Pier 39, home to the flagship Ghirardelli Chocolate Ice Cream and Chocolate Shop. I was on holiday, and felt entitled to a world famous hot fudge sundae. Actually, *every*day I feel entitled to chocolate and ice cream!

After I finished that delicious sundae, I headed southeast to Pier 33 to catch a ferry to Alcatraz Island, a. k. a. "The Rock." Alcatraz is a small island located in the middle of San Francisco Bay. For thirty years, it housed the most infamous federal penitentiary in the USA. Now a museum, it's a popular tourist attraction in San Francisco because of its history, and because of the curiously eerie feeling it still holds when one walks through it. On my arrival, a National Park Ranger provided a brief orientation, and then handed me a brochure for the self-tour. Strolling through the quiet, uninhabited, cement cellblocks, I flipped through the pamphlet. I stopped abruptly when I read the following:

#5, ALCATRAZ PRISON RULES AND REGULATIONS, 1934
You are entitled to food, clothing, shelter, and medical attention. Anything else you get is a privilege.

Wow! These notorious criminals had entitlements! These "bad guys" who were too dangerous to be held anywhere else, were "entitled" to food, clothing, shelter, and medical attention. My immediate thought after reading this statement was: *If prisoners were entitled these basic human necessities, isn't everyone else on the planet entitled to the same?* These are indeed the things charities around the globe work to supply the world's economically less fortunate people.

So, it occurred to me, if you and I have enough food to sustain us, basic clothing and shelter to protect us from the elements, and essential medical attention, then anything above and beyond these things is, honestly, a privilege. The hot fudge sundae I enjoyed earlier in the day had been a privilege, not an entitlement. Just as it was a privilege to have seven pairs of jeans hanging in my closet at that very moment, a privilege to live in a three-bedroom home, and a privilege to have medical attention beyond what was essential—like wearing braces when I was twenty-four. When I consider my life beyond my basic human rights, and I focus on my privileges, I see that I am flooded, bombarded, and overwhelmed with things to be grateful for!

So, the easiest way I've found to have a grateful mind is to ask myself this simple question, "Beyond basic food, shelter, and medical attention, what do I have in my life?" Ask yourself this, and get ready for the answers to flood your mind.

A GREAT MIND

A grateful mind is a great mind, which attracts great things. But why is a grateful mind great? In the Bible, the disciple John writes,

God is love.

1 John 4:16

As you can see on THE ART OF HAPPINESS SCALE, the highest thoughts are those of happiness, *love*, gratitude, and joy. Because God is love, **when we have thoughts of gratitude we are closely connected to the mind of God.** Isn't that wonderfully amazing?!

Because God is love, highest on the emotion's Top 10, then the furthest you can be from the mind of God would be an emotion at the bottom of the scale, such as No. 2, hate. Ungrateful thoughts, such as hate or jealousy, take us far from God and make our mind anything but great.

Fill your mind with gratitude, joy, and love, and you will have a great mind that most closely connects with God's intentions for our best selves.

Attract Great Things

In 1991, writer Sarah Ban Breathnach (pronounced Bon Brannock) sat at her dining room table determined to make a list of 100 things she was grateful for. Six hours later, not only had she completed her list, but she had discovered the key to happiness...cultivating a grateful mind!

In her inspiring book *Simple Abundance: A Daybook of Comfort and Joy*, Ban Breathnach encourages the reader to begin a gratitude journal. One of those readers was Oprah Winfrey. At Ban Breathnach's suggestion, each night Oprah jots down 5 things she can be grateful about that day. Regarding this habit, Oprah said, "What you focus on expands, and when you focus on the goodness in your life, you create more of it. Opportunities, relationships, even money flowed my way when I learned to be grateful no matter what happened in my life."

Everyone has positive, neutral, and negative events happening in their life, all within the same day! What we choose to focus on, we create more of. God hears all our thoughts, not just the thoughts we classify as a prayer. *All* our thoughts are prayers. Whatever we are focusing on, we are asking God for more of, whether it's positive, neutral, or negative.

You simply will not be the same person two months from now after consciously giving thanks each day for the abundance that exists in your life. And you will have set in motion an ancient spiritual law: the more you have and are grateful for, the more you will be given.

Sarah Ban Breathnach

Sarah Ban Breathnach, by: Annette Hackney Evans

Many of us continuously think about the problems in our lives, and the material things we wish we had. This is an excellent thing to do if we want to create more *lack*! To create more abundance, we can focus on what we have to be grateful for, no matter how small. **Each moment we choose to focus on the good, we reinforce the habit of gratitude.** The benefit is we will feel good now, while at the same time expanding the good.

Sir John Templeton, billionaire investor and philanthropist said,

> *If you're not grateful, you're not rich—*
> *no matter how much you have.*

Here's a man who has tons of money, and he's telling us happiness doesn't come from being financially rich, it comes from our feelings of gratitude for the money and things we do have. Until we learn to be grateful for the money and material things we have now, right now, God knows we won't be happy with more. Feel grateful and rich with the money and objects and people you have in your life, and you will experience joy watching them expand outward all the time!

The concept of "God is love" can also be applied in a scientific way. Stephen Post, Professor of Bioethics at Case Western Reserve University's School of Medicine, created a research group to test and measure the effects of love and other positive emotions on people. The findings surprised even him. He commented about his experiment writing, "Our studies have shown that love-related qualities—like gratitude—actually make us physically healthier." He was even able to see in the tests where health can be improved from having conscious loving feelings. Feeling love and gratitude:

1 defends – By focusing on things they are grateful for fifteen minutes a day, the people in the study were shown to increase their natural antibodies.
2 sharpens – Consciously grateful people were found to be more focused and have less clinical depression.

48

3   calms – The people who consciously participated in gratefulness tested healthier in their blood pressure and heart rate.

4   strengthens – These grateful people were shown to be physically healthier.

5   heals – A grateful attitude appeared to help bodies heal faster.

It's wonderful to see science consider and show that we can increase our body's natural antibodies, be more mentally focused and less vulnerable to clinical depression, have a healthier blood pressure and heart rate, and have bodies that are stronger and heal faster, all by being more grateful. A healthy body is definitely a great "thing" to attract.

Being grateful for what you have now, and enlivening your mood and your health from that expression, does not mean you have to maintain the status quo. If you want more, God will give you more opportunities to create more for yourself and those you love. Like creates space for like. And as long as you are

If the only prayer you ever say in your whole life is "Thank you," that would suffice.
Meister Eckhart

grateful for whatever you have, at any given time in your life, you can act in kindness and love as you grow emotionally, financially, and spiritually, because you will always remind yourself of what you are thankful for and why. Saying "thank you, thank you, thank you!" out loud is really a path to the realization of what you have to be thankful for, and God hears that and responds, in a multitude of ways.

I AM GRATEFUL!

Beyond the human necessities of food to sustain you, basic clothing and shelter to protect you from the elements, and medical attention, what do *you* have to be grateful for? Go ahead…get to 50!

1 _____

2 _____

3 _____

4 _____

5 _____

6 _____

7 _____

8 _____

9 _____

10 _____

11 _____

12 _____

13 _____

14 _____

15 _____

16 _____

17 _____

18 _____

19 _____

20 _____

21 _____

22 _____

23 _____

24 _____

25 _____

God gave you a gift of 86,400 seconds today.
Have you used one to say thank you?
William Arthur Ward

26 _____

27 _____

28 _____

29 _____

30 _____

31 _____

32 _____

33 _____

34 _____

35 _____

36 _____

37 _____

38 _____

39 _____

40 _____

41 _____

42 _____

43 _____

44 _____

45 _____

46 _____

47 _____

48 _____

49 _____

50 _____

Give thanks for unknown blessings already on their way.
Native American Saying

5

Love the Body You're With

Starting today,
if you can't be with the body you love,
love the body you're with.
Sarah Ban Breathnach

On a scale of 0 – 10, how beautiful are you? Take your time…then circle a number.

0	1	2	3	4	5	6	7	8	9	10
Ugly					Average					Beautiful

The number you circled is an indication of your body image. The number may be dramatically different from how other people perceive you. We all have parts of our body that we think could be improved, but it's a mistake to think that being more physically beautiful will solve a negative body image. After reading this chapter, without doing one sit-up, running one mile, or getting one Botox injection, I am almost certain you will love the body you're with a little more and rate yourself more beautiful.

Writer Carol Robidoux explained, "Body image, by definition, is not based on fact. It's more influenced by self-esteem than mirror image, according to the experts. It's not imbedded in your DNA; it's something you learned—from your family, your peers and mostly, from your culture." Body image is your perception of your own physical appearance. It's a self-portrait you carry around in your mind, something you picked up from your family, your peers, and your culture.

My family had a big impact on my body image. Like many families, my siblings and I were labeled by our perceived positive qualities. Of the girls, my oldest sister Teri had the "good personality," next in line was my "pretty" sister Sandy, and I was the "artist." Thus, it was only Sandy who was supported in her body image by my family, which led me to believe she must be more special than the rest of us, me especially.

At sixteen, Sandy started taking modeling classes and soon entered a beauty pageant. On a Saturday morning, my mom, Sandy, and I, headed over to a high school where the competition was to take place. I had nothing better to do that day and thought I could be useful retrieving changes of clothing, makeup, curling iron, etc., from the car. When we arrived, the high school gymnasium was bustling with girls; some were younger than me, some were my age at thirteen, and some older. They were all different from me, I thought, because they were there representing the "beautiful people," and I was not part of that group.

Yet, on one of my gopher trips back from the car, I was stopped by one of the pageant coordinators rushing through the gym. Seeing me she said, "You're not supposed to be out here. You should be in a classroom getting ready with the other contestants."

I blanched. *What…? She thinks I'm a contestant? Does she need glasses? Can't she see I'm not pretty enough to be in a beauty pageant?* In my mind at that time of life, I was about a 5 on the beauty scale, and I was sure you'd have to be at least an 8 or 9 to compete. Looking back, that was a message I internalized from my family. My place was behind the scenes, or in an artist studio. Whether this message was accurate or not in terms of a contest doesn't matter, it only matters that it was my perception. I didn't think I could compete because I didn't think I was part of the "beautiful group."

What message did you get from your family regarding your body image? Would your family think you should be a contestant in a beauty pageant, strutting your stuff down the catwalk, or a gopher like me, working behind the scenes?

While I picked up a mediocre body image at home, I actually

faired better at school with my peers. How has your body image been shaped by what you learned from your peers? Were you popular in school? Were you in the small percentage of girls that a large percentage of the boys were after?

And lastly, how is your body image affected by what you are continuing to learn from your culture? Most of us would agree that a Victoria's Secret model would be scored a "10" on the beauty scale. The official written rules to be a Runway Angel in the *Victoria's Secret Fashion Show Television Special* are: you must be 18-30 years old, 5' 8" or taller barefoot, and be in excellent health. Unofficial, unwritten rules, which we can infer from the contestants who are chosen, are that you need to be extremely lean yet have large breasts (an unlikely natural gift), full lips, and long hair (natural or artificial through extensions). To complete the sexy, sultry look, body make-up can be applied to create the illusion of perfect skin, in all colors.

Cultural expectations of beauty change over time. I know from my study of fashion design that the sense of what makes a "beautiful" American female body is relative to economic class, ethnicity, legal changes in women's social independence and access to healthy food. It's an issue about material ability in this way—how does an American woman *appear* to the public as wealthy, socially important, sexy, strong, demure, successful and capable of bearing children with regard to her current social and economic factors that identify people as "rich" and "successful" and essentially desirable? That's a long idea, and puts a lot of pressure on women, as we know. As economies and availability change, so do the expectations of body beauty in all of these elements of what "makes" a woman attractive. Victoria's Secret sells "sexy" as it is idealized today, not as any individual woman may be found sexy to her individual partner.

But why, you may ask, are we even talking about body image? Why do we spend so much time and money trying to improve it to match what we are told by economic and social trends to believe? Even if our family, peers, and culture were all accepting of our looks, why do we still desire to "look pretty" outside of our local experience, to other people on the street, whom we don't know?

In part, we can look to biology! We were born this way; we're hardwired with a yearning to be genetically desirable. Nature wants to continue our species, so sex is a basic human drive. Our idea of what is "sexy" is also meant to identify a description of the most fertile females. But as our economy and material accessibility change, so changes what "sexy" may be.

Ru·ben·esque (roo͞'bə nesk') *Adjective* full and shapely; voluptuous: said of a woman's figure, referring to the art of Peter Paul Rubens, a 17th Century Flemish Baroque painter.

Venus at a Mirror by: Peter Paul Rubens

A woman's fertility peaks between the ages of 19-24. No surprise that a Victoria's Secret model must be 18-30 years old. That range includes the fertility range, and sexiness sells a lot of lingerie! It is biologically understandable that men are physically attracted to women between ages 19-24 because they are the most fertile. (Not that men have babies on their mind when picking up women! What the body wants is not always relative to what people are emotionally and financially prepared for!) Women's fertility declines after the age of 30 and is almost zero after 43. By her 43rd birthday, a woman's eggs are much less efficient at being fertilized and women miscarry at a higher rate. And while it's very true that ideas about sexiness, as well as science and advanced health care today, enable women in their 40s to have babies, and be on the cover of *Vogue* (which is a magazine that works to inform us about sexiness, and other trending attractive qualities in women), in general biological terms, men are often attracted to women who look like their genes will make them good breeders. Women, however, are often attracted to men who look like they may be good providers, and/or have healthy genes to make healthy babies.

I'm in my late 40s now, and I have no desire to forever be someone who looks like a baby-making machine. I am, however, still very interested in building and maintaining a strong, beautiful body image for myself. I want this for myself because loving how we look makes us happier and more satisfied with our lives. We can't stay young forever. But we can always be beautiful on our own terms. Following are ideas on how to build a better body image that positively affect how we think, feel, and live our lives.

YOUR REALITY IS BETTER THAN A CELEBRITY'S IMAGE

Even I don't wake up looking like Cindy Crawford.
Cindy Crawford

Not only do you and I not wake up looking like a supermodel, but a supermodel doesn't either! Their image is not even *their* reality. As we are bombarded by images of celebrities every day, through television, newspapers, magazines and the Internet, sometimes we forget they have *many* professionals working to make them look the way they do: hair stylists, makeup artists, wardrobe stylists, photographers, lighting technicians, and digital editors. It genuinely takes a huge team of people to make a celebrity look the way they do, in the flash of a film moment.

Now in her mid 40s, Cindy Crawford voices the truth she's known all along—even she doesn't wake up looking like her image. And while we may admire the way she looks on camera, because honestly, that's where most of us see her rather than in real life, we can appreciate that we could look darn "pretty" to society too if we could afford all that help. But if we keep our sense of self-beauty intact for and to ourselves first, we are always beautiful to the world, because we shine with our own sense of it.

You don't have to be
born beautiful
to be wildly attractive.

Diana Vreeland
(*Vogue* editor-in-chief 1963-1971)

Diana Vreeland, by: Richard Ely

TALK NICELY TO YOURSELF

"Hello, Gorgeous."
Barbra Streisand in *Funny Girl*

In the 1968 movie *Funny Girl*, Fanny Brice, played by Barbra Streisand, said the above words to her image in a mirror. Because our mind has the incredible ability to believe what we repeatedly tell it, talking nicely to ourselves is essential for good body image.

When I was sixteen and my hair fell out, my body image plummeted so low I would have scored myself a 0 on the beauty scale. When one has alopecia, she or he spends a lot of time obsessing in front of the mirror. *Is the bald spot getting bigger? Wait, that's new hair growing in. I'm sure it wasn't there yesterday! It's coming back!*

On one such day, I invited my mom into my bedroom to see what I was sure was new hair growth. She walked in, took one look at the patchy hair on my head, and said, "You look spooky." Clearly, she didn't know how to appropriately communicate with someone suffering from alopecia! Her words weren't meant to hurt, and as a matter of fact she agreed and was excited that I had new hair growth. In support, she followed up the accidentally hurtful comment by telling me I was handling the situation well, much better than she herself could have if she were the one with alopecia. I heard all of her words, but the negative comment stuck. Now, at sixteen, the image I saw of myself in the mirror was that of a "spooky" creature in a bad B movie who climbs out of a black ocean with seaweed hanging on!

For years after that moment, I would look at my reflection and say, "Annette, you look spooky." Being the creative type, I added some of my own hurtful adjectives. "You are defective, damaged goods. How can anyone stand to look at you?"

As a conscious adult, I would never allow someone else to stand in my bathroom, look at me in the mirror, and whisper insults into my ear. Yet, for years I allowed myself to do just that, and of course, continually repeating these insults gave me a worse and worse body image. Can there be negative numbers on the beauty scale?

Yet, we must remember, the people we like the most are people we feel safe with; they are people we feel don't judge us. We can learn to change our internal voice to that of a beloved friend, someone who will soothe, strengthen and support us. Instead of scanning your image and finding flaws, scan your image and focus on your assets. Sometimes the list of cons can seem so long in our minds that we don't recognize that our list of pros is always far longer. Maybe your hair is *your* best asset. Or, do people compliment you on your beautiful eyes? Do your nails look fantastic with the new color you applied? If you catch yourself being your enemy and insulting yourself, pause, and acknowledge the thought. Then, be a great friend to yourself, and remind yourself of something to admire.

Everyone has insecurities about her or his appearance. Starting today, *right now*, be nice to yourself and become best friends with the person in the mirror. You are deserving of love from the most important person in your life: Yourself. **Treat yourself like someone you love.**

Although I felt awkward and embarrassed at first, I finally started talking nicely to myself and my body image has greatly improved. Now, in the mirror, I say, "Annette, you're looking good at 49! You have such a friendly smile! Hello, Gorgeous!"

Nurture Your Body

You are probably great at nurturing others –
don't you deserve the same quality care from yourself?
Gail McMeekin

One fall, my sister Teri's boss asked her to get a flu shot. She was so tired from all the work she had to do at her job, and in her life in general, her response was, "Are you kidding? Staying home in bed for a week would be the best thing that could happen to me!" If this sounds like you, maybe it would be nice to nurture yourself a little more, so that being sick in bed for a week doesn't begin to sound like a holiday.

Women are often great at nurturing others. Maybe because of

our response to society's perception of women as mothers, or maybe because we know ourselves to have giving natures, many women nurture our significant others, our children, sometimes parents, and even the "family" pet. Did you fall for the line, "Mommy, mommy, I really want a puppy. I'll feed it, I promise!"

I fell for it. I now nurture two Bichon Frises who get professionally groomed more often than I do. I used to even nurture the plants in my landscaping more than myself!

Because so many things are loudly calling out for our attention, we often miss the quiet voice of our own body asking for care. Sometimes it takes a week sick in bed before we listen. Yet, we can feel joyous and energized when we are doing a good job nurturing ourselves with the same energy we do others.

Nurture your body by making sure you get the amount of sleep you need. Eat wholesome foods, allowing for treats—if you eat good food most of the time, an occasional scrumptious dessert won't hurt you! Find a physical activity you enjoy such as walking, swimming or tennis. Learn to relax by soaking in a tub, practicing yoga, or meditating. Pamper yourself with a massage or pedicure. Talk nicely to yourself about your body. The more you nurture your body, the better you will feel physically and mentally.

Writer and humorist Erma Bombeck, who passed away from cancer, wrote that given another shot at life, "I would have gone to bed when I was sick instead of pretending the earth would go into a holding pattern if I weren't there for the day." She's no longer with us, but her words can still help us all. Nurture your body.

YOUR BODY'S FORM FOLLOWS ITS FUNCTION

"Form Follows Function" is a principle associated with modern architecture and industrial design. The principle means that the shape of a building or object should be primarily based upon its intended function or purpose.

Architects, interior designers and fashion designers begin each new creation by asking, "What is the intended function or purpose of this design?" The answer to this question shapes the building, room or garment.

Have you noticed that the form of our bodies follows the function that we expect of it? If an Olympic ice skater, marathon runner and swimmer were lined up and we were asked to guess their event, we could likely do it. The ice skater's largest muscles would be her legs, with large gluteals (buttocks muscles) to push off the ice. The marathon runner would be lean head to toe in order to carry her body 26.2 miles. The swimmer would have large arm, shoulder and chest muscles to thrust through the water.

Your body is also taking the form of the activities *you* do each day. And, unless you are spending hours training like professional athletes, it's not reasonable to compare your body to theirs. We can appreciate how our body functions for us and carries us through our day, regardless of its form.

Appreciate your body's ability to walk, swim, dance or cook a meal. Love your ability to play an instrument or paint a painting. Our bodies are vehicles for working and playing and they will look like what they do, so if you really, honestly love without regret or guilt the activities you do with your body, your body will be beautiful to you. By appreciating all the functions our body performs for us each day, we learn to become less critical of its form and much more loving of all its functions. And remember, if we want our bodies to perform a new function, all we need to do is start those activities—our body will follow in form to do them!

WEAR CLOTHES THAT COMPLIMENT YOUR FIGURE

Don't get hung up on size. If you feel bad about yourself because a 12 is what fits, take a Sharpie and write 6 on the label.
Stacy London and Clinton Kelly

I'll admit, before watching "What Not to Wear," hosted by Stacy London and Clinton Kelly, I didn't know a woman could look stylish, sexy and confident no matter what her size. Watching the two do makeover after makeover has made me a believer.

I commonly hear friends say, "I don't have any clothes that fit because I've gained weight," or "I'm not going to buy any clothes that fit *until* I lose weight!" In either case, the person wears clothes that are too tight, which emphasizes weight gain, or clothes that are too big, meant to camouflage their size, but such garments end up making them look bigger.

Stacy London understands a woman's dilemma when she helps them choose a new wardrobe. "I have been every size in my life. I've been smaller than a zero, up through a size 16. I've had lots of issues with body image and weight my whole life and it really took a great deal of work to recognize that at all those weights, no matter how I felt, I could still find a dress that made me feel sexy and powerful."

You *can* find beautiful, stylish clothing designed to fit your shape. Learn what looks best on you. Tops and jackets that cinch in at the waist make your waistline appear narrower. Boot-cut jeans make your thighs look smaller. And wearing high heels under pants that are hemmed to the ground make your legs look longer. Above all else, wear clothes that fit you, and ignore the size on the label. No one can see the label, they can only see your confidence in the comfort and attitude of what you feel good in.

Remember, we can't get what we want in life until we appreciate what we already have. If you think you would feel better thinner, work towards that, while appreciating where you are today. Wearing clothes that compliment your figure now will improve your body image no matter what size you are.

Maintain Good Grooming

Please brace yourself before reading the following quote. It may be painful for you.

> *There are no ugly women, only lazy ones.*
> Helena Rubinstein

Ouch! If you ranked yourself a 0, 1, 2 or 3 earlier, it may make you feel better to know that with a little discipline on your part, you may groom yourself right up your beauty scale.

Considering ourselves "ugly" can become a self-fulfilling prophecy. Negative thoughts drain us of energy and may lead us to take poor care of ourselves. Without a doubt, looking our best to ourselves requires effort. When we have the discipline to groom our hair, skin, teeth and nails, we may discover that we like our appearance and people respond to us more positively, and this will genuinely increase our energy.

American icon Jackie Kennedy is remembered for her style and elegance. She knew that the discipline of good grooming was more important than beauty when she said, "...the health and cleanliness of hair, skin, teeth, and nails are the basis of any beauty care. If these are attended to regularly and with a little discipline it should be possible to achieve what is more important than beauty, ...namely, good grooming."

I believe my words and actions are much more important than how I look, but now I know *both* are important. I've always noticed and admired women with impeccable grooming. Like I mentioned previously, my dogs get groomed once a month, so shouldn't I? When I get a manicure or pedicure, I do feel better about my body, prettier and more confident, which enhances what's more important to me... my words and actions.

To a certain extent, we are responsible for our own beauty. When we devote time and energy to our grooming, we are announcing to the world, and ourselves, "I am valuable. I'm beautiful and worth spending time and energy on."

THE OPINIONS THAT MATTER ARE YOURS, THOSE WHO LOVE YOU, AND YOUR DOCTOR

I'm going to share a story that will show you just how shallow I can be: When my girls were younger, we were at the grocery store pushing our cart through the refrigerated section. An employee in his twenties had half of his attention on stocking a freezer and the other half watching women pass by. I observed him "checking-out" two twenty-somethings as they walked by, and I couldn't help but be curious if he was going to turn and watch me, a mom in my 30s, trailed by two children. I strolled past him thinking my curiosity would never be satisfied, when I unexpectedly caught his reflection in a mirror at the back of a refrigerated food case. *He was looking at me!* I am ashamed to admit, I felt a little reassured. I had nothing to gain from his checking me out, so why did I care, when it made absolutely no difference in my life?

A portrait client of mine, who was also a plastic surgeon, once told me, "Most of the women I see as patients are those that were the 'best looking woman at the party' when they were younger." These women were used to having a good body image because they knew they turned heads. As they aged, they felt they saw those heads turned instead to younger women. They chose plastic surgery to regain a body and face shape they thought would bring back the attention they used to get.

It's not healthy to use strangers as a barometer for our body image. The people whose opinions matter in our life care about us for the right reasons. Loved ones care about what we do and who we are more than how we look. I want to look my best for myself and my family, but I know I'm loved for much more than my outward appearance. Being healthy is important, so beyond my family, my doctor's opinion also counts.

I'll have to make peace with the knowledge that Hugh Hefner will never ask me to pose for *Playboy*. Frankly, I would feel silly in bunny ears anyway. We don't need objectification to confirm our beauty to ourselves.

Be Happy!

*Happy people are beautiful. If somebody walks in the room
and they're drop-dead gorgeous, they're fun to look at. But
if someone is giving of their spirit and they make you laugh
and feel good, that's a whole other level of beauty.*
Drew Barrymore

We desire to be more beautiful so we are accepted and loved by others. People *are* attracted to us if they find us physically beautiful, but they are *more* attracted to us if we make them feel good. We are limited in the amount we can improve our external beauty. *Improving our internal beauty is limitless.* True happiness comes from being loved for our inner beauty, and that can last our entire lives.

Believed by Orson Welles to be "the most beautiful woman in the world," Dolores Del Rio was an actress who reached star status in 1928. She was also aware that external beauty is only skin deep. She wrote, "Take care of your inner beauty, your spiritual beauty, and that will reflect in your face. We have the face we created over the years. Every bad deed, every bad fault will show on your face. God can give us beauty and genes can give us our features, but whether that beauty remains or changes is determined by our thoughts and deeds."

If you want to improve your outer beauty, first improve your inner beauty. It sounds inside out because it is! **Beautiful people aren't always happy, but happy people are always beautiful.**

Now that you appreciate and love your body a little more as it is right now, *how beautiful do you think you are?*

0	1	2	3	4	5	6	7	8	9	10
Ugly					Average					Beautiful

Good for you! I'm optimistic that you scored yourself higher than you did at the beginning of the chapter.

Our calling in life is to use our gifts to create joy for ourselves and others. If we can do that looking out from a body that is a work of art we love, great! If not, that's okay too, because you only need a positive attitude to love the body you're with.

Lovely on the Inside

*Any female with the capability of seeing and developing her
inner self as well as her outer self is rather, well, lovely.*
Lori Borgman

E lle Woods, a blonde California sorority girl, knows her
boyfriend Warner Huntington III is proposing tonight. Why
wouldn't he want to marry her? She is impeccably groomed,
wears couture clothing, is from the expensive Bel-Air neighborhood
in LA, and loved by everyone. What's *not* to love?

Reese Witherspoon plays Elle in the 2001 movie *Legally Blonde*.
The conflict arises on this warm spring evening when she and Warner
dine at an Italian restaurant and her expectations are not exactly met.

"I plan on running for office someday," Warner says. "One of the
reasons I wanted to come here tonight was to discuss our future."

Both college seniors, Elle is aware that after graduation Warner
will move back East to be near his family and attend Harvard Law
School. Elle is certain that "discussing our future" means he wants
her in it, and will be presenting her with an engagement ring any
moment.

Warner says, "I think it's time for us Elle...Pooh Bear..."

Simultaneously they say,

WARNER	ELLE
"I think we should break up."	"I do!"

Shocked and wide-eyed, Elle says, "What?! I thought you were proposing!"

Warner raises his eyebrows, laughs nervously and says, "Elle, if I'm going to be a senator, well I need to marry a Jackie, not a Marilyn."

Elle is devastated! Her life has been spent developing her outer self, and up to this moment, being a "Marilyn Monroe" blonde and bubbly-sexy type has gotten her everything she wanted. Her broken heart leads to a week of over-eating, TV watching, and maybe worst of all, letting her nails go.

Then, Elle devises a plan. She will become the person Warner wants to marry...a "Jackie," as in the educated, demure, serious and dedicated Jacqueline Kennedy type of woman she thinks Warner means. She will invest time and money on her internal self and enroll in Harvard Law School, too!

> *You have to wonder what the ratio is between the time and money we invest in our external selves and the time and money we invest in our internal selves.*
>
> Lori Borgman

Elle studies hard, passes the LSAT, and miraculously gets into Harvard. She makes the move across the country, seriously stretching her comfort zone. At law school, Elle's pretty face and charming personality don't earn respect from her peers. But, Elle begins working like never before, starts to believe in herself, and gradually rises to the top of her class.

Because Elle is pretty and stylish on the outside, yet also smart and kind on the inside, she is one of my favorite fictional characters ever!

Do you invest as much time and money on your internal self as on your external self? Feeling lovelier on the inside does require effort, but the return on investment is huge. Here are some suggestions to more fully develop our inner-selves.

CHANGE CHILDHOOD LABELS

Several years ago, I was commissioned by a woman named Ann to create a portrait of her son and daughter-in-law for their one-year anniversary. Soon after I delivered the artwork, Ann sent me a card:

It was special for me to have such a unique gift to
present to the couple and I feel grateful also for having
a chance to meet you. I felt very connected with you…
Your gracious demeanor is lovely!
    Thanks for sharing your soul in so many ways!
    Fondly,
    Ann

After reading the card, I simultaneously wanted to cherish…and destroy it. I loved the compliments, yet I also resisted them. Why did Ann's kind words make me feel so uncomfortable? I felt like I was a fraud for making her think good things about me.

As a child, I was often told I was a "good artist," so I was comfortable with this label and confident Ann's son and daughter-in-law did indeed like the gift. Besides "good artist," I had another label. In my family, I was sometimes called a "smart aleck." This label did *not* refer to my intelligence! Synonyms for a smart aleck are "obnoxious, sassy, or smarty pants." How could I, a smart aleck, also have a "gracious demeanor?" Was it possible all the self-help books I had devoured over the years helped me camouflage my innate rudeness and that's how I had tricked Ann?

As children, we are vulnerable to believing the judgments of authority figures in our lives. To be honest, as adults we are too. The people who have made the biggest contribution to our self-image might have been parents, caregivers, other family members, friends, and teachers. If the labels they gave us were positive, they help us in life. If the labels were negative, they hurt us. The labels we internalized in our youth often affect how we think and act as adults today.

Think back to your childhood labels. Are they serving you in life today? Labels are good if they are positive, and make you feel lovely on the inside. Keep the ones that do and replace the ones that don't.

Childhood Label:	'good artist'	I'll keep it.
Childhood Label:	'smart aleck'	I'll replace it.
New Label:	'lovely demeanor'	I'll embrace it!

Repeat Positive Affirmations Daily

When I first became a stockbroker, I made up a mantra,
"I am young, powerful and successful." How ridiculous is
that? I wasn't so young. I was certainly not powerful. And I
was not successful. Still, I mentally repeated my mantra 25
times a day, and within six months it became a reality.
Suze Orman

A positive affirmation is a positive label you give yourself. Your subconscious accepts all words and emotions as facts, no matter if they are based in reality. Instead of letting other people, or your negative beliefs, dictate your self-esteem, why not shape it consciously yourself?

Make a list of things you are *going* to like about yourself. If you find this difficult, simply think of things you don't like, and write down their opposite. "I never finish anything," becomes, "I finish every worthwhile project I start." "I'm getting older and still haven't fulfilled my dreams," becomes, "I work consistently on my dreams and they are coming true!"

Put the list somewhere you can see it often throughout the day. Or do what Suze Orman did, memorize your mantra and repeat it 25 times a day. Focusing on the traits you like, or are *going* to like, about yourself makes them grow larger, and eventually these positive affirmations will crowd out self-defeating thoughts.

Focus on Your Successes

Success breeds confidence.
Beryl Markham

Feeling lovely on the inside requires confidence. To attain confidence, we need to notice and focus on our successes. Many of us habitually focus on our failures, which breeds insecurity.

For example, I have yet to meet a woman who feels she is successful during the holidays. Somewhere along the way, many women bought into the idea that we need to find the perfect gifts for our loved ones, and make the gifts look as though they were professionally wrapped. We may feel a desire to decorate our homes beautifully, and cook our family's favorite traditional foods. We *should* fill out stacks of gorgeous holiday cards, and swear that this year, they will arrive before January 1st. Also to be successful, we should want to entertain friends, and attend their functions. While doing all this, we think it would be best to be thin, well dressed, and look stunning!

My feelings of failure to accomplish this list last December seeped into January. I really felt like a loser when my holiday cards turned into *Happy New Year!* cards instead. Adding this to my other holiday failures I vowed, as usual, that next year would be different.

Then, unexpectedly, my focus changed when friends and family began sending e-mails expressing how much they enjoyed receiving our "New Year's" card. Unlike previous years, in this card I had enclosed a brief family newsletter and while addressing the cards, said a prayer for each recipient. My daughters even told me how proud they were to have their photo on the cards. Author Wayne Dyer says, "When you change the way you look at things, the things you look at change." I had not failed at creating the perfect holiday after all; in some ways I was more successful than ever!

Moving through the holidays, or any season of our life, focusing on our failures is a sad way to live. Instead, we can change the way we look at things, focus on our successes, and breed confidence. Confidence makes us feel empowered and lovely on the inside.

COMPARE YOURSELF TO WHERE YOU'VE BEEN

What I am is how God made me.
What I am not is how God made somebody else.
Jan Battenfield

One of our favorite forms of self-abuse is comparing ourselves to others. It's just mean to do this to ourselves. There will always be someone who was born more physically or mentally gifted, someone who was born into money, someone who had more loving parents, and someone who had the advantages of the best education. By comparing ourselves to anyone who seems "born with" what we don't have, we are sure to feel we come up short.

Instead of asking ourselves, "How do I compare to her?" a better question is, "How do I compare to where I've been?" God gave us the materials we have to work with; our only job is to make the most of them. No one, including you, should expect anything more than that.

Measure yourself according to how far you have come. Are your talents more developed now than five years ago? Are your relationships better now than one year ago? Are your living conditions slightly better than two months ago? If so, good for you! If not, today is a great day to begin!

When you can look back, and feel you have done the best with the talents and strengths God gave you to work with, then you *are* lovely on the inside.

Focus on Others

If we worry too much about ourselves,
we won't have time for others.
Mother Teresa

Imagine Mother Teresa waking up one morning, looking in a mirror, and thinking, "I don't have time to help the poverty stricken of Calcutta, I have to do something about these thighs. Next week, a film crew is coming to do a segment on me, and the camera puts on ten pounds. I can't let the homeless, starving people lying in the gutters look thinner than me. I better forget what God would have me do today and hit the gym!" Did I take it too far? As ludicrous as this sounds, this is the way some of us live our lives. We can't focus on the important things because we worry too much about how we appear to others.

We all want to look good. Being well-groomed and maintaining a healthy lifestyle are legitimate desires. The problem comes when we spend so much time focusing on ourselves in relation to how we think it will appeal to others that it consumes all our thoughts and actions. Whatever we focus on in our lives expands, so the more we focus on ourselves for other people's interests, *the more we focus on their interests instead of our own!* When we switch our focus to others in relation to being helpful, rather than trying to impress, we develop our inner self, and make a more important contribution to society.

It's wonderful to take the time to apply makeup, get manicures, and play tennis. It is *also* magnificent to make time for others when we want to share good things and help create success for everyone to grow. The former makes us lovely on the outside, while the latter makes us lovely on the inside.

Take Action Towards Success

Success is like a vitamin. And if you don't get enough of it when you are growing up, you suffer a very severe deficiency that could have long term impacts in your life.
Mel Levine, M.D.

Success in childhood could mean getting good grades, excelling in sports, or even being well liked by your peers. If your caregivers didn't make sure you had some form of success as a child, you didn't get your vitamins.

Sometimes we need to supplement our positive affirmations with concrete results. For example, if your current proactive mantra is, "I am a gifted public speaker," but you froze every time you gave an oral report in high school, you'll need to take some action. Joining a group such as Toastmasters would be a concrete step towards success in this case, as Toastmasters helps people practice public speaking.

Don't let a "vitamin deficiency" from childhood hold you back. Of all the above suggestions to develop your inner self, this is the only one that may involve spending money, and you are *so* worth it! Take action and watch as your new successes have long-term impacts in your life.

I see parallels in the lives of the fictional character Elle Woods, and the non-fiction person, Ivanka Trump. Like Elle, Ivanka is impeccably groomed, wears couture clothing, and is blonde! Born in 1981 in New York City to parents Ivana Trump and business magnate Donald Trump, Ivanka's first career was that of a model. At 16 she was on her first magazine cover. She has since graced the cover of many magazines and even strutted down fashion runways for top fashion designers.

Not content to rely only upon her outer beauty, at the age of 23 Ivanka earned a B.S. in Economics from the Wharton School of Business at the University of Pennsylvania. Working hard, she graduated summa cum laude (with highest honor). Investing time and money on her external *and* internal self clearly paid off. Ivanka Trump is *not* notorious for being an heiress behaving badly!

Words to describe Ivanka today are not only heiress, but businesswoman, writer (she published a book at 28), wife and mother. She has said, "I have a tough skin and enough confidence not to worry too much about being misunderstood because of my last name, my relative youth, or my modeling background."

In *Legally Blonde*, when Elle invests time and money on her internal self, she becomes lovely inside and out. She also begins dating a guy who really loves the person she is—the *whole* person. Want to know what happens to Warner? Because of Elle's new successes and confidence, he wants her back.

"I was wrong. And...you are...the girl...for me," says Warner.

"Really?" says Elle.

"Yes, Pooh Bear. I love you."

"Oh Warner. I've waited so long to hear you say that." But Elle has become so much more than the girl he knew and who wanted him to want her. She now realizes he isn't worthy of her, and dumps *him*! Elle continues, "But if I'm going to be a partner in a law firm by the time I'm 30, I need a boyfriend who's not such a complete bonehead!"

Elle's life is fictional and right now, so is your future. It is up to you to create it any way you want. Invest time and money developing your inner self and it will take you to real success.

Ivanka Trump, by: Annette Hackney Evans

To Be Loved...Love

To be loved, love and be lovable.
Benjamin Franklin

Our deepest desire is to feel loved. Period. And the only path to feel loved is to love yourself first. Then you can be lovable and love others with equal truth and dedication. The answer is so simple, yet can be a real challenge to practice on a daily basis. There seem to be so many things the world shouts at us to undermine our self love, to generate inside of us a deep feeling of lack, so that we have to buy things, or become things, to get the love we want. But practicing feeling good, and feeling loved is a worthwhile pursuit, even if it takes us a lifetime to master. When we have the conviction that we love ourselves, we are lovable. When we value and thank those who love us, we have the courage to be vulnerable and show the world our authentic self.

How to get to a place of feeling love is hard to think about in a practical way because love is an emotion, it's not something we can purchase. Over and over again, we try to change things in our external world, such as our bodies and our material possessions, hoping this will bring us more love. We are convinced that we will be more loved if we are just more beautiful or more rich. Einstein said, "The definition of insanity is doing the same thing over and over again and expecting different results." Beauty and money may bring us lust from others, or admiration, but until we begin to love ourselves for us, and become lovable to ourselves, we won't feel love as it's truly meant to be felt from the deepest part of the heart.

The definition of love is:

love (luv) *n.*
1 strong affection or liking for someone or something
2 a passionate affection of one person for another
3 the object of such affection; a sweetheart or lover

My personal definition of love includes all of the above plus a 4th, much broader meaning:

4 to want the best for every person I've known in my past, present, and future

My added definition of love isn't referring to a romantic love, but a love that means wanting the best for all people. I will share a secret with you. A *big* secret. A *life-changing* secret. When we want the best for others, we are telling God we also want the best for ourself, and *we* are the one who feels loved! To allow yourself to be loved…love. Don't hold it back like it's a prize someone must win from you. Love *all* people: family, friends, neighbors, co-workers, acquaintances, and anyone whose path crosses yours. I include people I may never meet such as those on television: actors, politicians, or ordinary people.

"But why," you may ask, "do I have to love *everyone*?"

This is how it works. Our mind is always entertaining a dominant thought. And we know from THE ART OF HAPPINESS SCALE that if we are thinking a loving thought, we put ourselves in a good mood. When we think a loving thought about another person, we are the one who feels loved.

Walt Whitman wrote,

The love is to the lover and comes back most to him,
The gift is to the giver and comes back most to him-
it cannot fail.

The love comes back to the lover! How simple and beautiful. I will share with you a second secret. This one may make you a little uncomfortable. When we want the worst for someone, and are unloving towards her or him, *we* are the one who feels unloved. Walt Whitman could also have written,

The hate is to the hater and comes back most to him.

Whatever we think or feel towards another, *we* feel most. **By extending love to another, we feel more love in our lives. By inflicting pain on another, we feel more pain in our lives.**

This means loving others is a selfish act. Selfish in a fantastic way, because everyone benefits! If we are serious about wanting to feel good, and feel loved, we need to start feeling love towards others now. Here are some simple ways we may love others:

BE A "THERE YOU ARE!" PERSON

I've always believed that there are two kinds of people in the world:
those who say, "There you are!" and those who say, "Here I am!"
Abigail Van Buren (a.k.a. Dear Abby)

My windshield wipers slapped the rain off the windshield on my way from Indiana down to Uncle Donnie's funeral in Kentucky. It was morning, and if all went well, I would be back home in time to greet my girls off the school bus. Uncle Donnie and I had always lived in different states, so I never knew him or his family well. He had been divorced from his first wife many years. They had three daughters together, and the oldest died in a car accident. That left his middle daughter, Susie, to bear the main responsibility for the family at his funeral.

I don't do well at funerals, and thank God I haven't had a lot of practice. The few I have attended have also been the few times I openly wept in public. The only reason I was attending this one was to support my mother while she mourned her brother's passing.

My tires crunched across the gravel parking lot leading up to the church and my dad greeted me at the door. I hadn't seen my cousin Susie, five years my junior, in many years. After quietly saying hello to my mom and a few relatives, Susie and I were face to face. I thought she would be devastated, first to learn of her father's death, then to travel a thousand miles to his funeral, and now to be the hostess for this somber family reunion.

"Annette! It's so good to see you!" she said. We hugged and then she took my hands in hers. "How are you? I've heard so many good things about you!"

> *I've learned that people will forget what you said, people will forget what you did, but people will never forget how you made them feel.*
> Maya Angelou

I had heard many wonderful things over the years about Susie, too. To be truthful, I thought I wouldn't like her very much. Anyone who is said to be that friendly and loving must be phony. Plus, I was jealous my mom said kinder things about her than she said about me. But at this moment, I could feel Susie was genuine. Because of the circumstances, I wasn't expecting such love to be directed towards me, but she sincerely wanted to hear about my life, even though her father lay still in the next room. We continued holding hands, sharing and catching up, until it was time to take our seats. Approximately fifty of us sat and listened as the minister talked about Uncle Donnie's life. We were then asked who would like to come forward and say a few words. According to most studies, people's #1 fear is public speaking; #2 is death. Our family was no exception. Although she later said it wasn't easy for her, Susie was the only relative to approach the lectern and deliver a eulogy. She shared beautiful memories of her father as a dad, grandfather and truck driver. I felt so proud of this cousin I'd never really known.

Susie Lawyer Briggs, by: Annette Hackney Evans

The sky was still gray and it drizzled as we gathered at the gravesite to say our final goodbyes to Uncle Donnie. The gathering then moved to the shelter of a local restaurant, where a buffet lunch was spread out for our group. From afar, I studied Susie, and was awed by her loving personality. She wasn't brought up in a family that was verbally or physically affectionate, yet she was passing out hugs and I-love-you's like she was raised that way. The miracle was everyone returned them to her.

Driving home, I thanked God for bringing Susie into my life. She became a model to me of how I aspire to love others. Instead of being jealous of her, I loved her, and that made me feel good.

Which type of person are you? When you see someone you know, do you say, "There you are!" Or, are you a Me Monster, and think, *Here I am!* If you want to be loved, love people and be a "There you are!" person, like my cousin Susie. I hope you get to meet her someday. When you make people feel you are glad to see them, you'll be the kind of person everyone is delighted to see.

TREAT EVERYONE WITH POLITENESS

In the 1939 classic movie, The Wizard of Oz, Dorothy meets two opposing characters along the yellow brick road. Glinda, the Good Witch of the North is nice, helpful, and speaks to Dorothy in a comforting, sweet voice. The Wicked Witch of the West, however, is mean, intends harm, and speaks to Dorothy in an annoying, screechy voice. Let's not even mention the contrast in their physical appearance!

Treat everyone with politeness, even those who are rude to you – not because they are nice, but because you are.
Author Unknown

I've witnessed many people, myself included, behave like Glinda most of the time only to become the Wicked Witch when we perceive someone has done us wrong. When we start spewing out mean things about another, our face becomes distorted, our voice sounds harsh, and we feel ugly on the inside. "Well, they acted like the Wicked Witch (or Wizard) first!" you may say. And you may be right, but our deepest desire isn't to be right, it is to be loved. To be loved, we must love.

Choose to be kind like Glinda, and banish the Wicked Witch from your Oz. Treating *everyone* with politeness is loving, and makes us feel good on the inside.

SEE THE DIVINE IN OTHERS

The inspirational book, *Discover the Power Within You*, by Eric Butterworth, changed my life. The author reveals Jesus' astounding message, "The Kingdom of God is within you." Jesus saw a Divine dimension in every human being and Butterworth reveals that the existence of the Divine within each one of us is the greatest discovery of all time.

This Divine power is within you, me, and everyone else, whether we are aware of it or not. Some of us choose to act from this godly place within, and some of us don't. Those who don't, aren't happy people, nor are they satisfied with any positive thing that happens to them.

"Namaste," a Sanskrit word, is a common greeting in South Asia. Today the term is associated with yoga and spiritual meditation all over the world. Some meanings and interpretations of this word are:

~ I salute the God within you.
~ I honor the Spirit in you, which is also in me.
~ That which is of the Divine in me greets that which is of the Divine in you.

The easiest way for us to love others is to look for and relate to that which is Divine in them. Some people act from this place of Divinity within them and it is easy to see and love the Divine in them. Other people are not kind, and we have to search for their Divinity because it's not as evident. When we take the time to discover it, and relate to that place in them which is of love, integrity, wisdom, and peace, we both feel the Divine, just as we both feel it when people see the Divine in us.

Do you have someone in your life who makes you feel like you are better than you think you are? That person in my life is my dear friend Bernadine. When I'm talking with Bernadine, I feel smart, wise, talented, and pretty. She helps me feel like I'm an excellent mother, with two extraordinary daughters. Bernadine sees the best in me, the Divine in me, that I sometimes can't see myself. Her presence calls forth my best. And it's not just me, Bernadine has a natural gift of seeing the Divinity in everyone around her. Her seeing the Divine in me makes it easy to see and feel the Divine in her – it's always mutual. So look for the Divine in others. Lift people higher and be lifted yourself. See and be the Divine. Namaste.

> *The key is to keep company only with people who uplift you, whose presence calls forth your best.*
> Epictetus

Don't Judge, or You Will Feel Judged

Excited about an upcoming dinner party I was hosting in 2 weeks, I began a guest list. When I came across the name of one friend, I had some judgmental thoughts about how she had been conducting her life lately. Still, I greatly enjoyed her company, and wanted her to attend.

Day 1: In the morning, I called to extend my invitation to her via voicemail. The day passed with no return call. *Oh well,* I thought, *Maybe she needed to check the day and time with her date. She usually doesn't reply promptly anyway.*

Day 2: Still no RSVP. Now I was thinking *and* voicing judgmental comments. I said to my husband, "It's been almost 2 days and she hasn't called me back. That's just flakey. I would really like to know if she will be able to come or not."

Day 3: As you've probably guessed…still no call. That night, as I brushed my teeth, my judgmental thoughts turned to feelings of guilt. *I wonder if she is mad at me? I don't think I've said or done anything to upset her. Maybe she just doesn't want to get together.*

Over that three-day period, I had thought and said judgmental things about my friend, and now my mind was directing these judgmental thoughts towards *me*. In Matthew 7:1-2, Jesus says, "Do not judge, or you too will be judged. For in the same way you judge others, you will be judged, and with the measure you use, it will be measured to you." I don't believe Jesus is saying if you judge someone, God is going to judge, or punish you. He is saying if you judge someone, you will be the one left with the feeling of being judged. When you feel judgment towards others, you feel it towards yourself.

Day 4: I received a phone call from my friend. "Annette, Hi! How are you? I've been sooo busy. Sorry I didn't call back sooner. We'd love to come to your house for dinner!"

Turns out, she wasn't mad at me after all. She was being her usual self—something I had long ago accepted. In fact, she was so friendly, I felt even guiltier! The guilty feeling was so negative, I wanted to get to the bottom of why I judge people in the first place. Getting out a piece of paper, I wrote her name at the top. Then as quickly as I could, I wrote down the names of nine other people I had judged harshly in the last month. I'm ashamed to say the list was surprisingly easy to come up with. I saw that two of the people were friends, five were relatives, two were television personalities, and one was a pop culture icon.

Next I asked myself, *Why do I judge these people?* Here is what I came up with:

~ *I sometimes or always feel unloved by this person.*
~ *If I point out this person's faults, maybe it will make me look better.*

~ *If this person knows of or feels my judgment, it might motivate them to act differently.*

~ *I am jealous of this person; either I am afraid of losing affection to them, or I envy their success.*

~ *They do things I won't allow myself to do.*

Whoa! Very revealing. Looking at this list a few times, I realized I had an insightful list of *my* shortcomings, not the shortcomings of those I have judged. I saw it then: **The better we feel about ourselves, the less need we feel to judge others.**

Have you judged anyone in the past month? It might not be as easy for you to come up with ten people as it was for me, but write down on a piece of paper (that you can later shred so that no one else sees) as many as you can. Now, next to each person's name, write down why you judged her or him. Look back to my list of five reasons if you need some help.

Learn anything? The next time you think or say a judgmental thing about another, ask yourself *why*. The answer will reveal more about you than it will about them, and that's self-reflection.

BE A GOOD LISTENER

*Sincere, total, nonjudgmental listening happens
all too rarely in any of our lifetimes.*
Mary Pipher, Ph.D.

Actions speak louder than words. We can say to someone, "You are important to me. What you think matters." But we can tell them even louder with sincere, total, nonjudgmental listening. When we listen, we are *showing* them they are important to us, that they matter, that what they say counts to us.

Being a good listener is a learnable skill. The following is a comparison list of positive and negative listening skills.

Good listeners...	Poor listeners...
give you their full attention.	are preoccupied with their own thoughts.
resist the impulse to "chime in".	start talking during pauses and bring the focus back to themselves.
have good body language. They face you and make eye contact.	avert their eyes from yours, are distracted by the television, their cell phone, another person, etc.
place themself in your shoes and try to see things from your perspective.	see everything from their perspective and think of how they would have done things differently, and tell you so, sometimes brashly.
ask about your interests.	talk about their interests.
empathize with your feelings.	tell you how you *should* feel.
don't give advice unless asked directly.	are quick to give advice.
are safe people to confide in. They don't criticize or judge in painful ways what you are saying. You know what you share will stay between the two of you.	are not safe people to confide in. They criticize and or judge what you say in short strokes. They may share what you say with other people.

My friend Barb, the therapist, is the best listener I have ever known. Yes, she had training in how to listen well, but she is also naturally good at it. She enjoys it. She gives everyone sincere, total, nonjudgmental listening. Her clients love her, and have been known to call her answering machine just to be reassured by the sound of her voice.

Thinking of the previous chart, we can all become a little more like Barb. Because we come across good listeners so rarely in our lives, when we do, we feel seen and heard. Isn't this something we all crave from the loved ones in our lives? Listening is a loving gift. Show love to others by being a good listener.

BLESS THOSE WHO ARE FINDING ABUNDANCE

Bless those who are finding abundance. And in your blessing of them and their abundance, you will become abundant, too. But in your cursing of their abundance, you hold yourself apart from it.
Abraham-Hicks

Artist Thomas Kincaid, "The Painter of Light," was unusual in his ability to be admired by the general public and yet disliked by many fellow artists. The public continues to love his pastel colored paintings, which typically feature a cozy cottage with his signature warm light glowing from the windows. Many artists are turned off by his idyllic subject matter and the mass marketing of his images on canvas, calendars, stationary, collectables, home furnishings and puzzles. Like his work or not, he was a financially successful artist.

Why are artists so tough on Kincaid, and judge him so harshly? Referring back to the reasons I have judged others, there are three reasons an artist might unkindly judge Kincaid:

- ~ They think by pointing out what they perceive to be Kincaid's artistic faults, their artwork will look better.
- ~ They are jealous; he was a full-time, financially successful artist. Many people love his artwork and will spend their hard earned money on his work, but maybe not theirs.
- ~ He does things they won't allow themselves to do. If they too create non-confrontational, pleasing art that is also commercially successful, peers may call them a "sell out."

To be successful in our chosen field, whether as an artist, a realtor, or a stay-at-home mom, it can only help us if we bless those who are finding abundance; in doing so, we may become abundant also. When I catch myself cursing the abundance of someone else, I stop, reset, and exclaim, "Good for them! Way to go. Bravo!" In part, this works because at the end of the day, if I am successful in my pursuits, I'd want people to be happy for me.

One gorgeous Sunday afternoon last year, strolling down a sidewalk in Laguna Beach, CA, I passed a gallery and a painting caught my eye. I stopped, and on closer inspection, saw it was titled *Tinker Bell and Peter Pan Fly to Neverland*, by Thomas Kincaid. The colors were fresh and the feeling whimsical. The painting did what it meant to do—it created a beautiful visualization of a land many of us know in our imagination. If Thomas Kincaid were alive today, I would love to tell him, from one artist to another, "Well done, Mr. Kincaid. I find your painting to be utterly delightful!"

MAINTAIN INNER PEACE DESPITE DIFFICULT PEOPLE

Think of a difficult person in your life. Someone who walks into a room and says, "Here I am!" then proceeds to act like the Wicked Witch (or Wizard) of the West. This person doesn't bring out your best, doesn't listen to you, and he or she is *not* excited about your successes. If we desire to be loved, and feel good, we must learn to have positive, or at least neutral, feelings towards them. Otherwise, their selfish behavior will destroy our inner peace.

Let's say the holidays are approaching, and you are already dreading seeing _____ (fill in the blank). Even though you hope for the best, you know from past experience that when you get together, it is unlikely to be pleasant. How can you make yourself love, or accept, someone who is difficult? It may not be easy, but with some mental preparation, you can do it.

~ Pray for this person. You don't have to get down on your knees, but when you catch yourself thinking bad things about them,

say to yourself, *I only want the best for* _____.
At first you may be lying; you might not truly want the best for her or him. Keep praying and you'll start to feel it. Prayer may or may not change the other person's behavior, but it will soften how *you* feel.

~ Ask God to reveal to you the Divinity in this person. Everyone has good and bad qualities in varying degrees. Only focusing on the bad is not fair to people, and worse, it makes you feel bad. It is not your job to change other's negative qualities; it *is* your job to see their good. Try to see what God sees. Remember, you don't have to take on the job of loving others, but you will if you are serious about feeling good. And "loving" here doesn't have to mean anything more than respecting they exist as humans, and that you love and appreciate human life. **To the degree we can love and have compassion for an "imperfect person" is the degree to which we feel others can love imperfect us.**

~ Think of this person as part of a valuable experiment, and you are collecting data. When in their presence, make a mental note of their behavior you don't like. Don't respond to their negative words or actions. Just observe. Now, think of what the opposite of their behavior would look like. This good behavior will become the standard you can set for yourself in your future.

~ Whether you are keeping company with this person in your mind, or they are across the room at the party, ask yourself why she or he is getting all of your attention. Do you enjoy feeling bad? Some people are not capable of giving us the love we need; don't take it personally. Focus on the people in your life who do care. Don't they deserve more attention than the difficult person? Focus on people who love you.

~ Lastly, if someone is intentionally out to get you, there's only one thing to do. Take the advice of Plato, "When men speak ill of thee, live so as nobody may believe them." That simply means, be the best person you can be, and criticism will not stand against you.

These suggestions will take some practice, but they will get easier with time. We feel empowered when we no longer let a difficult person affect the mood we are in. If you've tried, and you still dread seeing this difficult person in your life, give yourself more time. Skip the holiday get together with her or him this year. The holidays aren't always a great time for us to work on our relationships. Spend the time doing something you enjoy, instead.

Do not let the behavior of others destroy your inner peace.
Dalai Lama

Our deepest desire is to be loved, and becoming masters at loving others can truly help us attain this. When we love others, we are the ones who benefit the most. Feeling love in our lives gives us supreme happiness and confidence to be our authentic self. To be loved, *love.*

8

To Be Loved...Be Lovable

*You cannot make someone love you. You can only
make yourself someone who can be loved.*
Derek Gamba

Our culture in the USA would often have us believe that we can make people love us. The message we receive is, all it takes is to create an outward appearance that fits with current trends of "beauty," and to acquire more expensive material things. The truth is, no matter how "beautiful" or "rich" we are, we can't make someone love us. Either people feel love for us...or they don't. It's not within our control.

What *is* within our control is to make ourselves someone who can be loved. When we eliminate thoughts and behaviors that make us resistant to love from others, we can allow love in, and make it easier for others to love us. Better than striving for an unattainable outward perfection, we are more lovable when we become more inwardly authentic.

The definition of lovable is:

lovable (ˈlə-və-bəl) *adj.*
1 having characteristics that attract love or affection

Following are some specific thoughts and behaviors we can develop to attract the love that is all around us now, waiting for us to claim it.

Why, when we know that there's no such thing as perfect, do most of us spend an incredible amount of time and energy trying to be everything to everyone? Is it that we admire perfection? No – the truth is that we are actually drawn to people who are real and down-to-earth. We love authenticity...

Brené Brown

Brené Brown, by: Annette Hackney Evans

Open Your Arms to Receive Love

Someone once told me that if you fully open your arms to receive love, you'll get some scratches and cuts on your arms, but a lot of love will come in. If you close your arms, you might never get cut – but the good stuff won't come in either.
Quincy Jones

Are your arms fully open to receive love? This question may take deep self-reflection. However, for a quick indication ask yourself, "How do I respond when given a compliment?" Take a moment…and think back to the last time you received a compliment. Did you:

a. Smile, look the person in the eye and say, "Thank you."

~ or ~

b. Shrug your shoulders and say, "Oh, it's really no big deal."

If you answered "a," your arms are fully open to receive love. If you answered "b," your arms are closed and, while protected from scratches and cuts, you are missing all the good stuff.

Often, the reason we resist love is that someone hurt us when we tried to give it. At some point in our life, we fully opened our arms to receive love and got deep scratches and cuts…and it hurt! We learned that sometimes it hurts when love is not returned.

We've all been wounded like this in some way, and will likely be again. We will survive our wounds, but we may not survive living a life without love. It's time to be vulnerable! Be open! Be brave! Don't give anyone else the power to make you want to walk through life with your arms closed. Denying ourselves of the available love around us doesn't feel good, and it denies others the good feeling of giving love. Fully open your arms to receive love. When someone gives you a compliment, a gift, or offers an act of service, simply say, "Thank you," and let it all in.

FIND GOOD IN YOURSELF

The more you find good in another,
the more you'll find good in yourself.
Mike Dooley

When my daughters were young, I used to tell Barb how frustrated I was with what I accomplished each day. I started the morning with a "To Do" list, and by evening most things went *undone.* Come to think of it, I didn't feel I had accomplished much on my *life's* "To Do" list, either!

Barb asked, "But wouldn't you be happy if your girls turned out just like you?"

I took a moment to think about it and said, "Well...*no!*" And that definitely gave me pause for thought.

As a child, I learned in church I should love myself, and I thought I did, generally speaking. But I didn't want my daughters to turn out like me. I wanted them to be better educated and reach their full potential, which I felt I had not.

A few days after talking about this with Barb, my family and I went on a kid-friendly, long weekend getaway. Several extended relatives were going, including one person who had always been hard for me to love, a relative whom I'll call "Lisa."

Lisa is that person who always reminds you how accomplished her children are, how she herself is much too intellectual to watch television, and similar "snooty" things. Hardest to tolerate, she is also an incessant complainer.

To prepare for my time with her, when I thought of past conflicts and inevitable conflicts coming on this trip, I said this prayer, "God, please take away the tension between us and help me get along with her."

At first, it seemed God hadn't listened.

On the first day, tension between us was high. And on the second, we had a full-scale blowout. Days three, four and five, we were both better behaved, but the atmosphere was strained. I thought, *I can't wait for this "fun family getaway" to be over!*

Back home the following week, I woke up at 4:30 one morning to a request from God. "Get up, go to your computer, and type a list of Lisa's good qualities." *What the heck?* I thought. *Why should I have to do that?* I knew I was supposed to look for the good in others, but I never thought I'd be asked to literally write it down. I rolled out of bed, made some coffee, and sat down at my computer. As I stared at the blank, white screen, I asked myself, "What are her good qualities?"

A few seconds passed.

I had nothing.

> *Pain doesn't stem from the love we're denied by others, but rather from the love that we deny them.*
> Marianne Williamson

Then suddenly, one of her good qualities popped into my mind, and I listed it. Then I thought of another, and *another.* The list grew much more quickly than I imagined it could. For years, I had carried around a mental list of what I considered her shortcomings, and now that burden was dissolving with the goodness I could also find. Elated with the three pages I built up, I decided to send them to her as a peace offering. I felt *good* about it, and I felt good about *her.*

Later that morning, after the girls were safely on the school bus, I carried the letter down our drive and put it in the mailbox. Raising the red flag on the side of the box I wondered, "Could I fill three pages with things I like about myself?" Tears came to my eyes as I realized I *could* fill three pages. For the first time, I could see I had good qualities in abundance! In Matthew 22:39, Jesus said, "Love your neighbor as yourself." I had loved Lisa as myself. I had not loved myself very well, or her either, but I was starting this moment to change!

I thought God hadn't looked out for me on the long weekend getaway, but He had a bigger plan. If we didn't have the blowout, I wouldn't have been motivated to find the good in her, and be open to finding the good in myself. Seeing the good in her, I saw it in myself. Now I believe if my daughters grow up to be just like me I will be one, proud, mom.

Then, the best part—it worked. After receiving the letter, Lisa wrote me back listing the good qualities she saw in me. This interaction was *extremely* healing in our relationship. We still aren't BFFs, but we have since treated each other much more respectfully. That is what opening yourself to *loving* can do. It can bring peace, understanding, and smooth even the oldest bumps on the road we travel.

FORGIVE

*Forgiveness is above all a personal choice, a decision of the heart
to go against the natural instinct to pay back evil with evil.*
Pope John Paul II

On March 28, 2010, nineteen-year-old Conor had been fighting with his fiancé, Ann Grosmaire, for two days. On this day, he went to his father's closet and took a shotgun down from a shelf. After more arguing, he fell into what he called a "wrathful anger." He then pointed the gun at Ann and pulled the trigger.

Ann's father, Andy Grosmaire, stood beside her bed in the intensive-care unit, praying that she would survive. Later, Mr. Grosmaire said on the *TODAY Show*, "I felt like my daughter was asking me to forgive Conor, and I just told her I couldn't." After four days, Ann's condition did not improve, and her parents chose to remove her from life support. Mr. Grosmaire explained, "I felt like my daughter was joined with Christ and that He and her were asking me to forgive and I had never said 'No' to them, so I wasn't going to say no this time. And so, it was just an uplifting of joy and peace."

How did Mr. Grosmaire do it? And how do others, who have a heinous crime committed against them or their loved ones, choose to pay back evil...with love? Somehow, they manage to forgive the criminal.

Forgiveness is a personal choice about our own emotional balance. We know we can hold a grudge, especially about deeply horrible experiences we have had. That makes logical sense. The thing is, when we keep that grudge, *we* also continue to feel miserable. Forgiveness is part of the process of letting go of what makes us unhappy, even the unhappiness that comes from severe trauma. At some point in your life someone hurt you. She or he may not deserve your forgiveness, but *you* deserve to be free from pain. While you are angry, while you are busy thinking of revenge, you are also allowing yourself to be consumed by that serious negativity. You are hurting yourself. **Not forgiving is a form of self-abuse.** Will you let this person take one more minute of your happiness? One more week…or year? It is your personal choice. You need not forget, but forgiving will heal *you*.

The question to ask when we have been wronged is, "How much negative energy am I willing to invest to hold this person accountable?" Holding a grudge comes at a high price. Physically, it causes an increase in heart rate and blood pressure, and may account for loss of sleep and appetite, create fatigue, ulcers, headaches and skin rashes. Emotionally, we are robbing ourselves and the people around us of the love we are able to give in this moment. Thoughts of bitterness and love cannot occupy our mind at the same moment and allow us to be our fully loving best.

Psychologists say that when we think forgiving thoughts, we have no negative health or psychological side effects. Yet, forgiving is not something we should force ourselves to do so that God will save a place for us in heaven. Saying we forgive because the Bible tells us to, but still holding onto negative feelings, is *not* fooling our body. Forgiving is something we must do willingly, so that we may feel love in this moment, which is heaven here on earth.

The only people with whom you should try to get even are those who have helped you.

John E. Southard

Give up your worry that the past could have been any different. When you feel tempted to get even with someone who wronged you, change your focus and use your time and energy to "get even" with those who have helped you. Cherish the good people in your life.

Andy Grosmaire and his wife Kate helped get Conor's prison sentence reduced to twenty years, a much shorter sentence than is usual for his crime. Mr. Grosmaire said, "It frees us. The forgiveness frees us. It keeps us from going to prison with Conor." Take inspiration from Mr. Grosmaire and his family.

If Needed, Get Help

You may be reading this chapter and think, "I would like to open my arms to others, find the good in myself, and forgive those who have hurt me. I've tried, but I just can't do it!" Sometimes the thinking patterns we acquire as children are so habitual it is difficult to change them on our own. If we acquired poor eating habits in childhood we would have no issue seeking help to learn about good nutrition. If we emulated a sedentary lifestyle we saw modeled in childhood, we would have no shame seeking out a personal trainer. And if we established negative thinking patterns when we were young, being good to ourselves can easily include asking for help. We may need a professional to shake up our thinking so we can see things differently.

As a child, I learned to hold my feelings in, to appear stoic and strong. This strategy worked until 16, when my hair fell out. I had so much built-up, unexpressed pain over this experience, my emotional baggage became too heavy to carry. Getting relief meant going to therapy, where I learned new ways of thinking.

How do you know if you need therapy? For me, I couldn't find peace of mind at sixteen, and for many years afterward, I was often negative. When I got together with my friends, I wouldn't talk about the pain of my hair loss, because I was afraid I would start crying, which for me would be embarrassing. So, I would start spewing out other negative things that happened, or were happening, in my life. My friends would usually match my negative stories with their own stories. So, getting things off my chest felt temporarily good, but my friends were not professional therapists, who are trained in how to listen and help people with deep-seeded issues.

We all know if the car needs to be fixed, we talk to a mechanic, like my dad, who trained and practiced daily car mechanics. When we want to know what clothes are in style, we look at fashion magazines because they have professionals who spend their day scanning the world for trends in fashion. Yet, when we need help with a deep personal problem, and we seek out advice from friends, they can often be just as clueless as we are. They give us love, which we need, but they may not always be able to give us tools to help us love ourselves. Professional therapists practice teaching the tools of exploring and enlivening our own psychology.

The goal of therapy is not to make all our problems go away. As long as we are living, we will encounter challenges. Therapy does not make these challenges nonexistent. The goal of therapy is to give us insights, and learn coping skills. Therapy challenges the way we think, our "knee-jerk" reactions. They suggest useful ways we can learn to react differently, more positively. Past hurts can heal quicker, and we can feel good now with such knowledge.

People are more difficult to love, and sometimes not even approachable, when they are carrying baggage from past hurts. If you can't heal on your own, if you talk and hear your friends' support for you, but it's not helping, try talking with a professional therapist. Try talking with more than one to find someone who is the right fit for you and your personality. The ultimate success of therapy is to learn to love and have compassion for yourself. Therapy can help us lighten our load when good family and friends aren't enough, and we can begin to live the joyous life we are meant to live.

STOP COMPLAINING

Nobody wants to take along a complainer. Nobody wants to promote a complainer. Nobody wants to live with one. Nobody wants to be a partner of one. Nobody wants to have one around.
Jim Rohn

It's hard to love a complainer. When we consciously desire to love and be lovable, we need to stop complaining!

One afternoon, I tuned-in to Dr. Phil and heard him "tell it like it is" to a female guest. He suggested to her, **"It's time to stop complaining about what you don't want, and start asking for what you do want."** Whoa...what a mind shift. So many of us, myself included, know exactly what we *don't* want from others, but we're foggy about what we *do* want.

Since the day I watched that episode, instead of complaining about what I don't want, I try to identify what I *do* want, and ask for it. It is difficult for me, but I've gotten much more skilled by just practicing. In the workplace and at home, others are relieved when we make this shift. By communicating exactly what we want from others, we set everyone up for success because we have made our expectations clear.

Start today. When you catch yourself complaining, stop and rephrase your complaint as a request. A work complaint might be, "I deserve a raise!" Now, think about what you specifically want. Your request might sound like this, "I am an asset to our company because I have generated X amount of profit for us, so I deserve to make X amount of money now."

A complaint to your child might be, "You should have told me you had homework this weekend before 10 o'clock Sunday night!" She or he will be much more receptive to your request, "When you get home from school this Friday, let's look together at the list of all your weekend homework so I can help you get it done and we can have time to play too."

Another complaint at home might be, "Why does everyone dirty up the kitchen, and then leave the mess for me?" What is it that you do want? Rephrase your complaint as a request, "I would like for everyone to clean up after themselves. Don't leave the kitchen until you have put your dirty dishes in the dishwasher."

Many of us feel we shouldn't have to ask for what we want. Others should just know! Yet, people are not mind-readers. The clearer we are about our expectations, the more likely they will be met by others.

And it's okay if we don't know exactly what we want. The first step to requesting is simply to become aware of what we are complaining about. The second step is to think of the opposite of the complaint. The third step is to verbalize what we want to others, in a clear, plain way, so we can be easily understood.

Don't be a complainer, a downer, or a drainer. When we quit complaining, and ask for what we want, we are happier in ourselves, and we are much more lovable to the people in our lives.

WALK AWAY FROM NEGATIVE PEOPLE

In every person we meet there's this little piece of God in them and that's who you talk to. And that's the only person that you allow to talk to you. When something else is speaking, you walk away from that. If it's not good, if it's not love, you walk away from it.
Terrence Howard

While living in Pennsylvania, my daughters went to Sunday school every week. I loved Sunday school when I was a child, and decided I too, would begin going to the Sunday school adult class forming. I believe the reason for attending church is to grow into a more loving person. Yet, when I attended this class, it seemed the teacher wanted to teach us how to be more judgmental.

During the third week, the instructor began class by telling us, "Golfers should be in church on Sunday morning, not out on the course." I wondered, *Is he implying that because he is at church, he is better than them? Is he jealous he isn't golfing, but thinks he is pleasing God by being at church?*

After judging golfers, he started in on wealthy people, by quoting Matthew 19:24. "The Bible says, 'It is easier for a camel to go through the eye of a needle than for a rich man to enter the kingdom of God.' I suppose that means Bill Gates won't be getting into heaven!" *What?* I thought, *Does he personally know Bill Gates? Did they meet at the local diner for pancakes before church?* My guess is God is pleased that Mr. Gates employs hundreds of thousands of people and has given billions of dollars to charity!

By the time I got home that day, I was fuming. As I changed out of my church clothes into casual daywear, I realized that every week it took me an hour to get over being upset after this class. I don't like to be a quitter but this was not how I wanted to spend my Sunday mornings. What was being taught in class did not make me feel good. It was not love. So, I did quit, and although I encountered a few awkward moments in church when asked why I stopped going to class, I knew I made the right choice to walk away.

BEWARE, negative people suck the positive mental attitude right out of you and drain your energy. Whether it's a boss, co-worker, family member, neighbor, friend, or Sunday school teacher, be very selective about whom you choose to associate with. Negative people will bring you down.

A negative person can be difficult to convert to a positive thinker, and trying to do so is often futile. 1 Corinthians says, "Bad company corrupts good character more than good character influences bad company." I feel that means, in the time you spend with negative people, they will have more success bringing you down than you will have bringing them up. It is usually best to just walk away. Appreciate that they are human, and you love humanity, but don't let their experience drag you down.

On the eve of World War II, curators at the Louvre sent the *Mona Lisa* painting to the French countryside for safekeeping. They couldn't risk her being injured in the combat zone of Paris. For her own good, they had her "walk away" from negative people. She stayed in six different safe houses, hanging on bedroom walls so there would always be someone to keep her company. In 1945 she returned safely to her home in the Louvre. *Mona Lisa* now hangs in a bulletproof box kept at a constant 68 degrees. I bet she's glad she wore long sleeves for her portrait!

Mona Lisa, by: Leonardo da Vinci, created from 1503-1506, possibly continuing until 1517

Surrounding yourself with happy people improves your own chance of being happy, and being happy makes you oh, so lovable.

Don't Take Things Personally

*Others are going to have their own opinion according
to their belief system, so nothing they think about
me is really about me, but it is about them.*
Don Miguel Ruiz

Many people (again, myself included) try to live their lives being approved of by everyone. But politicians know that with two in the race, they only need an approval of 51% to win an election! And once they win, they still plan to work for as many people as they can, while knowing their work won't please everyone. Other people's opinion of you will be based on their belief system. It's not about you pleasing everyone. It's about what you can do for the people and situations that are important to you.

Here's a more local example: When my young family moved from Los Angeles to Columbus, Indiana, our good friend Kelly volunteered to help us unpack. In the kitchen, Kelly and I were knee-high in newspaper from unpacked dishes. Looking at the full countertops, I was proud of all the nice things I had acquired. There was the Noritake China and Waterford Crystal we received as wedding gifts, and our everyday dishes, trimmed in yellow and blue, which were replicas of those used by Claude Monet.

Kelly began unwrapping my set of vintage 1950's Fred Press bar glasses with fish motifs in metallic gold. I bought the retro set at a cool antique shop in Long Beach, CA. My plan was to someday throw a swanky dinner party, with Frank Sinatra playing in the background, and serve my guests cocktails in the tumblers.

As Kelly looked around, he commented, "Wow, you sure have a lot of dishes and glasses."

The tone of his voice was not that of someone impressed with my stuff. Kelly was a thirty-year-old single attorney who rented space above a storefront. His tone conveyed that all these "things" were excessive, even a burden. I saw then that my desire to accumulate things I thought were beautiful as a testimony to my sense of style and accomplishment was not universally understood, or admired, even by people I liked and who liked me. Everyone wants something a little different than others in their circle of loved and admired folk. What might have impressed my hip fashion design friends in L.A. might not impress my friends in the Mid-West. Suddenly the large amount of things fighting for space on the counter was a bit embarrassing because, if I looked through Kelly's eyes, I might be thinking, "Who needs all this 'stuff'?" But the truth was, I liked what we had, and it was okay, too, if Kelly didn't like it all as much as I did.

Everyone enjoys receiving compliments and being admired, but whether people approve of you or not depends on their belief system. Don't take it personally. I like popular and classical music. You might like country. I like fluffy white Bichon Frise dogs. My sister Teri likes black Dobermans. I like romantic comedies. My brother Dennis likes gross-out comedies. I like art museums. My friend Sue likes football stadiums. None of us are right or wrong, we just have different likes.

Spending our precious energy defending our choices makes us hard to love. Be lovable. Whatever someone's opinion of you might be, don't take it personally, especially when the difference in likes is with someone you love, who loves you too.

Now, finally, do you have to be loving and lovable all the time? No! There is a time and place for everything. I taught my daughters to be so kind that it was difficult for them on the soccer field. They wanted to "share" the ball. I loved them for their effort to be truly good-natured, but I had to embellish the lesson by explaining it's totally right to go out there and be assertive too, when the occasion calls for it. Go ahead and compete! Just play by the rules of the game and be loving off the field.

This applies to business, too. Don't let promotions pass you by because you are too "nice" to compete with or manage people. Giving someone a warranted poor review doesn't *mean* you are mean. As long as you are honest, fair, and respectful, you are doing your job. You can still be loving and lovable.

At the end of our lives we want to know two things:

"Have I loved?"   &   "Am I loved?"

One year from today, we will either be more loving and loved and therefore feel better, or less loving and loved, and therefore feel worse. In order to be assured that the answer to both of those questions above is yes, love people and be lovable today and keep building on that for a lifetime.

Nat King Cole, in 1947, two years after WWII, recorded a version of the song "Nature Boy," written by Eden Ahbez. These lyrics below, from that song, are just as true today as then:

The greatest thing
    You'll ever learn
        Is just to love
            And be loved
                In return

STEP #2

BELIEVE
YOU ARE
DESERVING

We are all a masterpiece with infinite
worth. When we genuinely believe
this, our life will change forever.
Susie Lawyer Briggs

Believe You Deserve Your Masterpiece

*Your chances of success in any undertaking can
always be measured by your belief in yourself.*
Robert Collier

During the years I attended Orleans Elementary School in Indiana, my mother drove the school bus. Early in the morning, my siblings and I were the first ones on the big yellow bus. Then on her route, Mommy would first pick up the kids who lived on the rural route out in the country, and next, the kids who lived in town. In town, on Center Drive lived a brother and sister, the boy a year older than me, the girl a year younger. Only God could have known that fifteen years later, Jonathan and Tammy would become my husband and my sister-in-law.

One morning, Mommy brought the bus to a stop in front of their large home (by Orleans standards) and Jonathan and Tammy ascended the bus steps. I remember nothing about my future husband from that day, but I vividly remember his sister like it was yesterday. As Tammy walked down the aisle of the bus, it became to me a fashion show runway. The ringlets of her perfectly curled hair bounced with each step. Sitting atop her head was a large bow made from the same blue floral fabric as her dress. And the dress...my goodness, the dress! It had a fitted bodice, and a full...*really* full, flouncy skirt. It was the perfect "twirling" dress. *If I had a dress like that*, I thought, *I would twirl around in circles so fast the skirt would swing waist high around me. I wouldn't care who saw my underwear.* Oh, the joy!

Mommy didn't have time to curl my hair in the morning. With five kids and a bus route that started when it was still dark outside, curled hair was not a priority. My clothes were adequate. Some new, some hand-me-downs, yet they didn't inspire my imagination like Tammy's did. I wasn't consciously aware of it at the time, but because Tammy lived in a large home, had curled hair, and wore beautiful dresses, I thought Tammy was better than me.

Because I attended middle school, high school, and college in Los Angeles, I forgot all about the girl with the twirly dress. However, Jonathan moved to L.A. after he graduated college and, as fate would have it, we began dating. We decided to spend our first Christmas together back home, in Indiana. His sister Tammy was coming home too. She was flying in after spending a semester studying abroad in England.

I desperately wanted to visit England…and France, and Italy. An art history course in college gave me an intense desire to see in real life the masterpieces from my textbooks. But with a small scholarship, student loan, and wages from my part-time job, I was lucky to just pay for college. A European vacation was out of the question.

Tammy's flight arrived just after ours, so we awaited her at the gate. We could barely see the top of her head over the holiday crowd. This time, Tammy wasn't wearing a twirly dress; she was instead wearing the latest styles from Europe. Although I wasn't consciously aware of it again, it had happened once more. I thought Tammy was better than me, and I was envious. She didn't have to work her way through college. She didn't have to live at home to save money. She got to study abroad. And, the salt in the wound, she was wearing clothes from Europe!

While in Orleans, I stayed with my cousin Susie (I have two cousins named Susie, this one is from my dad's side) and her beautiful family, and also spent a lot of time at Jonathan and Tammy's family home—the big one, from childhood. I observed how Tammy's mom doted on her; Tammy was her only daughter. She brought her coffee in the morning, gave her a hug before bedtime, and never let her walk out the door without telling her, "I love you."

As I said before, ours was not a physically or verbally affectionate family. Because Tammy was hugged and told she was loved, subconsciously I thought Tammy was more deserving of *being* loved. Subconsciously, *I thought Tammy was better than me!*

> *The person we believe ourselves to be will always act in a manner consistent with our self-image.*
> Brian Tracy

Before and after Jonathan and I got married, Tammy and I had a strained relationship. It takes two people to have a good, neutral, or bad relationship, and I came to understand my contribution to ours. Anytime Tammy said anything that I perceived as condescending, I got defensive, and set out to prove I was not inferior. Eleanor Roosevelt said, "No one can make you feel inferior without your consent." I gave Tammy my consent.

After years of soul searching, finally the thought that I was inferior slipped from my *subconscious* into my *conscious* mind, and I had an "aha" moment. *OMG, I **believe** Tammy is better than me.* Oh…what a horrible thing to admit to myself. (And what a horrible thing to admit to *you*.) But also, it was a relief to uncover this buried belief. I logically didn't believe myself inferior, but what counts is how we *feel*.

After my realization, I began noticing I didn't feel inferior to just Tammy, I felt inferior to *many* people. I had given more than a few people consent to make me feel inferior. I felt inferior to almost anyone who had more expensive clothes, a more expensive car, a bigger house, better education, more success in their career, or appeared to be more loved than I was. I also felt inferior to almost anyone who had hair. This made me feel inferior to basically everyone on the planet!

When I had this "aha" moment, I realized these beliefs had cost me precious energy trying to convince others, *and myself*, that I was just as good. Once I acknowledged these beliefs, and challenged them, I could see that I *was* just as good as anyone else. **When I had nothing to prove, my relationships improved.**

If you desire a friendship or romantic relationship with someone, but deep down don't feel you are worthy of them, then guess what, they won't feel you are worthy either. Believing consciously or subconsciously that we are inferior to anyone will not only sabotage our personal relationships, but we will also sabotage ourselves from reaching our dreams. Do you believe you deserve the relationships of your dreams? Do you believe you deserve to live the life of your dreams? Do you believe you deserve to live your life as a masterpiece? If you can't answer yes confidently right now, it's time to start believing.

We are what we believe we are.

C.S. Lewis

A few years ago, I didn't believe I deserved to live the life I dreamed of. While flipping through a magazine, I saw a photo of a talk show host in one seat and guest in another. The camera's point of view was behind the host and guest, so the photo showed the backs of their heads and the expansive audience looking at them. I had already begun writing this book, and imagined myself as a guest on this show discussing it. Knowing the power of visualization to manifest my dreams, I took a moment to see *myself* as the guest in the photo and imagined the audience looking at *me*. Suddenly, a surge of adrenaline shot through me and my heart rate spiked. I was nervous, and experiencing stage fright! *Why am I having this reaction?* I wondered.

As mentioned earlier, most people's number one fear is public speaking. Was this the cause of my anxiety? Yes, partially. Imagining the audience looking at me felt intimidating. But it was also something deeper. The more I thought about it, the more old beliefs came to the surface. *Who do I think I am, sitting on the stage like I'm someone special,* I thought. *My place is in the audience, listening to a guest who is more deserving than I.*

I knew that for me to finish this book, and perhaps someday be interviewed by a talk show host in front of a live audience, I would have to *believe* I deserved to be there. If I didn't, I would subconsciously sabotage my efforts so that I would never get in that uncomfortable position!

Take a moment and let the dream you have for your life come to your mind. Who are the people you see? What is your job? How do you feel? After your initial excitement, do you feel comfortable, or uncomfortable? This will give you a good idea of how deserving of this life you believe you are.

There are days when I myself think I am over-rated. But not today. Meryl Streep (Emmy acceptance speech)

What we believe we are, we become. Look around yourself. Look at your relationships and your environment; including your car, home, and workplace. Your beliefs about yourself put you there. It's not what we wish for in our life that manifests. It's not what we believe is possible that manifests. *What manifests is what we really believe about ourselves!*

How can we, starting now, begin believing we deserve fantastic relationships? How can we believe we deserve our wildest dreams to come true? Let's find out.

How to Believe Your Dreams Can Come True

1   Become conscious of why you *don't* believe you are deserving. Chances are, you picked up this belief in childhood.
2   Heal the belief that you are undeserving. When we match up feeling good today, with the belief that we are deserving of the best in life, then our dreams are allowed to become our reality.
3   Base your thoughts, words, and actions in believing. Rhonda Byrne, author of *The Secret*, writes about this: "To master believing, all you have to do is tip the balance of your thoughts, words, and actions, from 'not believing' to believing. The ONLY thing that can ever get in the way of manifesting what you want, is having more thoughts of 'not believing,' speaking more words of 'not believing,' and taking more actions of 'not believing,' than you are of believing. Base the majority of your thoughts, words, and actions in believing, and the law of attraction must obey you."

The mind is the limit. As long as the mind can envision the fact that you can do something, you can do it, as long as you really believe 100 percent.

David Hockney

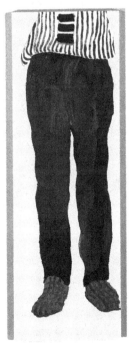

Self-Portrait, by: David Hockney © 1984/2005
Collection the David Hockney Foundation

Everything we want in life is because we think if we attain it, we will feel good. Whether that undertaking is a material object, a relationship or attaining a goal, our chance of success can be measured by our belief in ourselves. My relationship with Tammy improved dramatically when I no longer felt she was better than me, or that I had to attain what she had to feel good about myself. Attaining my goal of being a guest on a talk show discussing my book has yet to manifest. But believing I deserve to be there has given me the confidence to finish writing this book.

Believe you are as worthy as anyone ever born.
Believe you are worthy of receiving love.
Believe you deserve to be treated with dignity and respect.
Believe you are here for a purpose.
Believe you deserve for your voice to be heard.
Believe when you base the majority of your thoughts, words, and
    actions in believing, your dreams will become your reality.

When we master believing in ourselves, we master our lives.

10

Have a Happy Childhood

It's never too late to have a happy childhood.
Gloria Steinem

S itting on my sofa eating lunch, I tuned into a daytime talk show. The episode was about a sixteen-year-old runaway named Chloe. As the camera panned the outside of a run-down apartment building with bars covering the windows, menacing music played in the background. The talk show host's voice-over told me this is where Chloe lives with her physically abusive, twenty-something boyfriend.

Next, the camera took me into the television studio where Chloe and the talk show host were perched on tall chairs. With slouched shoulders, Chloe answered questions in a whisper, while trying to disappear behind her long, stringy hair. Through their dialogue, it was established that Chloe's dad was an alcoholic who emotionally and physically abused her. Home life was so painful that she felt she would have a better future by quitting school, running away, and living with her loser boyfriend.

How tragic!

I wanted to set my potpie on the coffee table, extend my hand into the television, and invite Chloe to sit down on the sofa next to me. We needed to have a conversation, she and I.

"Chloe," I would say, "When your dad calls you names, and hits you, it's not your fault. Make sure you hear that. *It's not your fault.*

His actions have nothing to do with you. His parents probably treated him this way. **He doesn't know how to do better. But you deserve better.** You deserve to be treated with love and respect from your dad, your mom, your boyfriend...*everyone.* You deserve to be loved as much as any child ever born. You deserve a blindingly bright future!" I would give her a big hug, and then help her climb back into the television to sit upon the tall chair in the studio.

At the beginning of this book, we talked about how artists must learn to develop solid drawing skills to begin to create masterpieces. A good drawing is the foundation upon which to build a successful painting. To create a masterpiece with our lives also requires a good foundation. Part of that foundation consists of having solid self-esteem. A happy childhood is the foundation for a child to successfully transition into adulthood with good self-esteem that is built through learning self-love, confidence, and the tools to make a positive contribution in the world.

If you didn't have a happy childhood, or there are areas that could have been improved upon, I have good news. It's not too late! No matter what your age, you can start today to build the same foundation a happy childhood gives you. Learning that you deserved to be loved, you can take responsibility for your happiness now and give yourself all you needed to have a happy childhood.

The supreme happiness of life is the conviction that we are loved.

Victor Hugo

Like Chloe, many of us have deep emotional wounds from our childhood. We may have grown up noticing other children who were being treated with love and respect by their parents, and wondered why those children received those positive energies when we didn't. "Why do they deserve to be loved, and not me?" we may have asked.

When we frequently hear or observe the message that we are not good enough, or *don't* hear the message that we *are*, we begin to believe we don't deserve better, and we carry this low self-esteem into adulthood.

Off we go into adulthood, and when we encounter people or

circumstances that make us feel the way our family did, it feels familiar, like home, like we deserve it. Is it any surprise that Chloe broke free from the hands of her abusive father, and ran straight into the arms of an abusive boyfriend? What else might we expect? This is what she has come to think she deserves, and sadly, what feels familiar.

People create the results they think they deserve.
Dr. Phil McGraw

If your family loved you, and showed it through their words and actions a majority of the time, you grew up likely believing you deserved to be loved. Chances are you treat yourself with dignity and respect and expect others to do likewise. You probably create positive results in relationships and your work, and believe that you deserve this success.

Parents have the privilege of assisting God in a miracle when their children are born. The fact that God created you, the fact that you were born, makes you deserving of your parents love. You deserved for your parents faces to light up every time you entered the room. You deserved to be hugged and to hear, "I love you." You deserved to feel safe, to know an adult was there protecting you. You deserved praise for doing good and to be told you contribute to this world in a way that no one else can. You deserved to have a future with no limits.

If you didn't receive these messages as a child, you are not alone. Jack Canfield, author of the *Chicken Soup for the Soul* books says, "A lot of people feel like they are victims in life, and they'll often point to past events, perhaps growing up with an abusive parent or in a dysfunctional family. Most psychologists believe that about 85% of families are dysfunctional, so all of a sudden you're not so unique." If you were a member of the 15% of functional families, thank your lucky stars *and* your family! If you belonged to one of the 85% of the dysfunctional families, let go of resentments that it should have been different. It's not too late to *parent yourself.*

Although Disneyland defines anyone ten years or older as an "adult," and charges you accordingly, the age at which one is typically considered a legal adult in the United States is eighteen. If you are over eighteen, *you have been raised.* Whether good or bad, your family's job is done, and now it's your turn. What do you choose to do? Will you blame your family for all that isn't right in your life and continue being a dysfunctional person? There's nothing unique about that. Like it or not, if you want to feel good, you have to get over it. You're an adult now. You can *choose* to be happy!

There is an expiry date on blaming your parents for steering you in the wrong direction: the moment you are old enough to take the wheel, responsibility lies with you.
J.K. Rowling

Look back at THE ART OF HAPPINESS SCALE. When you were growing up, what was the typical mood of your family? You may discover that it is the same as your typical mood as an adult. Was everyone usually in a good mood, and your family often compared to the Brady Bunch? Was the mood in your family neutral, sometimes good, sometimes bad, but usually hovering in the middle? Or, were members in your family typically in a bad mood? If this last experience seems like yours, you may be blaming them for why your life isn't better today. Depressed, angry, pessimistic thoughts can begin to be learned in childhood. Thinking negative thoughts will keep you feeling bad today, and your negativity will be a burden on you and everyone in your life. It's time to take responsibility for your own happiness. If you're over eighteen, tell your family in person or just in your own mind, "I am responsible for my own happiness and success. It is my job, not yours. You are hereby absolved of responsibility." Then, practice it. Practice being happy and successful regardless of what they did that may have been hurtful.

It's so much fun to have a happy childhood *now.* We're not a child anymore, waiting to be walked to the playground. We're an adult, and the *world* is our playground. Think back to your youth and recall the things that you wanted but didn't get. Don't let these thoughts make you feel bad; instead feel excited. You are responsible for your own happiness, and have the rest of your life to make your childhood dreams come true. Here are ideas to get you started fulfilling your childhood wishes:

FAMILY

The family you came from isn't nearly as important
as the family you're going to have.
Ring Lardner

Maybe the family you came from was wonderful and you wouldn't change a person. Or maybe, you needed more family members who demonstrated their love for you with their words and actions. Search out people who treat you the way you *wish* your family had. Healthy relationships come with love, joy, companionship, satisfaction, fun, adoration, and appreciation. Family members don't have to be limited to those who share your DNA. The people you call your family today may include anyone who supports and wants only the best for you.

PETS

When you were a child, did a friend have a pet that you wish you had? Did you want a Siamese cat that would look at you with her beautiful blue eyes? Did you want a golden retriever who greeted you with his wagging tail when you got home from school? Or maybe you had a pet, and don't want that responsibility as an adult. Because I had asthma and allergies as a child, having an indoor pet wasn't an option in my family. Now, playing with my two hypoallergenic Bichon Frises shoots me to the top of THE ART OF HAPPINESS SCALE!

MATERIAL THINGS

I first saw the *Gene Marshall Doll* in a glass display case in New York City's famous toy store FAO Schwartz. Inspired by Hollywood's Golden Age, she is a fictitious movie star from the '40s. Also offered was a wardrobe for Gene based upon movie-styled fashions from the '30s, '40s, and '50s. How *glam*orous!

I received her for Christmas during my adulthood because my family appreciated that I was so fascinated by her. My daughters and

Gene Marshall Doll
These "Mandarin Mood" Chinese silk pajamas are circa 1946. The ensemble will be perfect poolside for the dragon boat races at Gene's upcoming dinner party. The star's coveted invitations have been mailed out from the palm-tree-lined entrance of the Hollywood Station Post Office. Expect to receive yours any day!

I have had hours of fun changing her outfits to match the seasons. Showing my neighbor Carol the ensemble Gene wore for an exotic, Oriental themed dinner party she threw, Carol exclaimed, "Your doll has more fun than you do!" She was right. I needed to play dress up *myself* and throw a dinner party!

Was there some *thing* you wanted as a child? A special doll, perhaps? Or, the Slinky toy spring that makes that "slinkety sound"? Maybe a kite, a Lite Brite, or Shrinky Dinks? I wanted prettier clothes, which I now give myself when within my budget. I also wanted a canopy bed, and am grateful every night when I climb into mine now.

Sometimes material things *can* bring us a degree of happiness, especially when we are fulfilling a yearning from childhood.

TRAVEL

*My adult life has been dedicated to the fulfillment of
my childhood dreams…I dreamed of Africa.*
N. A. Noel

Nancy Noel is a beloved Indiana artist best known for her sensitive portraits of Amish children and ethereal angels. In 2000, Nancy went on a trip to Africa. She stopped at a small hut, serving as the local preschool, looking for children to paint. The school's teacher declared "We would like to name our school after you because you are our first visitor." Nancy continues to support her namesake school and has watched it grow from 60 to 250 children and counting.

Maybe you dreamed of Europe, or a road trip across America, or simply driving across town to visit relatives. I'm guessing there is someplace that has been calling your name for years. It's only polite to visit someday and say, "Hello, I finally made it!"

OCCUPATION

Did you want to be an artist? If so, take a class in your area, or just pick up some pencils and paper from the store and start drawing! Place something to draw in front of you, such as fruit, a jar, or a vase. Pay attention to the light source, and how it creates a shadow on the opposite side of the object. Begin your sketch with a simple outline of what you see, then start adding a bit of shadow and light. Have patience and *enjoy* the process. Similarly, did you want to be a psychologist, a teacher, or an entrepreneur? God gives us desires, and we won't be truly happy if we spend another day ignoring our longings. You don't have to quit your day job. Fit the study of your pursuit into your life in any quantity you can.

EXTRACURRICULAR ACTIVITIES

Participating in extracurricular activities while in school is not only fun but, among other things, develops social skills, which college admissions officers and employers are looking for. As adults, we can become so busy in our everyday lives that we don't make time to explore new things for ourselves. Perhaps it may be too late to win a gold medal in gymnastics, but it's not too late to excel at and enjoy other extracurricular activities.

Sports
   Participating in sports can provide exercise, camaraderie, and fun. Join a weekly hiking group or tennis league. Take a yoga class or swim at a public pool. My friend Shari recently ran her first marathon at the age of 46. She said, "Accomplishing this makes me feel like I can accomplish anything!"

*It took me four years to paint
like Raphael, but a lifetime
to paint like a child.*

Pablo Picasso

Self-Portrait with a Palette, by: Pablo Picasso © 2013 Estate of Pablo Picasso / Artist Rights Society (ARS), New York

The Arts

While in school, many of us were exposed to a variety of the arts. Now that we are adults, there are many ways we can still enjoy them. It's fun to be an observer and attend plays, musicals, music concerts, dance recitals, and poetry readings. And it's even more fun to participate! Try a painting workshop, writers group, or a photography class. One of my favorite success stories of enjoying art as an adult is my friend Jane Shauck. I met Jane when we were in our 20s and she was in management at Sylvania. Jane began dabbling in photography and it took off. Now in her 40s, the Wedding Photojournalist Association (WPJA) in 2007 ranked Jane No. 1 in Connecticut and No. 20 in the world!

Volunteer

When self-help author and motivational speaker Anthony Robbins was a boy, one Thanksgiving Day his family was going to, "at best, scrape together a meager meal on this day of feasting." There was an unexpected knock on their door, and a man delivered to them, "a huge basket brimming with every conceivable Thanksgiving delight: a turkey, stuffing, pies, sweet potatoes, canned goods— everything for a holiday feast!" In that moment, he learned that people really *can and do* care about other people they don't know, who need help. He swore to someday give back to others in a similar way. The Anthony Robbins Foundation's International Basket Brigade now provides baskets of food and household items to approximately 2 million families in need every year.

You and I may not be able to give on the grand scale of Anthony Robbins, but we can always give back within our means and time. Look back to your childhood and think of acts of kindness people showed you, *or* a need you had that *wasn't* fulfilled. Emulating the positive, and helping others in ways you once needed help will give you a great starting point of how to make a difference in other people's lives that is meaningful to you. Volunteer work is an extracurricular activity that heals our soul as well as benefiting the community.

PLAY

Play keeps us vital and alive. It gives us an
enthusiasm for life that is irreplaceable.
Lucia Capacchione

The essence of childhood is play, and it seems too often the essence of adulthood is work. We can maintain our enthusiasm for life if we put "play" on our "to-do" list.

To this day, I actualize my sense of play, and the hope that comes with it, when I make a wish and throw a penny in a fountain, when I make a wish and hold my breath while driving through a tunnel, and when I make a wish before blowing out candles on my birthday cake. Yes, I've made a lot of wishes! Wishes are fun! And they bring positive ideas into our conscious thoughts.

I also love reading the children's and young adult books my daughters bring home. I've never read an author more creative than J.K. Rowling in her *Harry Potter* series. And I enjoy Edward Cullen in Stephanie Meyer's *Twilight* series. He's *hot*!

I still actually roller-skate. I rarely pass a swing without swinging or a slide without sliding. Every Christmas Eve my daughters and I put on pajamas, fill our thermal travel mugs with hot chocolate, and drive around town looking at Christmas lights.

If all of these things I do are not similar to your sense of fun and play, be creative! Set up a weekly play date with your friends. Try board games, and serve Shirley Temples! (Fill the glass with ginger ale and add a splash of grenadine. Garnish with a maraschino cherry.) There *is* time in our schedule for fulfilling our adult responsibilities *and* playing and acting young forever.

Ralph Waldo Emerson wrote, "It is a happy talent to know how to play." No matter what it is, if it makes you feel happy, you're not too old to play, and playing makes us all more creative. Invite play into your life now.

When I was 14,
I was the oldest I ever was.
I've been getting younger
ever since.

Shirley Temple

Self-Portrait with Shirley Temple, by: Sir John Lavery

You may or may not have had an ideal childhood. Most people didn't. But it's not too late to have a happy childhood now. Take time to remember all the good and bad in your childhood and then see, whatever you lacked as a child, you can fulfill now! You deserved as a child, as you do now, to know that you are loved and worthy of all the goodness the Creator has to offer. You're an adult now. Let go of blame for lack in the past and find your fun and love now. A happy childhood is always available!

Fulfill the Dreams of Your Youth

Keep true to the dreams of thy youth.
Friedrich Von Schiller

List, in any order, the things you wish you had received in childhood but didn't.

_____

_____

_____

_____

_____

_____

_____

_____

_____

This is your valuable list of what to do for yourself to have a happy childhood today. You now have a bright and shiny plan for fun!

Happy Birthday to You!

The greatest gifts are those we give ourselves.
Sophocles

On my 34th birthday, I was not celebrating, I was doing laundry. The smudged window in my laundry room displayed a bleak, January sky in Pennsylvania. Leaning over to toss wet clothes from the washing machine into the dryer, I wondered, *What am I doing? This is my special day and I'm inside doing housework!* My husband had planned no extravaganzas. Our five-year-old was at kindergarten, and our two-year-old was napping; I could hardly expect these little ones to pull off a birthday bash. I lived three thousand miles away from family, and had only just begun to make friends in my new community; it seemed too early in those relationships to call for a party. So, I moved through the remains of the day folding clothes, taking care of the girls, and cleaning the kitchen floor. As a day I might recall from my past, this one was destined for the "Totally Unremarkable" folder. Ordinary days are nice and useful, and good in general, but wouldn't it be better if our *birth*days were memorable?

My birthday falls right after the holidays. It can be a hard time, a down time, for many people. Maybe you're like me: by the beginning of January, I have over-eaten, over-spent, and over-entertained myself. I also feel spoiled by the gifts I've received from loved ones.

The problem is, when my birthday arrives in January, I resent it when no one, including myself, makes an effort to celebrate my special day.

Getting into bed that night, on that unremarkable birthday, I realized the only person who could give me permission to take the day off from housework was *me*. The only one who knew what could make me happy on the day I grew a year older was *me*. *But, but, but...* I thought, *before having children I made myself happy on my birthday. Now I want to spend my energy making them happy on theirs.* Yet, honestly, aren't there enough hours in the year for both? It's not the job of family or friends to make my birthday a memorable one; it's a real pleasure when they do, but it's not really their actual *job*. I'm an adult. If I want a great birthday and no one has yet suggested plans to make that happen, it's mine to make it so by telling people, and of course the people I share love with will respond. Before falling asleep, I decided that in 365 days things would be different. I would look forward to the day with eagerness, not look back on it with regret.

Women are often fantastic at honoring the birthdays of others. When a baby is born, we often see a blue or pink balloon tied to a mailbox, and it's most often put there by a woman. I've even secretly tied balloons to friends' mailboxes on their birthday, and I've tied them to my mailbox for my daughters' birthdays. My girls have had Princess Parties, Make-Over Parties, Magic Parties, Tropical Parties (which included playing in the hot tub in 20 degree temperatures in February), Pool Parties, and Sleepover Parties. All of this was to make them feel good, because they are special to me. As adults, we deserve the same care and attention, and we can give it to ourselves—people we love will share in the joy and fun.

Children want to know the day they were born is special. When my friend's daughter Brittany was a little girl, one birthday she walked with her mother into a large department store. She looked up and saw helium balloons for sale, bobbing on the ceiling. She turned to her mother and said, "How did they know it was my birthday?!" She recognized that her family saw her birthday as special, and was happy to think the world might know it too.

For many children, their birthday ranks right up there with

Christmas, the most famous birthday recognized in history. Like the birth of Jesus, your birth was also a miracle. If your mother conceived one month earlier or later, you as you know yourself to be wouldn't even be here. Be glad God chose you as you are!

Another important point: when creating joy for your birthday, celebrate the day in a way that makes *you* feel special. Only you know what that is. What do you enjoy? Hiking in a park? Getting together with friends? A spa day, perhaps? Writer Sarah Ban Breathnach shares her birthday rituals in her book, *Simple Abundance*.

First, I take a soothing bath… Then I go alone to my bedroom… My favorite music is playing in the background…and beside my bed is a bouquet of my favorite flowers. I put on a brand-new nightgown and get comfortable in my freshly made bed. Then I offer a personal psalm of thanksgiving for my life… Next I ask for a birthday gift that only the Giver of Good can bestow: to conceive a wonderful new dream or plan; to realize a dream delayed; …to find a new friend; to achieve a long-sought goal… I sip a glass of champagne, then slowly open a beautifully wrapped gift from my authentic self. And of course, it's the perfect present.

Ban Breathnach doesn't wait for someone else to make her birthday special; she knows the greatest gifts are those she gives herself.

Happiness on our birthday does not fundamentally come from a mailbox full of cards, receiving expensive gifts, or planned festivities by a loved one. These things are nice, but not essential for our happiness. They are icing on our cake. (We all benefit, however, by learning to spread icing on someone else's cake. We teach people how to treat us, and it's important to teach those in our life to celebrate events that deserve recognition, to make others feel good. This helps us all become less self-centered and open ourselves to sharing joy.) Real happiness on our birthday comes from treating ourself with unconditional love, from knowing we deserve to be treated specially by ourselves first. It comes from celebrating being on the earth the past year and being eager to make our next trip around the sun.

Happy Birthday to You!

(Write in your birth date here.)

Today you are you! That is truer than true!
There is no one alive who is you-er than you!
Shout loud, "I am lucky to be what I am!
Thank goodness I'm not just a clam or a ham
Or a dusty old jar of sour gooseberry jam!
I am what I am! That's a great thing to be!
If I say so myself, HAPPY BIRTHDAY TO ME!

Dr. Suess

Theodor Geisel (Dr. Seuss), by: Everett Raymond Kinstler
© 1982 Collection: Hood Museum, Dartmouth College

Looking outside ourself for happiness sets us up for disappointment. Expecting people to *make* us happy is equally a setup for disappointment, because even people we love who love us are not going to "get it perfect" every time. Going inside ourselves to ask *what* fulfills us, wholesomely and beautifully, is how happiness is born. If you have expectations for your birthday, as I do, we can take responsibility to go to bed content on that day. And, when we make the effort to fill ourselves with self-love, we appreciate the caring gestures of our loved ones more deeply. Believe you deserve to have a truly *happy* birthday! The greatest gifts we receive are those that we give to ourselves.

My last birthday I thought, *I'm treating myself good this year. I'm getting a pedicure!* While relaxing in the messaging chair having my toenails painted, my phone buzzed with a new text message...

Amy:	happy birthday Annette! hope you're doing something fun
Me:	I'm getting a pedicure...right now!
Amy:	then why are you texting? Enjoy it!

STEP #3

ENVISION YOUR FUTURE

The best way to predict the future is to invent it.
Alan Kay

Tell Me What You Want

Yo, I'll tell you what I want,
What I really, really want.
Spice Girls

When was the last time you allowed yourself to want what you really wanted? When have you allowed yourself to want what you really wanted, and you wrote it down, or said it out loud? I know one thing about you for sure: you are reading this book because you hope to create a future that is more joyful than your life today. Step #1 is to Feel Good now, and Step #2 is to Believe you deserve all the good the Creator has to offer. Step #3 is Envision Your Future. To envision your future, you have to be very clear about what you want. You have to be honest about what you want, what you really, really want!

Most of us are good at knowing what we *don't* want. We don't want to be overweight and not fit into our favorite clothes. We don't want to be poor and unable to live the lifestyle we desire. We don't want to be unappreciated and ignored by our significant other. Think about it, during most of our conversations, we could be singing, "Yo, I'll tell you what I *don't* want, what I really, really *don't* want."

What keeps us from allowing ourselves to want what we really want? In one word…FEAR! Motivational speaker Les Brown says, "Too many of us are not living our dreams because we are living our fears." We shrink our dreams because we are afraid our dreams won't come true and we will be hurt. Some of us even fear success because we fear the stress it might bring to continue to be successful. If our dreams do come true, we fear some people may not like us, or we're afraid we will have to work 24/7.

I considered shrinking my dream of living in a large home while house hunting in Indiana. After seven years of home improvement projects, combined with a seller's market, we sold our home in Pennsylvania for double the price we bought it for. Relocating to a state where homes were less expensive meant that for the first time in my life, we could afford almost any size home we wanted. There was one drawback; I was afraid one of my friends would judge me for buying, or even *wanting*, a big house. I had heard her make condescending remarks about people who lived in large homes, and I was afraid if I were one of those people, I would lose her friendship.

But, I really, really wanted to live in a large home. When my magazine subscriptions arrived, it wasn't the art magazines that I couldn't wait to flip through, it was the interior decorating magazines. I dreamed of having my own studio with north-facing windows, a guest room for out-of-town family and friends, and a large kitchen, perfect for entertaining. After months of house hunting, I chose to fulfill my dream of living in a big house, even though I feared losing my friend. And, during the four years we lived on Eagle View Court, I was prolific! I wrote and painted in my studio, I hosted countless overnight guests, and threw many fabulous parties!

Are you denying or putting off your dreams because you are living your fears? Do you want to lose weight but are afraid you'll just gain it all back? Do you want your dream job, but are afraid of the public speaking it requires? Do you want to start working on your wildest dreams but are afraid your loved ones will just laugh?

A French fashion designer who lived her dreams, not her fears, was Gabrielle "Coco" Chanel. In 1895, when Gabrielle was 12, her mother died of bronchitis. Her father sent her two brothers to work as farm laborers and Gabrielle and two sisters to live at a convent that was, "founded to care for the poor and rejected, including running homes for abandoned and orphaned girls." From these humble beginnings

Chanel went on to create the high fashion Chanel brand. She said, "I invented my life by taking for granted that everything I did not like would have an opposite, which I would like." Chanel didn't want to be constrained by a corset, so she designed deluxe casual clothes suitable for sport and leisure. She didn't want her hands occupied carrying a hand held bag, so she created a purse with a stylish chain strap to be worn over the shoulder. She thought it distasteful to walk around with millions of dollars worth of jewelry around one's neck, so she popularized her own brand of elegant costume jewelry. By knowing what she wanted (and didn't want), Chanel became the only fashion designer to make *Time* magazine's list of the 100 most influential people of the 20th century!

One evening a few years ago, three girlfriends and I were at my house enjoying a stimulating conversation over a bottle of wine. I spontaneously asked them, "If you could have anything you want in your life, right now, what would it be?" Louise, Robin, and Julie immediately smiled and their eyes became wide with a mixture of excitement and fear, but they were game to play. We went around our circle sharing and learning fascinating things about each other.

Louise started us off and said, "I would like to go to Amsterdam in the springtime to see the tulips in bloom."

I was next and said, "I would like to go to New York in the springtime, and sit in the front row at a fashion show."

Robin said, "I would like to go to an Opera."

"I would like to go to Fiji," said Julie.

It felt liberating to tell others what we wanted. We enjoyed ourselves so much we went around our circle again, and again.

Louise: "I would like to truthfully know love."

Me: "I would like to bring inspiration and joy to huge numbers of women."

Robin: "I would just like to commit to something!"

Julie: "I would like to earn a six figure income in my business."

The most courageous act
is still to think for yourself.
Aloud.

Coco Chanel

Coco Chanel, by: Annette Hackney Evans

Louise: "I would like to work at an AIDS orphanage in South Africa. I'd be entirely focused on my work, with my hair only in a ponytail, and I'd wear a t-shirt and flats." If you knew Louise, you would know she rarely leaves home without her hair styled, cleavage showing, and high heels on!

A lot of people are afraid to say what they want. That's why they don't get what they want.
Madonna

Me: "I would like to finish my book and have it be on the *New York Times* Best Seller list."

Robin: "I would like to go to Buenos Aires. I would dance on the beach in a long, flowing, white dress, while bossa nova music played in the background."

Julie: "I would like to lose weight."

Louise: "I want an Aston Martin convertible."

Me: "I want a convertible sports car too. On Christmas Eve, I'd put the top down, pile it high with blankets, and my girls and I would do our traditional driving around looking at lights."

Robin: "I want to be able to trust other people more."

Julie: "I want to be a mom."

Our thoughts were honest, intimate and revealing. We were having so much fun and we continued through the evening exclaiming more and more things we really, really wanted.

Start thinking about what you want. Be fearless. The sky's the limit! To get you started, I'll share 25 things I want in true Chanel "say aloud what you want" style.

25 THINGS I REALLY, REALLY WANT...

1   Sit in the front row at a New York fashion show.
2   Bring inspiration and joy to huge numbers of women.
3   Be on the *New York Times* Best Seller list.
4   Own a convertible sports car.
5   Own a real, authentic, Chanel jacket.
6   Win an Academy Award (I'm not choosey about the category).
7   See both of my daughters graduate from college.

8   Have my hair grow back!

9   Have a meaningful conversation with Oprah Winfrey.

10 Own my dream home.

11 Have my dream studio where I enjoy painting and writing.

12 Weigh 125 pounds for the rest of my life.

13 Be a multi-millionaire.

14 Have lots of free time to play and create.

15 Visit Baden-Baden, Germany, where Grandma Frances' grandparents immigrated from.

16 Love openly.

17 Allow in love from others.

18 Grow closer and closer to God.

19 Do a portrait painting demonstration in front of an audience.

20 Make a lasting contribution to my hometown Orleans, Indiana.

21 Have family and friends who are happy, interesting and fun.

22 Stay true to me…and never give up my power.

23 Live in a way that makes my daughters proud to say I'm their mother.

24 Leave this world a better place than I found it.

25 _____

(Space for a new desire on its way!)

I WANT THESE THINGS, AND BETTER!

Wow! Saying what I truly want is huge. I feel exposed, vulnerable, and bold! I may never achieve all the things on my list. An Academy Award…come on, what's the chance? But hey, it would be fun! I would like a shot at being on the Oscar's Best Dressed list. **Even if my chances are practically nonexistent, without saying what I want, my chances are *completely* nonexistent.**

Now it's your turn. Write down what you really want in your life. Don't censor yourself. These aren't concrete goals; these are things you think would be fun and good for you. For more ideas, look back to your list of things you wish you had received in childhood. If the thought of someone picking up this book and reading your list makes you uncomfortable, make your list on a separate sheet of paper. Write down, as quickly as they come to you, 25 things you want in your life. Ready...Set...GO!

25 THINGS I REALLY, REALLY WANT...

1_____

2_____

3_____

4_____

5_____

6_____

7_____

8_____

9_____

10_____

11_____

12_____

13_____

14_____

15_____

16_____

17_____

18_____

19_____

20_____

21_____

22_____

23_____

24_____

25_____

I WANT THESE THINGS, AND BETTER!

How do you feel? Exhilarated? Scared? The fascinating thing about wanting what we really want is, the more we think about our dreams, and write them down and say them out loud, the more comfortable we feel with them, and the more real and attainable they seem.

Now that you have allowed yourself to want what you really want, you may be asking, "How on earth will I manifest these 25 things?" Here is one of my all-time favorite quotes that expresses that concern:

> *Most of us have never allowed ourselves to want what we truly want, because we can't see how it's going to manifest.*
> Jack Canfield

Yes! Hallelujah! During our lives, we tend to shrink our dreams because we don't know how they are going to manifest. Do you think Coco Chanel knew how she would rise from an impoverished childhood to be asked in 1931 to travel to Hollywood and costume starlets...for *$1 million?* No! She just had the courage to say, and go after, what she wanted.

It is not our job to have all the answers. Do we want to live our dreams, or live our fears? If we choose to live our dreams, we need to turn over how they will manifest to God. We must have faith that God will listen, and opportunities for us to take to help us make our dreams come true will become available.

Let me share an example with you. Last year, I became exceptionally lackadaisical in my eating. My sweet tooth was out of control and all the waistbands on my jeans felt two sizes too small. They were literally painful to wear. At that point, I saw three choices to correct this problem:

#1 I could shrink my dream of my body image, and resign myself to the idea that the older I got, the chubbier I would get. I could think, *I'll just sort through my closet and donate anything too tight to charity, so I won't be reminded every day of what I can't wear. Then I'll buy some new clothes for my chubbier body.*

#2 I could shame myself into action via my b - - - h voice to myself: *Have you looked in the mirror lately? You look six months pregnant! And my God, the muffin top...you're embarrassing me! Quit putting food in your mouth, get your butt to the gym, and burn off some of that fat!*

#3 Or, I could turn over my desire to lose weight to God, and have faith that He will show me how to manifest my desire through kind action to myself, rather than self-aggression and anger.

When you have choices, choose the path to your destination that will be the most enjoyable. I chose option #3 above. I went in my closet and pulled out my tightest, most suffocating jeans. I hung them on a hook so they were the first thing I saw when opening the door. I prayed, *God, I don't know how I am going to fit into these jeans, but I have faith that you will show me how to manifest my desire through kind action to myself.* I was calm and content as I left my bedroom and continued my day.

Nothing happened for a few days, but every time I went in my closet and saw my jeans, I no longer felt discouraged, I felt calm and optimistic. I would think, *It's going to feel so good when I can comfortably button you!*

I visited my friend J.P. in Los Angeles, and we walked from her home over to a popular outdoor mall for lunch. While there, we bumped into her neighbor, Ruth, whose little girl is also inflicted with alopecia. Ruth told me of a new diet her daughter's doctor put her on, one that was supposed to help with alopecia. The diet consisted of lean meats, fruits and vegetables. *Interesting*, I thought, as J.P. and I headed to a restaurant, and for dessert enjoyed a slice of flourless chocolate cake topped with a layer of chocolate cheesecake loaded with chunks of milk chocolate and finally a layer of chocolate mousse.

That same week, during my 7:00 am Tuesday Toastmasters meeting, fellow Toastmaster, Michelle, gave a wonderful speech in which she told of a new diet she was on. The diet mimicked what cavemen survived on, and consisted of eating lean meats, fruits and vegetables. Hmm…it sounded exactly like the diet that was supposed to help with alopecia.

I had forgotten all about the jeans hanging in my closet when I got home and ordered the diet book online. The diet, which is similar to a gluten-free diet, claims our immune system is compromised by the carbohydrates and sugar we consume. In an effort to improve my immune system, and grow hair, I went on the diet immediately. After two months, my hair was not growing back, but I did fit comfortably into my jeans! I didn't know how it was going to happen—how I was going to lose weight in a way I enjoyed and felt positive about, rather than felt tortured by. I just had faith that God would help me figure it out, and He did. All I had to do was ask.

God gives us desires and dreams for a reason. Don't downscale yours out of fear. Think about what you want, write down what you want, and say out loud what you want. Do this until it becomes a habit. Don't concern yourself with how it will manifest. Sit back, relax, and know that soon the day will come when you will look back in awe at how God rearranged things so you can have what you really, really want.

Find Your Calling

The place God calls you to is the place where your deepest gladness and the world's deep hunger meet.
Frederick Buechner

YOUR DEEPEST GLADNESS

YOUR CALLING

THE WORLD'S DEEP HUNGER

F inding our calling is the most important discovery we will ever make. Once we know what it is, we may let it shape our entire life. It will give us deep gladness, and feed a deep hunger in the world.

Aren't we all a little envious of people who have always known their calling? They seem comfortable in their own skin, and their lives have a focused direction. You can become one of these people now. It's never too late to find your calling.

WHERE YOU **WILL** FIND YOUR CALLING	WHERE YOU **WON'T** FIND YOUR CALLING
Inside yourself	Outside yourself
Looking for clues from your childhood	Looking for clues from society
Listening to your inner voice	Listening to your family and friends
Serving others	Serving only yourself

There are many reasons we haven't yet discovered our calling. Maybe our parents wanted us to do or be something other than what we naturally are. They may have wanted us to fulfill *their* dreams. Perhaps our friends and teachers influenced our dreams. It's normal to spend time doing things we get praised for, and that stroke our ego, even if it doesn't give us a deep gladness. Or, maybe we had to trade in our dreams to increase our marketability in the workplace. We've made our choices based on what can bring in the most money. If any of these examples resonate with you, and you have a gnawing feeling that you're not following your calling, keep reading...

In the Book of Exodus, God spoke to Moses through a burning bush. He said, "So now, go. I am sending you to Pharaoh to bring my people the Israelites out of Egypt," Exodus 3:10. God gave Moses his calling: to lead the Israelites out of Egypt and into Canaan. But what about you and I? I've done a lot of gardening and God has never spoken to me from within a bush, burning or otherwise. I have, however, heard from God in the following ways, and so can you.

156

LOOK FOR CLUES FROM YOUR CHILDHOOD

Our calling is something that has been with us all our lives. When we were children, we naturally gravitated towards it, it made us happy. Often, as adults we have forgotten our calling, and yet to find true happiness we need to remember it.

"The first story I finished was when I was six years old," said British novelist Joanne "Jo" Rowling. Although she always wanted to be a writer, her parents, both from impoverished backgrounds, thought that writing would never "pay a mortgage." To please them she went to college to study Modern Languages. Quickly, and without their knowledge, she switched her major to Classics.

In 1990, four years after graduating, Rowling was on a four-hour-delayed train trip when she conceived the character Harry Potter, a scrawny, bespectacled boy attending a school for wizardry. Sadly, in December of that same year, her mother passed away.

1993 was a bittersweet year for Rowling. She gave birth to a daughter, but 4 months later separated from her husband of 1 year. Rowling was diagnosed with clinical depression and saw herself as the biggest failure she knew. Referring to that time in her life, in her 2008 Harvard commencement speech, she said:

Failure meant a stripping away of the inessential. I stopped pretending to myself that I was anything other than what I was, and began to direct all my energy to finishing the only work that mattered to me. Had I really succeeded at anything else, I might never have found the determination to succeed in the one area where I truly belonged. I was set free, because my greatest fear had been realized, and I was still alive, and I still had a daughter whom I adored, and I had an old typewriter, and a big idea. And so rock bottom became a solid foundation on which I rebuilt my life.

I would like to be remembered as someone who did the best she could with the talent she had.

J. K. Rowling

Portrait of J. K. Rowling, by: Stuart Pearson Wright

Failing gave Rowling the courage to entirely devote herself to her childhood passion, writing. Pursuing her calling took Rowling from living off of welfare benefits to multi-millionaire status, and internal happiness, within 5 years. *Harry Potter* has been the best selling book series in history, and the movies the highest-grossing *film* series in history! Clearly, J. K. Rowling fed a deep hunger in the world that we didn't even know we had!

Pursuing your childhood passion may or may not earn you millions, but it might bring you a long, fulfilling life. When Ronnie Hackney, "Daddy" to me, was a little boy in Indiana, he enjoyed fixing any toy that was broken. Cap pistols and BB guns were his specialty. In his teen years, he fixed bicycles and motor scooters before graduating to automobiles. He often worked on his friends' bikes, scooters, and cars, and said, "I would do it for pay, but if they didn't have any money, I would do it anyway." By nineteen, he was a full-time employee at an auto garage. He couldn't believe he got paid to do what he enjoyed doing.

Daddy has been a mechanic his whole life, and his last job was working on police cars for the Los Angeles Police Department. When he retired from the LAPD, his title was Senior Mechanic and Garage Supervisor. To this day, he still works on cars, and at 76, his current project is restoring a 1930 Ford Model A Coupe.

What made you happy as a child? Think back, especially to the time you were ten-years-old and younger. I suggest this period because for many of us, this was likely a time before the outside world strongly influenced our behavior in terms of our habits and thoughts of a career. Did you play with baby dolls, and were fulfilled pretending to nurture them? Was math your favorite subject because you liked it when numbers seemed organized? Did you look into the mirror, singing into your hairbrush like it was a microphone, imagining yourself as a charismatic performer?

When I was ten years old, my schoolteacher announced that "Dress Up Day" was coming, which meant that we were to come to school *dressed* up as what we wanted to be when we *grew* up. When the day arrived, I went to school as an artist, wearing a white painter's smock (I borrowed my sister Teri's smock; they were very stylish in the '70s) with paintbrushes sticking out of the pocket. What would you have gone to school dressed up as on Dress Up Day?

Look for clues in your childhood to see what gave you your deepest gladness. Author J. D. Salinger wrote, "There are no big changes between ten and twenty—or ten and eighty, for that matter." Daddy can testify to that. Look back to when you were a child to find your calling. There have been no big changes in what activities make you happy between then and now. You were born with gifts, and you have them to bring joy to yourself and others.

LISTEN TO YOUR INNER VOICE

None of us will ever accomplish anything excellent or commanding except when he listens to this whisper which is heard by him alone.
Ralph Waldo Emerson

When other people tell us what we should be doing with our lives, that is from a source outside of ourselves, an *outer* voice. When we listen to the whisper heard by us alone, that is from a source inside ourselves, our *inner* voice. We may find our calling when we listen to this inner voice. So, how do we hear it? How does it speak to us? We can hear it by asking ourselves the following three questions:

Question #1: *Where do I feel most like me?*

Several years ago, my friend Bernadine e-mailed me the following, "Some people are **working backstage**, some are **playing in the orchestra**, some are **onstage singing**, some **in the audience as critics**, some are **there to applaud**. Know who and where you are."

I read this and thought, *Duh... doesn't everyone want to be on stage singing? Doesn't everyone want to be the star of the show?* I e-mailed her back and said, "Bernadine, which do you want to be...a stagehand, musician, singer, critic or an audience member?

Her response surprised me, "I want to be in the audience. I am there to applaud!"

What? That was her first choice? Bernadine is a talented person and would be wonderful at any of the other options. But she wants to be in the audience to applaud, because that's where she is comfortable, and feels joy. Bernadine is the friend I told you about earlier who has a natural gift of seeing the Divinity in everyone, so it makes sense she enjoys applauding. Thank God we all have different callings because the stage would get pretty crowded if we didn't.

In the production of life, what part do you play? Are you onstage singing a duet with me? Or are you sitting in the audience, with Bernadine, applauding? Know and *feel* who you are and where you feel best.

In an interview, singer-songwriter Pink was asked where she feels most like herself. Not skipping a beat, she turned to the interviewer, and with a mischievous smile on her face, answered, "On stage." No shocker there.

Question #2: *What activities give me energy?*

When we are participating in activities that are aligned with our calling, we get a big energy boost. Begin to pay attention to what activities invigorate you, and which activities are draining.

Take a look at your calendar. Do you look forward to attending the Board of Directors meeting on Tuesday? While driving home from the meeting, will you be happy you went, or will you wish you hadn't just wasted two hours? What about the presentation you are giving to the sales force on Friday? Will you enjoy preparing for and delivering your information, or do you procrastinate and dread the whole thing?

After observing your energy levels for a week, if possible, decrease activities that make it seem like the clock stands still, but definitely try to increase activities where you get in the zone and time flies.

Joseph Campbell said, "Follow your bliss." A synonym for bliss is happiness. What makes you happy? You are the only person who can answer that question. When we follow our happiness, we feel energetic, and the life force travels through our body. We can be sure our inner voice is telling us we are closely aligned with our true nature. Our bliss, our happiness, is our calling. **Follow your calling.**

Question #3: *What is my heart telling me?*

This morning I had *The Baroque Collection of Classical Music* playing in the background while I was writing. This collection has music by several classical composers, many of whom have names I cannot pronounce. They usually play in the background without my notice. But, when Pachelbel's "Canon in D" began, my fingers quit typing. I found myself sitting still, listening with my eyes closed to the entire four minutes and fifty-eight seconds piece. Of course, I heard the music through my ears, but I felt it in my heart. It created a beautiful aching in my chest. I began visualizing my daughters on their wedding day, walking down the aisle to "Canon in D," with me in the front row crying with joy. Katharine Hepburn said, "You can't change the music of your soul." This means, we can't change what our heart responds to. A classical music buff might tell me that clearly Albinoni's "Adagio" is a much finer piece of music. But my heart told me what I liked. And I listened. Mesmerized.

Another example of how we may hear our heart talk to us is while we're reading. Haven't you had the experience of reading along, and suddenly, a passage seems to *jump* off the page? It resonates with you? You pause, and reread it. And then reread it again. When this happens, our heart is telling us, "This is something very important. Consider this. Remember this."

Have you ever been with a loved one, maybe a child, or even a pet, and they do something so incredibly cute that your heart literally skips a beat? This is probably not a heart arrhythmia; this is the feeling of love. It is our heart's way of telling us what is important in our life.

Many of us have noise in our life from the time we get up until the time we go to bed. Which do you think we'll hear the loudest, an inner whisper, or the television? Will we hear an inner whisper, or the radio, or people talking? Whatever silence we can create in our daily life, whether that is one minute, or thirty minutes, will reward us with the ability to better hear our inner voice. Pay attention, listen, and we will hear this whisper, which is heard by us alone.

SERVE OTHERS

Each of us should use whatever gift he has received to serve others.
1 Peter 4:10

Sometimes we can get caught up in thinking our purpose in life is financial gain, or fame, or something equally big and dramatic. We may use the clues from our childhood and information from our inner voice to pursue material things that we believe will make us happy. Material things can be fun, but they will often only give us short-term pleasure. After our basic needs are met, accumulating more material things to fill holes in our emotions never provides lasting happiness. No matter how much we acquire, we soon want more because we are not listening to the inner voice. Most people work at making or selling things they don't see value in, in order to buy things that don't add value to their life. Love what you do and you will acquire things you truly value and love.

The truest fulfillment comes when we recognize our gifts, and then use them to serve others. Author Stephen King said, "If God gives you something you can do, why in God's name wouldn't you do it?" He is good at writing horror fiction. I personally think he writes it too well. I stopped reading his books when I was no longer able to pass by a dark window at night! Currently, the genre of romance is the largest and best-selling fiction category in North America. I'm guessing Stephen King doesn't wake up in the morning and say, "Well, I'd like more financial gain, so today I'll try my hand at writing romance." It's silly to imagine him thinking that! King writes what he is good at, what he is passionate about, and he is serving others who enjoy an adrenaline rush reading his books and watching his movies.

In 1997, Amy Wrzesniewski, Ph.D. and Professor of Organizational Behavior at Yale School of Management, researched the effects on people when they saw their work as a: a job, b: a career, or c: a calling. The people in the study were from various occupations, from so-called "menial jobs" to high-level professionals. It's not surprising to learn from the study that people who saw their work as "a job" did it only to earn money, and felt their work offered no other reward. People who saw their work as "a career" had a deeper, personal investment. They marked their achievements through the increase in money they earned and also through advancement in their field. People who saw their work as "a calling" showed passionate commitment to "work for its own sake." They focused on not only the money they earned, but also as much on how their work affects the world. Those people who felt their work was "a calling" had a significantly higher sense of well-being than those who saw it as "a career," and certainly those who saw their work as "a job." Those who saw their work as "a calling" were affected by that sense of purpose: they were happier.

To find your calling, take what you are naturally good at and makes you happy—your *gifts*—and use your gifts in a way that improves the lives of others. You'll improve your own life as you do.

LOOKING FORWARD TO YOUR PAST

We looked for clues from our childhood to find our calling, and we can also look ahead to our golden years to imagine what we want to accomplish in our lifetime. I've read self-help books in which authors encourage us to write our own obituary. That's too morbid! I don't want to think about my funeral. Let's have a party instead!

Imagine a party is being thrown in your honor to present you with a lifetime achievement award! The invitations went out, and 156 of your close, personal family and friends have RSVP'd that they are attending! The party is being held downtown at The Masterpiece Gallery. How will everyone fit?!

Lifetime Achievement Award!

Please join us for a
celebration in honor of life artist

_____
(your name here)

The *Masterpiece* Gallery
Saturday, June 12th, 6:30 pm

_____
City   State   Country

The night has arrived. It is Saturday, June 12th, and the party starts in an hour and a half. You go to your closet and pull out the dress you bought just for tonight's occasion. You shimmy into the dress, and then admire yourself in the mirror. Is the hemline a tad too short for someone in her eighties? Maybe. But who cares, you still have fantastic legs! Your gaze moves up to your face, and you wonder at the years that have passed. You have wrinkles, sure, but you have something else, too. There it is, that sparkle in your eyes that has never left. Your inner light is radiating out, which has only grown stronger.

You arrive at the gallery early, before anyone else. Standing outside, looking at the twinkling white lights hanging in the windows, and all the balloons within, your heart skips a beat. This is all for you. And tonight, you feel deserving. The front doors are swung open, awaiting your arrival, and you climb the steps and enter.

The Masterpiece Gallery has five rooms: The Health Room, The Legacy Room, The Philanthropy Room, The Material Things Room, and The Family & Friends Room.

The Health Room

Standing in The Health Room, you notice grass beneath your feet, and the calming sound of a tinkling fountain in the center of the room. On the walls are photos of you doing physical activities you have enjoyed throughout the years. People have always told you they admire your energy. In the photos, are you playing tennis? Are you walking along the beach? Are you cycling in a pack with other enthusiasts?

What are the physical activities you are participating in, in these photos in The Health Room? Write them below.

_____

_____

_____

The *Masterpiece* Gallery

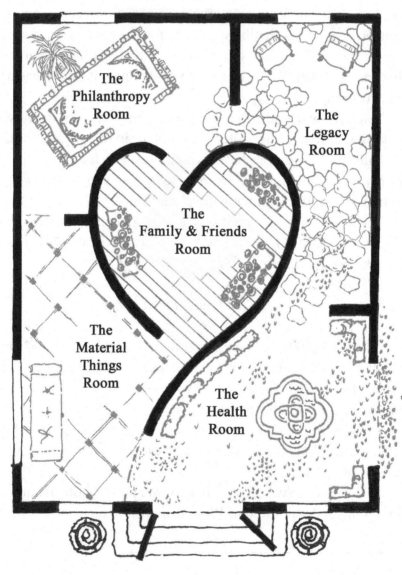

The Philanthropy Room

The Legacy Room

The Family & Friends Room

The Material Things Room

The Health Room

You feel a deep gratitude that these activities have contributed to your current excellent health. You fish a few pennies out of your purse, make a wish to enjoy continued good health, and toss them into the fountain.

The Legacy Room

Walking through the grass, a stone path appears. You follow it to The Legacy Room. You take a seat in the corner of the room to look at the photos of you lining the walls from floor to ceiling. There are images of your life's work. Your calling. You are awed. Did you really accomplish this much? What are you doing in the photos? Are you speaking to groups of hundreds? Do pre-school children surround you? Are you sitting behind a desk at your family's business?

What are you doing, and where are you, in these photos in The Legacy Room? Record below.

_____

_____

_____

You consider yourself blessed to get to spend so much of your life doing work that brings you happiness. You stand up...elegantly smooth your skirt...and walk to your right into The Philanthropy Room.

The Philanthropy Room

You stand in the middle of the room, on a lush, colorful, beautifully woven rug. You turn slowly to view images of all the people you have helped in your life. Through their photos, they gaze at you with grateful faces, all people whose lives have benefited because you exist. Your work, and your donations of time and money, have touched so many lives. What is the age range of most of these people? What is their nationality? Are there more girls or boys, women or men?

Who are the people in these photos hanging in The Philanthropy Room, and how have you helped them? Make some notes.

_____

_____

_____

You are humbled that your calling has brought happiness to so many. You say thank you to these beautiful people and step onto the marble floor of The Material Things Room.

The Material Things Room

Balloons are bobbing on the ceiling, tied with colorful streamers twirling down. On the walls are photos of all the things that money can buy that have genuinely encouraged and supported your vision of yourself and your happiness. You laugh when you see the photo of you and a loved one playing in the water on a vacation. Fond memories flood back inspired by photos of the homes you've lived in. What else are there photos of? What kind of cars, if any, have you owned that you really loved and enjoyed? Are there photos of family heirlooms you intend to someday hand down, such as jewelry, paintings, or antique furniture, each with its own special meaning and memory? Are any from the "25 Things I Really, Really Want" list?

What material items have you enjoyed during your life that are shown here in The Material Things Room? Write these below and use additional paper if needed.

_____

_____

_____

Yes, when taken in all at once, you have enjoyed a wonderful amount of abundance. You take a deep breath and appreciate all that you have now and had in the past. You say softly, out loud, "Thank you." Then, you walk across to the warm, hardwood floor in the heart of the gallery, The Family & Friends Room.

The Family & Friends Room

Standing in the center of the heart-shaped room, you feel the love surrounding you. Massive bouquets of red roses sit atop three tables and the smell is heavenly. The photos on the walls are all the loved ones you had throughout your life. Many you have loved for years, and a few are new arrivals. These are the people you have loved, and they have reciprocated by loving you. While the other rooms in the gallery were important, this is the one that gives you the most special feeling. These are the people who will show up tonight and celebrate you.

Voices and laughter coming from the gallery entrance bring you back to the moment. You smile broadly as you head towards the door. Who are the people walking in with gifts in their hands? Is it your significant other, your children, or new friends from the dancing class you're taking?

Who are the people pictured in The Family & Friends Room? Write down their names.

_____

_____

_____

As the party begins, you realize you have never felt so loved in your life. Yours truly is a life lived well and well lived.

By finding clues from our childhood, listening to our inner voice, serving others, and looking forward to our past, we can find the place

God has called us to. In the next chapter, "Your Definite Purpose," you will learn how to take your calling and make it the central focus in your life. Let's get started answering our calling and earning our Lifetime Achievement Award! It's all part of the plan to turn your life into a masterpiece.

Your Definite Purpose

Definiteness of purpose is the starting point of all achievement, and its lack is the stumbling block for ninety-eight out of every hundred people simply because they never really define their goals and start toward them.
Napoleon Hill

apoleon Hill was born in 1883 and grew up in a one-room cabin in Virginia. Despite modest beginnings, he became a best-selling author, an advisor to presidents, a motivational speaker and, to this day, an inspiration to millions.

At the age of 25, Hill was a young reporter at *Bob Taylor's Magazine,* a popular periodical at the time that gave advice on how to achieve power and wealth. He was given a golden assignment: to write a series of articles about famous and successful men and women. His first interview was to be with Andrew Carnegie.

Scottish-American industrialist Andrew Carnegie was the founder of the Carnegie Steel Company. In 1901 he sold the company for $480 million, which is the equivalent of over $13 billion in 2013. He was also a philanthropist, and I was surprised when just last month I discovered I have benefited from his good deeds. While in Indiana for a few days, I visited one of my favorite childhood places, *The Orleans Public Library.* I was looking for a few art or decorating books to feed myself visual food, when I saw a plaque above the fireplace that read, "This building the gift of Andrew Carnegie 1915." Researching further, I found that a Carnegie library is one built with money donated by him. When the last grant was made in 1919, there

There is one quality which one must possess to win, and that is definiteness of purpose, the knowledge of what one wants, and a burning desire to possess it.

Napoleon Hill

Napoleon Hill, by: Annette Hackney Evans

were 3,500 libraries in the United States, nearly half of which were built with construction grants paid by Carnegie. If he were alive today and standing in the middle of *his* imaginary Philanthropy Room, he would see a photo of me on the wall, a person who's life has benefited because of his existence, because he made available to the public a building full of books.

Meeting Andrew Carnegie was a turning point in Napoleon Hill's life. He found that Carnegie believed that the process for success was simple, something *everyone* could learn. Carnegie was impressed with Hill and asked him to interview over 500 *more* successful men and women, and put his findings together in a book. Hill accepted the challenge with gusto.

The final version of Hill's research was *Think and Grow Rich*, published in 1937, and now one of the bestselling books of all time. Hill found that the starting point of all achievement, the first step toward getting whatever it is you desire, is having a *definite purpose*. If we decide what we want most in our lifetime, and keep this definite purpose in mind on a daily basis, we will move towards the life we desire.

The Statue of David

Having a definite purpose (knowing what you want) and a desire to possess it is necessary to turn your life into a masterpiece. Having a definite purpose is also necessary in order to *see* a masterpiece.

Sitting in my dark art history classroom at CSUN, our professor projected onto a screen slide after slide of Renaissance art. Up came the *pièce de résistance*, Michelangelo's statue, *David*, looking like a modern day movie star. I sat up straight and thought, *Oh my, I have to go to Italy to see him in person!* I lived in Los Angeles, and David lived in Florence, Italy, so meeting him would have to wait until I could afford the time and money for the trip. But I was so infatuated with David, at that moment I developed a definite purpose: to one day see him *in person*. Happily, I could keep in mind exactly where he lived, to help the clear focus of my goal to visit him:

Gallery of The Academy
Via Bettino Ricasoli, 58/60
50122 Florence, Province of Florence, Italy
055 238 8612

Nine years passed, and when I was 27 years old, B.C., my husband and I were financially able to plan a trip to Europe. The package deal included stops in London, England, Paris, France, and Rome, Italy. Not included was Florence, Italy. But being 173 miles north of Rome, it was only a short train ride. I was so excited! My dream of seeing David was finally, after all these years, coming true.

Our first stop was London. Our sightseeing included the official London residence of the British royal family, Buckingham Palace. We even took a tour to their official country residence, Windsor Castle, in Windsor, County Berkshire, England. In Paris, we visited the maison of Da Vinci's Mona Lisa, The Louvre, the granddaddy of public art museums. Next stop, Rome. The first day, we visited the Vatican, home to the Pope, and The Sistine Chapel, with the glorious painted ceiling by Michelangelo.

The second day in Rome, the time had come. We were purchasing tickets to take a train ride 173 miles north to Florence. I was going to the home of

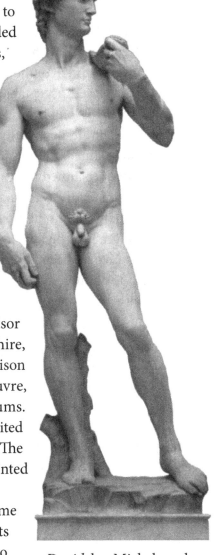

David, by: Michelangelo, 1501-1504

177

who I was there to see, the home of *David*. It seemed surreal that I was about to, on that very day, view him in person.

After disembarking the train, we quickly went to the Gallery of the Academy, located in the historical district of Florence near San Marco Square. My heart was beating out of my chest as we entered.

We walked in…turned a corner…then…I caught my breath. There he was.

Gorgeous.

As good-looking in real life as he was in photos.

Seventeen feet tall with six pack abs as hard as marble.

Throngs of fans surrounded him. We weren't allowed to touch him, but photos were acceptable.

I remembered, long before, in that art history classroom, I had developed a definite purpose, which became the starting point to getting what I wanted: this moment, this day, this sight. I had defined a goal, thought, planned, and moved towards it. Then, nine years later, I put myself halfway around the world, standing at David's feet, and I have photos of him to prove it, as the culmination of that plan!

Back in Rome, as our trip came to an end, I threw a coin in the Trevi Fountain. Traditional legend says this means I am ensured a return visit to Rome. My bags are always ready to be packed for a reunion with the statue of *David*, anytime! I know I will see him again, that's a definite purpose.

THE TWO ENVELOPES

Andrew Carnegie told Hill that he believed every person (that includes you and me) comes to earth with the equivalent of two sealed envelopes. One is labeled *Riches* and the other labeled *Penalties*. We get to choose which one to open and live by.

The Two Envelopes Given to You at Birth

This envelope contains the *Riches* you may enjoy if you take control of your mind and direct it to your clear purpose.

This envelope contains *Penalties* you must pay if you don't take control of your mind and direct it.

Riches	Penalties
1 Good heath	1 Ill health
2 Peace of mind	2 Frustration, discouragement
3 Labors of love	3 Indecision and doubt
4 Faith and confidence	4 Fear and worry
5 Hope, positivity, earnestness	5 Envy, angst, hatred
6 Material riches you choose	6 Poverty, lack, want

We have a great power under our control. It is the power to control our own minds and to direct our mental energies to whatever it is we want in our lives. Now that you know you have a choice, which envelope will you open? *Choose the Riches!*

YOUR DEFINITE PURPOSE

While there are many different kinds of success, Napoleon Hill studied how some people were able to become financially successful. He studied more than 25,000 people over the course of twenty-five years, and found that only 500 of these, or 2%, were wealthy. Interviewing these five hundred millionaires is what led Napoleon Hill to conclude that definiteness of purpose is the starting point for all achievement. These were the people who actually defined their goals and started towards them. They are the ones who opened the *Riches* envelope. That means that 98% of people will never achieve what they want in life, simply because they don't have a definite purpose. They opened the *Penalties* envelope. Are you one of the 2% of people headed towards what you want most in life, or are you one of the 98% without a plan?

My desire to see Michelangelo's *David* was a medium-sized goal. It took time to plan the trip, time to earn the money to pay for the trip, and time to go on the trip itself. Our definite purpose is a lifetime goal. Yet, achieving any goal, regardless of the size, works the same: we first have a desire, a focus, a definite purpose. If I hadn't desired to see *David*, I would never have *seen David*. The desire comes first, then belief, then action, then success.

When we think about every person we know who has achieved lasting success, we discover that each of these individuals had a definite, major purpose. Napoleon Hill's definite major purpose was, "Assembling and publicizing the principles by which great individuals achieve enduring success." At the time of his death in 1970, *Think and Grow Rich* had sold 20 million copies. He achieved his purpose, and more. Today is the day you and I begin achieving our purposes!

Up until a year ago my definite major purpose was to, "Provide my daughters the love needed for good self-esteem and the discipline required to reach their full potential. My purpose is to be a good mom and raise good citizens." Now, Camille is in college, and Isabella is a senior in high school. They are both in their last phases of childhood, so my definite purpose of raising them well is shifting. My new definite major purpose is to "Bring inspiration and joy to huge numbers of women through my writing, speaking, and art."

What is your definite, major, purpose right now? What do you want *most* for your life right now? Look back to Chapter 13, and revisit *The Legacy Room*. The photos on the walls were of you engaged in your life's work. What were you doing? This is your major desire in life, your calling, your definite major purpose. Write it down here again, and add more details if you like!

_____

_____

_____

You've done it! You've written down your definite major purpose. Congratulations! This is a milestone in your life. Stand up and clap for yourself. Jump up and down. Celebrate!

You have now opened the envelope entitled "Riches." I grant you official membership into the 2% Club, members who, according to Napoleon Hill, have a definite purpose. You have defined your current main goal for your life, that which is most important for you to achieve in your lifetime, and are ready to move towards it. Michelangelo said, "Every block of stone has a statue inside it and it is the task of the sculptor to discover it." You have a calling, a definite purpose inside you. It is your task to chisel to discover it, and then use your energy to move towards it.

The Crucifixion of St. Peter, by: Michelangelo, 1546-1550
Cappella Paolina, Vatican City, Rome, Italy
Michelangelo painted a self-portrait in this
detail of the fresco (man with turban).

Imagine

*Before a painter puts a brush to his canvas he sees his picture
mentally. It is the mental concept that he externalizes with the
help of paint and canvas. If you think of yourself in terms of a
painting, what do you see? How do you appear to yourself? Is the
picture one you think worth painting? You are what you think you
are. You create yourself in the image you hold in your mind.*

Thomas Dreier

Feeling good will draw good things into our life. Visualizing will
draw *specific* good things into our life. If we aren't intentionally
visualizing what we want, we will continue to get more of what
we are remembering from our past, or currently observing in the
present.

God is always answering our prayers, and our prayers are anything
we are thinking about. We may ask ourselves, are our thoughts asking
God to give us more of what we had in our past, to keep giving us
what we are presently getting, or to give us a new future full of the
things we *truly* want for ourselves?

Dr. Phil McGraw said, "If you live in the past then your past
becomes your future." Obviously we can't actually live in our past,
but if we are continuously thinking about it, it's the same as if we
are. Replaying, over and over in our mind, personal home movies
from our past will draw more of that into our present life. If the
home movies are good, and we don't want our lives to change, then
continuing to think about our past is a positive motivation for our
future. If we are recalling things we didn't like, it's time to create new
home movies.

A phrase that has become mainstream is "live in the now." This means, be conscious of what is happening around you and inside you…right now. Pay attention to the cooing turtledoves outside your window, the gorgeous floral arrangements you see through the florist shop window, or the warmth in your stomach after drinking hot tea with honey. It is also as simple as relaxing and taking three… deep…breaths. Living in the now is a healthy and spiritual habit. It is challenging to be present all the time. Our mind is eventually going to wander. So, it is our job to direct our thoughts towards a positive goal daily, regardless of what other thoughts get in the way. Learn to draw your thoughts back to your goals every day. After only a short time, it will be second-nature to do so, and the goals will manifest as successes.

When we learn how to intentionally visualize, we draw into our lives the image we hold in our mind, and we have the ability to imagine what *will* take us beyond our current circumstances.

LIFE'S COMING ATTRACTIONS

Imagination is everything.
It is the preview of life's coming attractions.
Albert Einstein

Between 8th and 10th grade, I took acting classes in North Hollywood with film and stage actor Francis Lederer. He taught an acting style that was an extension of the Stanislavski method. He asked us to notice that each of us has an internal dialogue, accompanied by images, constantly flowing through our mind. Mr. Lederer explained that to be a believable actor, we must create an internal *monologue* for our character, accompanied by images that would be flowing through her mind. Whatever character we are playing, we must, in our mind, conjure up the thoughts and pictures she would be imagining.

Let's imagine you and I are acting in a scene together. You are Anna, and I am Beatrice:

ANNA

Hey, how was that concert you went to? It was at the
Walt Disney Concert Hall, right?

BEATRICE

OMG, I forgot to tell you about it? The conductor...
um, what's his name? Gustavo Dudamel! He was
unbelievable!

ANNA

Really? He's as dynamic as people say?

These are simple lines. What's important is whether I believe
them well enough to convince the audience that Beatrice has been
to this concert hall and seen that conductor. If I'm just reciting my
lines without conviction, without earnest feeling that I have been
to this place and seen this thing, no one will be convinced. To be
believable, I have to imagine what Beatrice would be imagining.
Even if I, personally, have never been to the Walt Disney Concert
Hall, I would have to create images in my mind as if I had been
there to give Beatrice realism. In my short dialogue with Anna, I, as
Beatrice, imagine my memory of the Hall's exterior, with its giant,
shining, slanting shapes that look like silver shavings fallen to the
ground. I "remember" sitting in the dark theater, with lights shining
on the L. A. Philharmonic, illuminating the dark fabric of Gustavo
Dudamel's suit, while his arms swing through the air as he conducts
the music. I "recall" the violins, flutes, and oboes in the beautiful
music of ...perhaps...*An American in Paris.*

Along with the images, I have to give Beatrice feelings. Beatrice has
enjoyed the concert, therefore, she's happy. She's elated to remember
it as she recalls her experience to Anna. It was a magical evening that
she will remember the rest of her life. If I were able to stay in character
and use my imagination and emotion in this way, my performance
of Beatrice would be believable to an audience.

185

Using this acting technique, we can also create the future life we desire. We can imagine all the details of the life we want—you can imagine yourself as the person you know yourself to be right now, comfortably buttoning your jeans at your ideal weight. You can imagine the view out of the windows of your dream home. You can imagine holding hands while taking a walk with your soul mate. To make these things realities, we must be intentional about the positive images we hold in our mind, or negative ones may automatically take control.

I used to be a worrier. I could take an innocent situation and with my imagination, I could see it turn tragic. Maybe you can relate. Pretend your significant other isn't home when he said he would be. You think:

He said he would try to be home by 6:45 tonight, but he's not here yet. That's okay. I'm running a little late myself. If we leave by 7:00 we'll still have plenty of time to make it to the 7:35 movie.

Okay, now it's 6:53. Where is he?! It's Friday night, and if we're late, we'll be stuck sitting in the front row of the theater! The movie has been out awhile; maybe the theater will be empty. But just standing in line to buy the tickets can take ten minutes on a Friday. Where is he? He always does this. Why hasn't he called? Why does he always think it's okay to keep me waiting? He knows I hate missing the beginning of a movie.

> Worry is a misuse of the imagination.
> Dan Zadra

Now it's 6:58. Oh my God...I wonder if he got in an accident. He certainly wasn't texting and driving, because I haven't received a text! But, many other people text and drive. Did he get hit? ...What was that? Do I hear a siren? Is he in an ambulance right now being rushed to the hospital? Are his injuries permanent? How long will he need to be in the hospital? Do we still have time to make the movie???

At 7:00 pm sharp you hear the garage door go up, and then the laundry room door opens. In he walks with a bouquet of flowers.

"Hi Honey," he says, "It took a little longer than I thought to stop and buy you flowers. Are you ready? I don't want to miss the previews."

Worrying is using our imagination to create images in our mind of what we don't want. Worry leads to anxiety, which can lead to a host of negative physical and emotional side effects. Worry and stress can cause a loss of energy, insomnia, and over-eating. Psychological side-effects may include panic attacks, low self-esteem and obsessive thinking. Socially, anxiety may have a negative effect on our relationships and even cause us to avoid people. If what we imagine is a preview of life's coming attractions, is this what we want to attract?

Let's use our imagination to intentionally create images in our minds that make us feel good, that make us excited to be alive.

IMAGINATION IS MORE IMPORTANT THAN KNOWLEDGE

In Chapter 12, when you made your list of "25 Things I Really, Really Want," I did not ask you to determine *how* you might get them. When we use our imagination to visualize something we want to manifest in our life, *first* comes the desire. Second comes the knowledge of how we will acquire it.

For the past two years, in my imagination I could visualize this book completed. I could see my self-portrait on the cover. I could feel the weight of the book as I flip through the pages. I could envision myself at book signings in local bookstores. Did I have the knowledge needed to make these things happen? The answer is a resounding… NO! My college education is in fine art and fashion design. I was urged several times to quit writing, to stick with what I know. I have heard, "You're a better painter than a writer." And, "If you must write, choose a subject you have schooling in, such as art and fashion, *not* self-help." These comments were logical, but every time I was at my easel painting, sentences ran through my mind like the ticker & news band at the bottom of a CNN show. The more I resisted these unwritten thoughts, the less enthusiastic I became about my art, and life in general.

*I am enough of an artist to
draw freely on my imagination.
Imagination is more important than
knowledge. Knowledge is limited.
Imagination encircles the world.*

Albert Einstein

Albert Einstein, by: Max Wulfart

Reminding myself *daily* that my imagination to create this book was more important than my lack of knowledge, is what made it possible for me to finish. While a bachelor's degree in writing, or a Ph.D. in psychology, would have been helpful, they weren't essential. Life events, such as living with alopecia, have caused real pain in my life. You have been through hard times too. I believe by sharing with you the life lessons I have learned, I may help make your journey more joyful. That's what motivated me to write.

From where I sit now, at the table in my dining room, I have learned the steps to write and publish this book. I learned them by hearing God's desire for me to write the book, beginning the process, and then listening for God's guidance throughout the journey. I don't yet know the steps I will need to take to sit behind a table at a book signing. I just have the faith that my imagination and God's help will pull me closer and closer. Draw freely on your imagination. Don't limit your dreams because of limited knowledge. Knowledge comes *after* we begin pursuing our dreams, not before.

Carry the Picture in Your Mind

No one is an artist unless he carries his picture in his head before painting it, and is sure of his method and composition.
Claude Monet

We cannot give birth to anything that we haven't first conceived. In Chapter 4 and 11, I shared with you Sarah Ban Breathnach's writing from her wonderful book *Simple Abundance*. This book was her third, and it was conceived while on her own personal search for happiness. Thirty publishers rejected the book, and Ban Breathnach cried herself to sleep many nights. Then one afternoon in 1994, she took a *New York Times* Best Seller list, whited out the title in the number one spot and typed in *Simple Abundance*. She then changed the date to read "June 1996," and pinned the list up on the bulletin board above her desk, where she looked at it every day. *Simple Abundance* hit number one on *The New York Times* Best Seller list two months before her prediction, and went on to sell five million copies.

As life artists, we must conceive the life we desire, and then carry these pictures in our mind. (Or pinned to a bulletin board above our desk.) When we don't allow our imagination to defeat us, we allow God to use our imagination to help us succeed and accomplish our dreams.

Mrs. Ban Breathnach had a clear image in her mind of not only her finished book, but also its ultimate success, and her dream was fulfilled.

When we think of our future life in terms of a painting, we must make sure it is an image worth painting for ourselves. We can use our imagination to dream big, and have faith that the knowledge needed to fulfill our dreams is on its way.

Industrialist and philanthropist Andrew Carnegie not only built libraries, in 1891 he built one of the most prestigious venues in the world for both classical and popular music, Carnegie Hall, located in New York City. There's an old joke that goes something like this:

One day, after a disappointing rehearsal, a violinist was leaving Carnegie Hall via a backstage door. He was approached by two tourists who were looking for the Hall's entrance. When they saw the musician's violin case, they asked, "Excuse us, sir, could you tell us how to get to Carnegie Hall?" "Yes," said the violinist, "Practice, practice, practice."

Your character Anna and my character Beatrice might have a similar dialogue:

ANNA
Could you tell me how to get to The Walt Disney Concert Hall?

BEATRICE

Yes. Practice, practice, practice.

This is the same process for any goal we choose for ourselves.

ANNA

Can you tell me how to imagine my future life in my mind and move toward it?

BEATRICE

Yes. Practice...*practice*... **practice**!

Your Self-Portrait Reference Materials

*Our subconscious minds have no sense of humor, play no
jokes and cannot tell the difference between reality and
an imagined thought or image. **What we continually
think about eventually will manifest in our lives.***
Robert Collier

hat we continually think about will manifest in our lives,
Robert Collier, a well-known self-help author, tells us. His
point is that it is crucial to direct our thoughts to images
of how we would like our lives to look. We must form a clear and
definite mental image of the things we want to have, do, or become.

Our subconscious is the part of our mind below the level of
conscious perception. It is running the show in our lives. Therefore,
it is essential to impress upon it how we envision our future. When
we do this, we will have unconscious impulses, behaviors, and actions
that draw us closer and closer to the life of our dreams.

A large part of an interior decorator's job is visualizing. When
she walks into a room, in her mind she can create a space that suits
the purposes of the room. She may replace flooring, and add drapes,
furniture and accessories. She may change wall color, and even *move*
walls, all in her mind! We will use this same "re-decorating" approach
to re-visualize any part of our life.

To turn our lives, our self-portraits, into masterpieces, we will
visualize in our minds the lives we want. We will see our life's
potential. If visualization doesn't come easily to you, or if you like
to visualize but need to practice staying focused, there are many

visualization tools to help. I've offered them below as Reference Material Tools for your Self-Portrait Plan.

There are artists who create purely from their imagination, but most of us use some form of reference materials. Reference material is anything one refers to during the process of creating. Reference material for a portrait painter might be something directly in front of the artist, such as a person sitting. Or, it could be a photo, or several photos that she took and would like to capture on canvas. An interior decorator will often create a design board. On this large board she may collect reference materials such as colors, fabric swatches, photos of furniture, and possible floor layouts. This keeps her vision for the room crystal clear. To create our life self-portrait, we may also use reference materials to help shape our masterpiece.

Energy flows to thought. By directing our thoughts, with the help of our reference materials, we direct our energy. We are telling our subconscious mind what we want, and expecting it to be delivered in the best way possible. The words and images occupying our mind are what we are asking for in life.

Let's start asking!

REFERENCE MATERIAL #1: SELF-PORTRAIT PLAN

In Chapter 13, you visualized yourself at your "Lifetime Achievement Award" party. There were five rooms in the Masterpiece Gallery, each displaying images of the full, rich, juicy life you have lived. The five rooms are taking up valuable square footage in your life today, and how we choose to fill them creates our self-portrait. Looking at the following Self-Portrait Plan, in the Definite Purposes column you can write in more details about what you imagined in the five rooms:

"Health" = The Health Room images
"My Calling" = The Legacy Room images
"Serving Others" = The Philanthropy Room images

"Material Things" = The Material Things Room images
"Family & Friends" = The Family & Friends Room images

Fill in the boxes on the left with your definite main purpose in each of these areas of your life. Remember, we're not carving this in stone, just sketching it in pencil. The important thing is to have a purpose to move towards.

SELF-PORTRAIT PLAN	
DEFINITE PURPOSES	WHAT I WILL GIVE
Health	
My Calling	
Serving Others	
Material Things	
Family & Friends	

Good for you! You have supplied your subconscious mind with a clear purpose to move towards in these 5 areas of your life! This is the same as declaring, "God, these are the desires You have placed in my heart, and I am asking You to help me accomplish them in the best way possible."

Next, look at the column on the right labeled, "What I Will Give." God will help us accomplish our purposes, but we also must do our part. We may be waiting on God's help, but He is also waiting on us to do our part and take action. The action we take will be things that align with our natural gifts, our values, and that which we enjoy. What are you willing to give to manifest your definite main purposes?

What will you give to have optimal health? You might use a pedometer and commit to walking 10,000 steps a day, while enjoying the outdoors.

What will you give to fulfill your calling? Would taking a class to become more educated in a specific subject be beneficial?

What will you do to serve others? Is there a charity dear to your heart that you can volunteer your time to?

What will you give for the material things you would like to enjoy? Are there actions you can take that align with your gifts to increase your current income?

What will you give to have loving relationships with your family and friends? You may decide to simply make spending time with family and friends a priority.

Everything in the What I Will Give column will be unique for you. While not Bible scripture, I believe the common phrase, "God helps those who help themselves," is true.

With your Definite Purposes and What I Will Give columns penciled in, you now have a concise list of what a successful life looks like for you. Right now, from wherever you are in your life, it is time to work on what you will give to achieve your goals!

I have one copy of my Self-Portrait Plan taped to my bathroom mirror and another copy in my "Self-Portrait Notebook" (Reference

Material #3). This makes it easy for me to read it daily. Place copies of yours anywhere you will be able to refer to it daily. Whatever our mind is fed is what is attracted to us. Do you want to think about and move toward your definite proposes, or, whatever has possession of your mind at the moment? Read your Self- Portrait Plan daily to move towards the life you choose.

REFERENCE MATERIAL #2:
COMING ATTRACTIONS AND HIGHLIGHT REEL

Let's revisit now your list of "25 Things I Really, Really Want" from Chapter 12. As Einstein said, imagination is a preview of life's coming attractions. What images do you want to occupy your mind? Did filling in your Self-Portrait Plan give you new ideas of what you would like to add to your list, and other things you would like to take off? Fill in "Twenty-Five Coming Attractions" that illustrate what good things are going to happen in your life coming soon. If you don't get to twenty-five, that's okay. This list is meant to evolve.

TWENTY-FIVE COMING ATTRACTIONS

1_____

2_____

3_____

4_____

5_____

6_____

7_____

8_____

9_____

10 _____

11 _____

12 _____

13 _____

14 _____

15 _____

16 _____

17 _____

18 _____

19 _____

20 _____

21 _____

22 _____

23 _____

24 _____

25 _____

Good job!

Okay. Before we go further, let's take stock of what we have clarified to ourselves so far. We have a Self-Portrait Plan in place, and we have a list of "Coming Attractions" we are excited to make happen and which we will be happy to look back on as great accomplishments. We know these events and experiences are going to happen for us because we visualize ourselves accomplishing them. So what's next? Every time we make something awesome happen, it will go on our

"Top Twenty-Five Highlight Reel" so we see all the great things that we have already manifested in our life.

Pastor Steve Furtick said, "The reason we struggle with insecurity is because we compare our behind-the-scenes with everyone else's highlight reel." Hallelujah! What do all your friends post on Facebook? Their highlight reel! While I look at photos of my friend Laura wine tasting at the best wineries in Napa Valley, which it appears she does every other weekend, I'm usually home drinking a glass of whatever wine was on sale at the grocery store. What are celebrity news magazines? A highlight (and sometimes lowlight) reel of celebrities lives. It seems that while the stars are skiing in Aspen during the holidays, I'm homebound with Christmas decorations to clean up and a stack of new bills.

But *our* lives have highlights too! We just need to remember them. If someone made a highlight reel of your life *so far*, what would be up there, flashing on the screen? I'll start you off with your first one. Write down more, now. Remember to save some spaces for things you will accomplish off of your "Twenty-Five Coming Attractions" list.

TOP TWENTY-FIVE HIGHLIGHT REEL

1 I was born!

2_____

3_____

4_____

5_____

6_____

7_____

8_____

9 _____

10 _____

11 _____

12 _____

13 _____

14 _____

15 _____

16 _____

17 _____

18 _____

19 _____

20 _____

21 _____

22 _____

23 _____

24 _____

25 _____

Don't you feel good about yourself? Filling out mine, I have more highlights than I was aware of. I included the five-foot-long chocolate peanut butter candy bar I won at church when I was a young girl. My brother Dennis remembers it as being the all-time best tasting candy bar he's ever eaten! And even though much of middle school and high school sucked, I included on my list learning to ride a unicycle in 7th grade, and being voted Class Artist in 12th. Those are great highlights from my school days.

Now, when we cross an item off our "Coming Attractions," we can immediately add it to our "Highlight Reel."

REFERENCE MATERIAL #3:
SELF-PORTRAIT NOTEBOOK

*Choose to make your imagination your ally. You do have
a say about what pictures live in your head—and you can
choose the most positive images to shape your life.*
Jane Seymour

When painting my self-portrait for the cover of this book, I wanted the painting to give you clues about who I am. I am an artist who likes to get dressed up, and loves opulent settings. Your Self-Portrait Notebook will tell the story of who you are. For now, that story may be totally fictional. My self-portrait is; I don't even have a gold dress, *yet*. This Notebook is a portrait of how you envision yourself when you have achieved your goals. It is something for you to aim towards, your target.

In The Self-Portrait Notebook, store images of how you envision your life. Keep these all in one place so that you can look at them daily to help you make the images live in your head and heart, to shape the life you truly want for yourself.

Supplies needed:
    1 three-ring binder (1" rings are a good size)
    5 sleeve protectors
    5 sheets of paper
    1 roll of removable tape (This tape is clear and looks like regular
        tape, only it has a blue core.)
    scissors
    images – these may be gathered from magazines, photo albums,
        or downloaded off of the Internet

To begin, take the 5 sheets of paper and on the top of the first one write *The Health Room*. On the top of the second write *The Legacy Room*. On the top of the third write *The Philanthropy Room*. On the top of the fourth write *The Material Things Room*. And on the top of the fifth write *The Family & Friends Room*.

Now, start gathering images that represent these five areas of your life. For The Health Room, if you have committed to eating healthier, you might find a photo in a magazine of fruits and vegetables, or any foods you know are healthy that you enjoy. For The Legacy Room, if you dream of earning your MBA, download an image of a diploma off the Internet and put your name on it. For The Philanthropy Room, you might find a brochure of the place you'd like to volunteer every Tuesday night. For The Material Things Room, you could gather photos of places you would like to travel. For The Family and Friends Room, look through photo albums and add pictures of the people in your life who believe in you, those who lift you higher. Also, add people who you would *like* to be in your life. If you hope to meet Mr. Right, and he hasn't shown up yet, add a photo of your dream man to this sheet.

In his book *Illusions*, author Richard Bach wrote, "To bring anything into your life, imagine that it's already there. If you want to be with what you're magnetizing, you have to put yourself in the picture, too." Taking his advice, find the best, most flattering photos of yourself, and add them to the pages of your Self-Portrait Notebook. This makes it easy to visualize yourself among the things you are manifesting.

Spread your five sheets out on a table, or the floor, and begin adding your photos to each category. By sticking the images down with removable tape you will be able to easily add, move, or change your images to make a book you can really believe in.

When you are satisfied, and each sheet represents what you would like to manifest in that area of your life, slip the page into the sheet protector and put it in the three-ring binder.

Looking through your Notebook, are you excited about this life you are moving towards? Do you have positive expectations about your future? The goal of your Notebook is to create such a clear vision of your life in your mind that it will begin to show itself in your outside world. I believe God wants all those things for you, *and more*. All you have to do is show yourself and Him what these things are, and you'll be on your way to making them happen!

What we think about manifests in our life. Our subconscious mind cannot tell the difference between reality and what we are imaging. Look through your Self-Portrait Plan, Coming Attractions, Highlight Reel, and Self-Portrait Notebook daily. Your subconscious mind will work to make these imagined images a reality. Let the fun, and the life of your dreams, begin!

Don't part with your illusions.
When they are gone,
you may still exist,
but you have ceased to live.

Mark Twain

Mark Twain, by: Frank Edwin Larson

Focus

I don't care how much power, brilliance or energy you have, if you don't harness it and focus it on a specific target, and hold it there, you're never going to accomplish as much as your ability warrants.
Zig Ziglar

Have you ever put cookies in the oven to bake and thought, *Since I'm standing right here in the kitchen, I don't need to set a timer, I'll just take them out in 15 minutes.* While waiting, you washed the cookie dough off of your hands and dried them on your dishtowel. You then noticed the dishtowel had specs of pasta sauce on it, so you decided to throw a load of laundry into the washer before it stained. You went to your bathroom to gather towels, and then to your laundry basket to find other "lights" to make a full load. Now in the laundry room, while pouring laundry detergent into the tub, you remember you forgot to get the mail. Upon closing the lid, you head outside to check your mailbox. After retrieving your mail, you head straight to your outdoor recycle bin to sort through it all. When you enter your home, you smell something...something *burning.* OMG, *the cookies!*

Many of us know what we want in life, and we start out on course, headed in the right direction. But somewhere along the way we lose focus; we begin to live our life unconsciously, and simply go through the motions and react to what is happening around us. And then, in a moment of clarity, we look around and think, *I never accomplished my goal. What happened?* **How did I get here?**

The key to have ongoing clarity, and realize our definite purposes, is by harnessing our focus. We now have the reference materials to make this easier. They are our:

- ☑ Self-Portrait Plan
- ☑ Twenty-Five Coming Attractions List and Top Twenty-Five Highlight Reel List
- ☑ Self-Portrait Notebook

Check, check, and check. Now, take a deep, calming breath again. We must stay focused and let these specific targets occupy our mind a greater percentage of the time than things we recall from our past, or what we are currently observing in our environment. We have to be conscious of these goals, daily.

I'll bet sometime in your life you have seen someone become really successful, and thought, *Why is she so successful? She's not even that good. I can do a better job than she can!* And, you may be right. You may have more intelligence or talent than "she" does, but "she" has focused on a specific target. That's what you are learning now, to create a moment of calm, and focus, regularly, throughout your day, no matter what the day brings.

Many of us try to stay focused on our goals by concentrating on our desire for money, power, or recognition. These forms of motivation are fine, but what happens when our day to day routine starts to bog us down? I'm sure most of us have experienced New Year's Resolution Syndrome. We took massive action for a while (January) until it wasn't so easy anymore (February) and our old habits set in (the rest of the year). To ensure that our dreams come true, we must cultivate the habit of staying focused on our goals, and doing it in a way that feels good. Let's look at ways to stay focused.

BE A VIBRATIONAL MATCH TO YOUR GOAL

As I think, I vibrate. And it is my vibrational offering that equals my point of attraction. So it's always a match. What I am thinking and what is coming back to me is always a vibrational match.
Abraham-Hicks

As we think, we vibrate, says the Abraham-Hicks "Law of Attraction." This "vibration" is not about our body subtly shaking like when we are sitting in a massaging chair. It's about a feeling we send out: we might be said to give off a "good vibe," or a "bad vibe." Another way to say this is, the thoughts we are thinking are creating the energy we are sending out. It's an invisible current we are emitting. If we are focusing on positive things, we are giving off a positive vibration. If we are focusing on negative things, we are giving off a negative vibration. It makes no difference if what we are focusing on is how we feel when we observe our surroundings, or imagine something in our mind; what matters is if the feeling is positive or negative. Whatever feeling we emit, we attract that feeling back to us and draw more of into our lives.

We might think of our energy as a boomerang. We fling our positive or negative energy out, and the same energy comes back to us. Some people think of the world as being a giant mirror. The energy we give off hits the mirror, and is reflected back to us.

Imagine yourself looking at the pictures in your Self-Portrait Notebook. You are ruminating over the photos on your Legacy page and feel great. You are a vibrational match to living the dream. You may be asking yourself, *Well, I'm visualizing the life I dream of, and I'm feeling great right now. Why haven't good things started happening?* Simply, because it takes time, practice and patience to make our positive vibrations actualize into positive and productive life-improving outcomes. Charles Haanel put it this way,

You cannot entertain weak, harmful, negative thoughts ten hours a day and expect to bring about beautiful, strong and harmonious conditions by ten minutes of strong, positive, creative thought.

This is where many of us trip up. We lose our focus on the positive thoughts. We imagine the life of our dreams, feel good about it, and begin to attract good things. But then, we look around ourselves, feel negative about our current condition, and begin attracting more negative things. We attract positive, then negative, then positive, then negative, and that undermines our positive path.

Let's look at some examples.

GOOD FEELING GOAL	POSITIVE THOUGHTS	NEGATIVE THOUGHTS
Read the Bible, cover to cover	*Being knowledgeable about the Bible is part of a well-rounded education. Maybe God has messages for me that will only be revealed if I read it cover to cover.*	*It will take me too long. I have a stack of reading for work that I barely get to. I don't want to stay up till midnight for over 3 months to read "The Bible in 100 Days."*
Find my Soul-Mate	*I'll have a companion to go out and do fun things with. Plus, there is nothing better than the feeling of being in love.*	*All the guys my age like younger women. If I'm vulnerable and put myself out there, I might get rejected. Rejection hurts!*
Become a Millionaire	*I want the financial freedom to buy whatever clothes I like, to live in my dream home, and help others by donating to my favorite charities.*	*I don't know how I can make more money. I'm already working 10-hour days. Will I have to work 12+ hours a day? I don't want to work that hard.*

Whether we are spending more time focusing on the positive thoughts or negative thoughts will determine if our good feeling goal will manifest. The positive thoughts are a vibrational match to the good feeling goal. Therefore, in time, the goal will manifest. The negative thoughts are not a vibrational match to the good feeling goal, so we will eventually lose our motivation to attain it.

The more we focus on what we want, the more positive thoughts we are sending out, and attracting back. This takes us higher and higher on THE ART OF HAPPINESS SCALE. It's an upward spiral!

When we are consciously grateful, joyous and enthusiastic, a dominant amount of the time, we will become a vibrational match to the things we desire.

FOCUS ON SIGNIFICANCE

Have you ever climbed the proverbial ladder of success, and thought you would attain 24/7 joy once you reached the top? I have believed that.

While growing up, I often felt I had less material things, less opportunities, and heck, since I'm being honest, thought I was less *worthy* than many of my friends. I believed if only I had a lot of money, I could buy a lot of material things, enjoy better opportunities, and be a more worthy person. After high school, I leaned my ladder against the wall of being a famous fashion designer. I excelled at The Fashion Institute of Design and Merchandising, and after graduation, spent the next eight years climbing my ladder and building my career. I believed I was on my way to riches, an enviable lifestyle, and a flock of adoring fans.

During my eight years working in the fashion industry, I had a gnawing feeling I wasn't doing work that had significance to me. A question that ran through my mind was, *Does the world really need another clothing line? When I die, will any of this have mattered?* Don't get me wrong, I admire fashion designers. Many designers are following their calling by using their talents in a way that brings joy to themselves and their customers. I buy magazines dedicated to

The key to realizing a dream is to focus not on success but significance.

Oprah Winfrey

Oprah Winfrey, by: Simmie Knox

fashion and enjoy wearing current styles. I simply feel that I, in this season of my life, am meant to do something different.

Stephen Covey, who was an American educator, author, businessman, and keynote speaker, said, "If the ladder is not leaning against the right wall, every step just gets us to the wrong place faster." I had leaned my ladder against the wall of being a successful fashion designer, but I have learned that the only thing that can fulfill me is aspiring to my definition of significance.

In 1992, I climbed down from that ladder, and propped it against a different wall. I began working seriously on my portrait painting business and then, in 1993, Camille was born. For me, painting and parenting are both all about adding significance to the world. When my Grandma Frances passed away, I learned that on the back of her oil paintings hanging in her home, was a small label with the name of her daughter or son who inherited it. These were the most cherished keepsakes her children received. I believe a treasured painting brings joy to my clients, just as both of my daughters add joy in the world.

Now that my daughters need less parenting, I have a new focus. I am adding significance to the world through my artwork *and* writing. I am confident that now my ladder is leaned against the right wall again, and I am enjoying the climb.

Frequent Contemplation of Your Dream

> *Too much stress cannot be laid on the importance of*
> *frequent contemplation of the mental image, coupled*
> *with unwavering faith and devout gratitude.*
> Wallace D. Wattles

To move towards our dreams in the most enjoyable way possible, we must focus on our definite purposes daily. There are three ways to make this more effortless:

#1 Focus on the Mental Image

Focusing on your dreams by reviewing your Self-Portrait Notebook one time per day is all that's necessary. Five to ten minutes at a time is sufficient, but frequent contemplation is best. Remember, it's something you should look forward to doing, so put a lot of images in there you really enjoy!

#2 Focus with Faith

When we add positive emotion to the mental images in our mind, our vision is realized even faster. Fear and worry are negative emotions. Faith and confidence are positive emotions.

When we contemplate our dream, and have faith that it will come true, we are saying, "God, this is what I want in my life, and I know that if it is your will, and with your help, it *will* manifest."

If we contemplate our dream, and fear that it will not come true, we are saying, "God, this is what I want, but I don't trust that you heard me, and don't trust you will help me, so I'm scared it won't manifest."

God will respond to either request. Make sure you request with faith. Feel as if the life of your dreams is already yours. Feel it as much as you can. Get excited...*now!*

#3 Focus with Gratitude

Visualize your dreams, have faith they will come true, and dwell with gratitude upon the end result. Be grateful to God that all of your desires are being granted.

Frequent, focused contemplation of your dream just 5 – 10 minutes a day, combined with persistent faith and gratitude, is the process through which we imprint our subconscious mind. This is what sets creative forces in motion. When our mind is consumed with these positive images, it will become alert to opportunities. By having a target, we also gain energy that boosts our performance, and we are propelled into inspired action. When these things happen, we no longer need to look for more superficial forms of motivation. Focusing with passion will naturally move us forward in the right direction.

When we have more good feeling thoughts than negative, we become a vibrational match to our dreams. We can lean our ladder against any wall that has significance to us, and *enjoy* the climb! And by focusing on our Self-Portrait Notebook daily, with faith that our dreams are coming true, we will never have to look around ourselves bewildered and ask, *What happened? How did I get here?* We will know that we are exactly where our focus brought us, and we can enjoy the warm, gooey, delicious cookies in our life!

STEP #4

TAKE
DIVINE
ACTION

The world needs dreamers and the world needs doers. But above all, the world needs dreamers who do.
Sarah Ban Breathnach

Pray as though everything depended on God. Work as though everything depended on you.
Saint Augustine

Close the Gap Between Where You Are and Where You Will Be

If one advances confidently in the direction of their dreams, and endeavors to lead a life which they have imagined, they will meet with a success unexpected in common hours.
Henry David Thoreau

Mary Cassatt knew as a teenager that she wanted to be an artist. Cassatt was born in Pennsylvania in 1844, sixteen years before Abraham Lincoln moved into the White House at 1600 Pennsylvania Avenue. In America during the 1800s, only a small number of women became professional artists. Most women who came from families with stable incomes didn't pursue a career at all, mainly because it was expected in an upper-middle-class family like Cassatt's that she would "marry well" and have a family of her own. Yet, at the time of her death at the age of 82, she was known as one of the great American artists of the Nineteenth Century.

Mary Cassatt went against her family's intentions for her and used all of her advantages to make painting her career, not just a pastime. *How did she do it?!* How did she close the gap from being a fifteen-year-old girl with a dream, to achieving a lasting place in art history? True, she had talent, and true, she was born into a wealthy family, but the world is full of talented individuals, lucky to be born into affluent families, who never find success on their own. Using the blueprint of Cassatt's success, you and I can also close the gap from where we currently are, to where we want to be. Where we *will* be, if we take the appropriate action.

Portrait of the Artist (Self-Portrait), by: Mary Cassatt

First we have to determine our starting point, or Point A. Next we need to know our end point, or Point B.

You are Here   **Achieved Goal**

Point A   **Point B**

Cassatt's Point A was enrolling at the Pennsylvania Academy of the Fine Arts when she was 15. Her Point B was to make a successful career from her art, regardless of the fears of her family and friends at home.

We, too, have determined our Point B. We know from our Self-Portrait Plan the outcomes we want to achieve in the five main areas of our lives: Health, My Calling, Serving Others, Material Things, and Family & Friends. Our Point A is wherever we stand currently in these areas.

Whatever our goal is, the quickest route to Point B will always be the same. It doesn't matter if it's a large goal, such as leaving a legacy, or a small goal, such as losing ten pounds. (I know, I know, losing ten pounds might not seem like a small goal.)

Here is a formula that will determine the results we create in every area of our life. Although unaware of it, we are already using this formula. We might as well use it deliberately to get the results we desire. It is how Mary Cassatt, and everyone else, creates a successful life.

B	→	T	→	F	→	A	=	R
e		h		e		c		e
l		o		e		t		s
i		u		l		i		u
e		g		i		o		l
f		h		n		n		t
s		t		g		s		s
		s		s				

Beliefs lead to thoughts, thoughts lead to feelings, feelings lead to actions, and actions lead to results. Simple, huh?

If we don't sincerely believe we deserve or have the ability to attain our goal, we will not have thoughts about how to achieve our goal, which will lead to pessimistic feelings. These feelings will sap our motivation and energy and without those we will not achieve our desired results.

When we do, however, **believe** we deserve and have the ability to attain our goal, we will have **thoughts** about how to achieve our goal, which will lead to **feelings** of optimism, enthusiasm, and passion. Next, we will be motivated to take **action**, which will then lead to our desired **results**. This is the route Mary Cassatt took. Let's look at how she did it.

BELIEVE

Mary Cassatt was from her youth a free-spirited, restless, and determined person with a clear goal—to become a great artist.
Nancy Mowll Mathews, Author of *Mary Cassatt*

When Cassatt was seven years old, her family took an extended four-year trip to Europe. They stayed in Paris, France, for a while before settling in Darmstadt, Germany. This trip deeply affected Cassatt and may have been responsible for changing the trajectory of her life. Her exposure to the museums and art of her period, and before, encouraged in her a feeling that art was something worth devoting her entire life to.

Regardless of the time in which she lived and what was expected of her, regardless of insecurities she may have had, and regardless of where she lived, Cassatt believed she could achieve her goal of becoming a great artist. Clearly, she believed in herself and her goal because she achieved the results she desired!

Believing you deserve to get the results you desire is so crucial, it is Step #2 of this book! Before we take any action towards our goal, we have to *believe* we can achieve it. Whether we believe we can or can't accomplish anything is often an unconscious thought. Having positive thoughts *is* believing in a positive way. Negative thoughts are "limiting beliefs"—believing we *can't* achieve our goal before we even start often holds us back. It doesn't matter if these limiting beliefs are conscious or not. It only matters if they are present and stronger than positive beliefs about goals we hold very dear to us. Limiting beliefs will hold us back.

We cannot create a new future if we believe we don't deserve it, or believe we will fail, or believe there will be pain involved. We first have to acknowledge our limiting beliefs, challenge them, and then eliminate them. If we don't, it's like having one foot on the gas moving forward, and one foot on the brake, keeping us stuck where we are.

If Cassatt had limiting beliefs, they could have logically sounded like this:

"I'm a young, wealthy girl living in the 1800s. It's my job to find a wealthy husband and have children."

"There have been so few female artists the art world considers 'great.' The great male artists will never accept a woman as their equal or better."

"I may not be talented enough to be a great artist."

Cassatt's results show that she never let these limiting beliefs take hold of her. Her success shows she believed she could create the life she wanted, that she could move to Europe and show her paintings along side competitive men, and that she was talented enough to be a great artist!

Think / Feel

Dwelling from, not upon, the space you want to inherit
is the fastest way to change absolutely everything.
Mike Dooley

A leader is a person who leads a group, an organization, or a country. A leader is a person who is followed by others. We are the leaders of our lives. And if we don't use our thoughts to lead our own life, someone else will tell us how we should lead it.

In a Presidential race, candidates know they are not yet President as they make speeches and meet people. Yet, they also know if they want to get elected, they must look Presidential, they must act Presidential, and they must encourage people to imagine them as President, enacting their vision for the country. Essentially, they must *act* as if their Point B was already in motion, as if the votes were already cast, they had won, and now they are doing their job as President. That is how they convince everyone they can do the job— they already believe in their ability to do it.

The fastest way for us to reach our Point B is to think and feel like we are already there. We must, in any small or large way we can, look like we are already there, act like we are already there, and sell our vision to ourselves and the people around us.

One reason we don't have the results that we want in our lives is that we don't *feel* as though we already have them. When we are at Point A, and see our Point B as "way over there," it will continue to stay "way over there." But when we think and feel as we would if we already had the thing, then the law of attraction draws it closer and closer to us, and the gap closes.

It is natural and easy to wake up every morning and observe that things are pretty much the same as yesterday. The Point A that you are living today is the result of your past beliefs, thoughts and feelings. If we don't control our mind and see things from the vantage of Point B, then our future will look just like today. When you wake up tomorrow morning, do as they say, and dress for the job you want, not the job you have. Also, act as if you are leading the life you want, not the life you have!

How much of the day are you willing to believe, think and feel you have already attained your goal? If your answer is 5% of the day it will take a lot longer to be drawn to you than if you are dwelling in it 80% of the day.

How do we train our minds to stop thinking about what we don't want and to start thinking about what we do want? Keep the images from your Self-Portrait Notebook in your mind. Train your mind to hold these visions. You already made the decision of what you want, your Point B, now *believe* you are already there. When we have thoughts and feelings that dwell in the positive, we are there, instantly. There is no reason to suffer or struggle on our way there. This will get easier as each positive thought is imprinted in our subconscious. Our subconscious mind will begin work to bring into focus the life we desire.

We can be the leader of our lives. We can sell ourselves on the vision of the life we want and get excited about it.

ACTION

If you want to be successful, find someone who has achieved the results you want and copy what they do and you'll achieve the same results.
Anthony Robbins

Back in the states, four years after the Cassatt family's sojourn in Europe, Mary took action and enrolled at the Pennsylvania Academy of the Fine Arts. At the time, women made up only 30% of the Academy student body.

By the time she was 21, Cassatt had been studying at the Pennsylvania Academy and living on her own for six years. Faculty encouraged students to study abroad, but when Cassatt asked her parents permission to study in Paris, her father, a conservative banker, was not enthusiastic about the idea. Eventually, though, she convinced them to allow her to go.

While in Paris, Cassatt attended classes and also traveled throughout Europe studying and copying old master paintings. This is a common approach to learning painting and drawing skills that is still used today. By studying and copying masterpieces, an artist can more quickly achieve an understanding of technique.

In her 30th year, Cassatt settled permanently in Paris, where her work was regularly shown at the Salon de Paris, an annual government-sponsored art exhibition. Artists showing at the Salon were held in high esteem, but there was a trade-off: artists had to conform to the Salon's preferences for subject matter and style in their paintings. Many young artists eventually began rejecting the idea that great art had to be within these structures, which held underlying moral and ethical themes. Cassatt would become one of these alternative thinkers and painters.

The following year, Cassatt saw a pastel painting by Edgar Degas, a leader of the Impressionist movement, in a gallery window in Paris. Cassatt described the significance of this experience: "I used to go and flatten my nose against the window and absorb all I could of his art. It changed my life. I saw art then as I wanted to see it."

Coincidentally, while visiting the Salon de Paris, Degas saw and admired Cassatt's work! In 1877, he invited her to join and show her work with other Impressionists.

Of this experience, Cassatt wrote, "At last I could work with absolute independence without considering the opinion of a jury. I had already recognized who were my true masters. I admired Manet, Courbet, and Degas. I hated conventional art—I began to live."

Cassatt had painted her early Salon submissions in the darker tones of the old masters, but under the influence of the Impressionists, she took on their characteristics. Her palette brightened noticeably and she painted with broken, shorter brush strokes. She began painting common, ordinary scenes from her life and included a sense of movement in the composition. Up until this time, still lifes, portraits, as well as landscapes were usually painted in the artist's studio. The Impressionists, however, often painted *en plein air*, which in French means "in the open air;" they literally took their work outside and painted while surrounded by nature.

Cassatt found people achieving the results she wanted. She followed and at times copied the styles of the Impressionists she was inspired by, and achieved the same results.

Our society places a huge importance on being ourself, unique, and original. That is good, but while we are finding our voice, it is perfectly acceptable to keep our goal in mind and take direct inspiration from people who get the results we want. Once we find them, we may emulate them! We learn to do almost everything new by watching, observing, and imitating. This speeds up our learning curve and may cut years off of reaching and implementing our goals.

In 1995, I came across a book in the library, *Painting Portraits*, by Everett Raymond Kinstler. Like Cassatt "flattening her nose against the window" to absorb Degas' art, I couldn't get *my* nose out of that book! The images of Mr. Kinstler's portraits were the way I wanted to paint. His colors were fresh, the settings elegant, his brushstrokes lively, and his sitters appeared happy! He is the artist of the wonderful portrait of Dr. Seuss in Chapter 11. Several years later, I began noticing an emerging artist appearing in art magazines who had a very similar painting style as Mr. Kinstler. His name is Michael Shane Neal. I learned, not surprisingly, that Mr. Kinstler is Neal's mentor, and Neal his protégé. Along with Neal's thriving commissioned portrait business, he teaches painting classes in the summer near his home in Nashville, Tennessee. In 2006, I drove down from Indiana and attended his weeklong "Advanced Portrait Painting Workshop." Not only is Neal an excellent painter, he is also a charming Southern gentleman and gifted teacher. I enjoyed myself and made such great leaps in my painting ability that I attended his workshop again in 2008.

When we imitate someone we admire, someone who is getting the results we want, we never entirely stop being ourselves. Just like Cassatt, our unique personality will emerge, and we will achieve results faster, creating a version of our own success.

RESULTS

Degas and Cassatt became close friends for the rest of their lives and she was the only American who ever exhibited in the Impressionist shows. Cassatt was described by French journalist and art critic Gustave Geffroy in 1894 as one of *les trois grandes dames* (French for "three grand women") of Impressionism. She was alongside Marie Bracquemond and Berthe Morisot, both highly regarded in the genre.

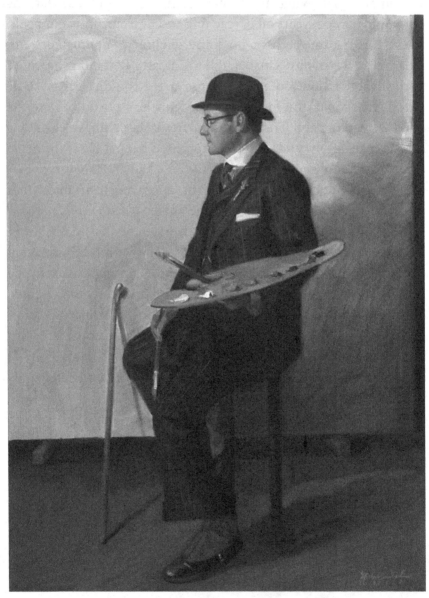

Self-Portrait, by: Michael Shane Neal

Cassatt reached her goal of "becoming a great artist" and is known today for her paintings of everyday scenes of women and children from life in the second half of the Nineteenth Century. Even after struggling with declining eyesight between 1912 and 1915, she remained active in the arts. In America, she worked hard to encourage collection of Impressionist paintings, emphasizing clearly this was an important movement in the fine arts. When you or I go into a major American museum, we can enjoy viewing Nineteenth Century Impressionist paintings, and this is due in no small part to Cassatt's tireless efforts.

From Mary Cassatt's life we can learn how to merge two worlds together, our present, and the one we imagine. We can believe the joy of the life we imagine far outweighs any pain our limiting beliefs cause. We can be the leader of our lives and think and feel as if we are already dwelling in the place we desire. We can take action by emulating role models who are getting the results we want. Advance confidently in the direction of your dreams, lead the life you imagine, and you will quickly find your way to success.

19

A Powerful Prayer

Prayer is mans greatest power!
W. Clement Stone

Prayer is aligning ourselves with the purposes of God.
E. Stanley Jones

We live in a time that people like to get results ... *fast!* In Chapter 18, we learned that if we **believe** we can accomplish our dream, if we have **thoughts** and **feelings** that our dream has already come true, and take **action** by emulating people getting the results we desire, we *will* see positive **results**. What if I told you that by adding one more factor into the B → T → F → A = R formula, you could get there even faster? Most people have heard of this one factor, but they don't take advantage of it. If I tell you what it is, will you try it? Do you want to know what it is?

Okay, turn the page...

PRAY !

B	→	T	→	F	→	**P**	→	A	=	R
e		h		e		r		c		e
l		o		e		a		t		s
i		u		l		y		i		u
e		g		i		e		o		l
f		h		n		r		n		t
s		t		g		s		s		s
		s		s						

PRAY! Pray to God for the life you desire! Pray to God to guide your actions. Remember, the thoughts we are thinking are going out into the Universe as a request. And whatever we are asking for *is* being delivered to us. It doesn't matter if the thoughts are conscious or unconscious, positive or negative; we are getting back what we are thinking about. This is why sending out conscious, positive thoughts, is so powerful!

Here is a powerful prayer that I challenge you to pray every day for *at least* the next 30 days. By the end of that time, I believe you will notice significant positive changes in your life.

> *Dear God,*
> *Spoil me with blessings!*
> *I desire a bigger life.*
> *Please be with me when it feels like my calling*
> *is too big.*
> *I will listen for your voice to guide my thoughts,*
> *words, and actions.*
> *Keep temptation away from me.*
> *Help me forgive myself for my mistakes and*
> *shortcomings and help me forgive those who*
> *have harmed me.*
> *Thank You for responding to my needs.*
> *I now feel the joy I will feel when my requests*
> *are fulfilled.*
> *Amen*

Spoil Me with Blessings!

Back in the '70s, my sisters, Teri and Sandy, accepted Jesus Christ as their personal Savior. This meant that they were publicly announcing at church that they believed in Jesus and wanted to live their lives as Christians. Tradition had it that they would be baptized the following week in front of the congregation at The First Baptist Church. In our church, babies were not baptized; baptisms were performed when people were old enough to choose for themselves and request it. In our family, that meant late elementary school. During the week, my mom bought Teri and Sandy each a new dress to wear after the baptismal, when they shook hands with the congregation in a receiving line.

A year or so later, my brother Ronny Dale, along with a few of his best friends, went through the same process. He accepted Christ, my mom bought him a new shirt and pants, and he was baptized the following Sunday.

In 1974, as the congregation sang "Just As I Am," I felt an inner nudging that it was my turn. I nervously walked to the front of the church and accepted Christ. My baptism was scheduled for March 31, the following Sunday. I was eager and excited...*to get my new outfit!* Of course I loved Jesus, I grew up going to church, so that was a given. I also was a ten year old who loved clothes! Monday came and my mom didn't mention shopping for a new dress. Tuesday and Wednesday came and went with still no mention of shopping. My eagerness and excitement were being replaced with doubt, and feelings of unworthiness. Was I going to get a new dress? I thought it was part of the deal. Was there something wrong with me? My siblings deserved new things, but I didn't? You might be wondering, *Why didn't you just ask your mom?* Well, with five kids in my family, I learned to not ask for much, to not be selfish. I also thought if I did ask, my mom might think the only reason I accepted Christ was to get a new dress. Even though this wasn't true, I didn't want that thought to enter her mind. Thursday, Friday, and Saturday passed and my mom decided that after I was baptized I would wear my pretty, yet old, pink dress to shake hands with the congregation in the receiving line. Mommy had made the pink dress for me, and maybe she thought it was lovelier than anything new we could buy. Or, maybe she forgot all about buying new outfits for my siblings for their baptism. Or maybe finances were tight at the time, and because I didn't ask for a new dress, she thought it wasn't important to me. I still don't know the real reason, because I still haven't asked!

Some of us (*me*) see and relate to God as our parent. Just as I didn't ask my mom for much, I didn't ask God for much, either. Because both of my parents worked very hard to support five children, they had limited time and resources. I learned that if I really wanted something, it was best to rely on myself to accomplish it or earn it.

But guess what? *God is not our parent!* He *wants* us to ask. Anyone who asks, receives! What if there are blessings you are forfeiting simply because you are not asking God for them? The blessings we are receiving are only limited by us. God has unlimited time and resources for us, and a willingness to give. He is waiting to say, "Yes." If we really want something, we can rely on God to help us accomplish it or earn it. Ask for material things that will truly add joy and ease to your life. Ask for internal gifts such as happiness, joy, and love. All of these things God is willing and able to give.

Ask God to spoil you with blessings today and your life will be bursting with miracles. Ask and it *will* be given to you.

I Desire a Bigger Life

My favorite animated children's movie is Disney's *Beauty and the Beast*. I can relate to Belle, the main character, strolling around town holding a book while singing:

> I want much more than this provincial life
> I want adventure in the great wide somewhere
> I want it more than I can tell
> And for once it might be grand
> To have someone understand
> I want so much more than they've got planned.

Do you feel this way? Do you want a bigger life? A bigger life than anyone else wants or expects from you? If this is your desire, then it is what God wants for you too. He is waiting for you to use your talents and education in a way that brings happiness to yourself and many, many others. He wants us to say, "God, take everything that you have made me responsible for, and make it bigger. Let me do more for You!"

And so I tell you, keep on asking, and you will receive what you ask for. Keep on seeking, and you will find. Keep on knocking, and the door will be opened to you. For everyone who asks, receives. Everyone who seeks, finds. And to everyone who knocks, the door will be opened.

Jesus Christ
(Luke 11:9-10)

Jesus Christ, by: John Howard Sanden

If you are living in a way that positively touches individual lives, the business community, or the world in general, God wants to expand your life. If you're making the world better, it's not only right to ask God for a bigger life, but He *wants* you to. When you ask, He will bring opportunities and people into your life so your influence grows.

PLEASE BE WITH ME WHEN IT FEELS LIKE MY CALLING IS TOO BIG

I was a stay-at-home mom for eighteen years. Taking care of my daughters, husband, house, and pets, was a labor of love, a choice I was fortunate to have. I did, however, still feel nudged to have a creative outlet and income, and painted commissioned portraits as time would allow. Many times I prayed, "Please God, give me a bigger life!" My prayers would be answered and I would start gaining clients. Then, I would get so overwhelmed with the amount of work it seemed I couldn't keep up with, I would beg, "Please God, give me less to do!" Many people can relate to a fear of failure, but I developed a bigger fear, a fear of success.

Looking back, I see that when I tried to do everything on my own, and I got overwhelmed, I cannot *ever* remember asking for God's help. Instead of asking for less to do, I could have been praying, "God, please be with me when it feels like my calling is too big!"

If God wanted us to have an ordinary, provincial life, we wouldn't need to lean on Him as much. We would just do things in a way that was familiar to us, the way, perhaps, our mothers and grandmothers did things. But because the desire for a bigger life is placed in my heart, and I believe it was placed in yours too, things are sometimes going to get overwhelming. We won't always be able to handle this unfamiliar, big life alone. We may need to pray, "I want a bigger life. I want to use my calling to help myself and many, many, others. God, I need your help. I can't do this alone!" It is at this moment that God gives us strength, wisdom, provides us with resources, and sends the people into our life whom we need to fulfill our calling. Being dependent on God's help is a positive way to manage a big life.

I WILL LISTEN FOR YOUR VOICE TO GUIDE MY THOUGHTS, WORDS, AND ACTIONS

We have five senses to take in information from our external world: sight, hearing, taste, touch, and smell. We may use our senses to protect ourselves, such as staying away from a large spider we see, throwing out spoiled food we taste, or pulling our hand away from something hot that we feel. Studies reveal that we may also have a *sixth* sense, which might be called instinct, intuition, or some may even say, the voice of God.

In the July 1, 2000 issue of *Psychology Today*, research psychologist Dean Radin, writer Colleen Rae and psychologist and noted skeptic Ray Hyman, discuss the possibilities of a "sixth sense" actually existing in humans. The article explains a study in which people were positioned in front of a blank computer screen and hooked up to electrodes to measure changes in their skin resistance and blood flow. The computer then randomly selected pictures of either potentially calm scenes, such as a tranquil lake, or potentially emotional scenes, such as a large spider. The studies revealed that the bodies of the subjects responded to emotional pictures *before* the computer even selected the photos. Our sixth sense can warn us of danger even before something bad happens!

Just as important as protecting us from something bad, our sixth sense can guide us to the life we desire. When we ask God to guide our thoughts, words and actions, He may work in a mysterious way to accomplish things we cannot do on our own.

> *Others call it instinct. Christians call it the voice of God.*
>
> Mark Burnett

The Beatles' Paul McCartney said he had the idea for the song "Let It Be" after having a dream about his mother. His mother, Mary, died of cancer when he was fourteen. He writes, "I had a dream where my mother, who had been dead at that point for about ten years, came to me in the dream and it was as if she could see that I was troubled. And I remember quite clearly her saying, 'Let it be,' and 'It's going to be OK. Don't worry.' You know, 'Let it be.' I woke up and I remembered the dream, and I thought, 'Well, that's a great idea.' And I then sat down and wrote the song using the feeling from that dream and of my mum coming to me in the dream."

We all experience intuition in different ways. Your intuition may speak to you by a picture flashing in your mind, or having a gut feeling about something, or give you Divine inspiration through dreams like Paul McCartney experienced.

When we have the intuition, and act on it, our intuition gets stronger. Imagine if you had two employees. One of them was joyful, and accomplished what you asked her or him to do. The other was pessimistic and never accomplished what you asked of her or him. Which employee would have favor? Which would you work with to get your job done? Which one would you want representing you? If we don't listen and act on what God wants us to do, with a joyful heart, He will move on to the next person who *is* willing. When we do listen, we are trusted with more ideas and more Divine interventions. Listen for the voice of God to guide your thoughts, words, and actions.

Keep Temptation Away from Me

When God answers the first two requests of our prayer—to be spoiled with blessings and to give us a bigger life—temptation naturally follows. Everyone sins, yet it does seem that with money and influence comes greater temptation. After all, the daily news is filled with wealthy and successful people doing some really appalling things.

The following is a list of what is commonly known as the cardinal sins, or seven deadly sins:

1. Lust - intense or unbridled sexual desire
2. Gluttony - excess in eating or drinking
3. Greed - a selfish and excessive desire for more of something (such as money) than is needed
4. Sloth - disinclination to action or labor
5. Wrath - strong vengeful anger

6   Envy - painful or resentful awareness of an advantage enjoyed by another joined with a desire to possess the same advantage

7   Pride - excessive self-regard

According to this list, I have done a lot of sinning. When we have greater abundance and a bigger life, we will have more freedom in how we choose to live. This means we will live with more temptation. All the good that we do can be spoiled by doing just a little bad. Ooh...how I could use the lives of a few politicians as examples.

We could try to deal with temptation with self-discipline and willpower. This method is the least effective. Those of us who have been on a diet know that sheer willpower *never* lasts forever.

Another way we could deal with temptation is by staying away from that which tempts us. A friend of mine is an alcoholic. He knows that to remain sober, it is not a good idea for him to be hanging out in bars. As he says, "If you keep visiting a barber shop, eventually you're going to get a haircut." Likewise, if you keep visiting a bar, eventually you're going to have a drink. He will be less tempted to drink alcohol when he meets friends for coffee, instead.

> *Remember that it is easier to stay out of temptation than to get out of it.*
> Rick Warren

A third way we could deal with temptation is by simply not focusing on that which tempts us. With practice, we can catch our mind thinking about the temptation, and then redirect our thoughts to something else. We don't get rid of a bad habit; we replace the bad habit with a good habit.

We may fight temptation with willpower, avoidance, and changing our mental focus, but there is a more powerful way, and it's simply this: we may ask God to keep temptation away from us. Ask God to not allow in temptation in the first place! "God, keep temptation away from me." Steering clear of temptation will keep sin from spoiling the abundance of blessings we are receiving. Remember...ask and you shall receive.

Help Me Forgive Myself for My Mistakes and Shortcomings and Help Me Forgive Those Who Have Harmed Me

When we look back on our life with regret regarding our mistakes and shortcomings, and we have anger towards those who have harmed us, we aren't free to move forward. We must release these negative feelings, *on a daily basis!*

God is love, and when we are feeling happy, loving and grateful, we are most closely aligned with God. It is only when we let go of unforgiving thoughts, and choose to allow love in, that God can fully work in our life.

As our life becomes a masterpiece, and we are spoiled with blessings and have a big life, we will begin to stand out in a crowd. We will no longer go under the radar; we will be out in the limelight. Unfortunately, this opens us up to the "haters," people who are living low on THE ART OF HAPPINESS SCALE. Haters don't like to see you being happy and joyous. It makes them jealous. This gives them two options: they can either raise themselves up to the level they perceive you to be, or tear you down to the level they perceive themselves to be. Which do you think is easier for them? Unfortunately, it's tearing you down!

Don't respond to them with anger. That is meeting them at their level. Respond to them with forgiveness. God has blessings stored up for you. Free yourself to be filled with those blessings.

Thank You for Responding to My Needs I Now Feel the Joy I Will Feel When My Requests Are Fulfilled

Thanking God in advance for responding to our needs is *having faith*. It is said that seeing is believing, but having faith is believing before seeing. Faith is visualizing and believing we have already attained that which we desire. Imagine you already have all the blessings you desire. Imagine you are already living a big life. Imagine you are currently so closely connected to God that your thoughts, words, and actions are Divinely guided. Thank God for having already responded to your needs. It is at this point that God will powerfully move all circumstances, people, and events, for you to receive! Once you begin saying the prayer, and are receiving abundantly, keep asking! Keep the circle going. You'll find your blessings keep increasing, and your influence enlarging, and you have a BIG life for God. You will know that all this has been given to you because you have aligned your desires with the purposes of God; you have prayed a powerful prayer.

Amen!

Take Action!

Not what she wishes and prays for does a woman get, but what she justly earns. Her wishes and prayers are only gratified and answered when they harmonize with her thoughts and actions.
James Allen

Have you ever done a Paint by Numbers? My cousin Susie, from my dad's side of the family, is 10 years older than me, and when I was little she bought one for us to paint. I enjoyed doing anything with Susie, and the painting was so…much…FUN! A Paint by Numbers kit includes a printed art board, paints, a brush, and a picture of the finished painting on the cover of the box. The only steps between the supplies and a finished painting are the time and action you need to take to complete it.

The same can be said of reaching any goal we have. The printed art board represents wherever we are starting from today. It is our Point A. The

Girl With Kitten (Paint by Numbers), by: Susie Dalton & Annette Hackney

paints and brush are the resources that we have available to us. The picture of the finished painting is equivalent to the images we have collected for our Self-Portrait Notebook. It is our Point B. The gap between where we currently are and the life we want is the time and action we must take to get there.

Wishing and praying are fantastic starts to get us headed in the right direction, but the only way to close the gap is through *action*. We must justly earn the life we envision.

We all know people, and are guilty ourselves, of saying we want something, yet take no action to make it a reality. We may say we want to complete a Paint by Numbers, *yet take no action to complete it!* Is what we are saying true? Do we *really* want what we say, if we don't take action? No matter how much we wish and pray, the paintbrush will not stand up by itself, dip into the paint, and begin moving around the canvas. (Unless you are a smart, overachieving magical person like Hermione Granger, of course.) If we really want the completed painting, we must pick up the paintbrush, dip it in the paint, and *begin painting.*

If we say we want to lose weight, yet we sit on the sofa every night watching television and eating potato chips, our actions say what we really want is to sit on the sofa every night watching television and eating potato chips!

Don't ask God to guide your footsteps if you're not willing to move your feet.
Anonymous

When we say we want something, whether it is losing weight, making more money, or improving our relationships, yet we take no action to make it happen, then it's not true. We really want something else *more*. Saying we want something is only true if we are taking action to get it. Here are ways to make getting up off the sofa easier so we can take action!

BE QUIET AND TAKE ACTION

The way to get started is to quit talking and begin doing.
Walt Disney

While a student at Art Center School in Los Angeles, Canadian painter Robert Genn was frequently called into the registrar's office. She wanted to talk with Genn about his late payments, but a few times also informed him, "Looking over the reports from your instructors, they are pretty well consistent in saying that you talk a good job and do a poor one."

Genn writes that at the time he was shocked to hear his instructors' assessment. He then decided to change, and committed to a vow of silence; going forward he would "understate and over prove." He came to realize that when he talked a good job, it took away his need and energy to actually *do* a good job.

We all know someone (and it may be ourselves) who is constantly telling us about her or his "big plans." Such people say they are going to take their mother on a vacation, or buy a new house, or start their own company. We *Well done is better than well said.* Benjamin Franklin may listen to them tell us their dreams for weeks, months, even years. Sometimes it even seems as though they want to get credit for their intended good deed before actually having done anything.

The thing we don't realize is, talking about doing something without actually taking action *dissipates* our energy. Robert Genn says, "When you talk, you gradually lose your need to do. Each word is a brick removed from the wall of your desire."

To make it easier to take action, quit *talking* about taking action. Simply take action! And when you catch yourself telling someone about your grand plans, quiet yourself down and use that talking energy to act.

PRACTICE FEELING GOOD

If we practice playing the piano, we improve playing the piano. If we practice speaking French, we improve speaking French. And if we practice feeling a feeling, we get better at feeling that feeling.

When we look at our future self in our Self-Portrait Notebook, we expect to feel good once we reach the life of our dreams. This means that in order to feel good once we reach our goal, we have to practice feeling good along the way. The feeling we will have when we accomplish our goal, and the feeling we have on a daily basis, must be a match.

Imagine you purchase a Paint by Numbers kit of Vincent Van Gogh's painting, *Starry Night*. You can imagine the finished painting hanging above your breakfast table, where you admire it and feel good every morning while enjoying breakfast. This good feeling inspires you to take action and begin working on the painting in your kit.

Quickly, this good feeling turns bad if perhaps you become frustrated that you can barely make out the faint numbers on the printed art board, making you pessimistic that you are choosing the correct colors to paint with. You might also become irritated that the bristles on the supplied brush are stiff and thick, which makes painting within the hazy lines very challenging. You thought this process would be much easier than it turned out to be. You force yourself to finish the painting, and stubbornly hang it on your wall. *There! Finished!* Then, while having breakfast, you look at the painting and relive the feelings you practiced while painting it: feelings of frustration, pessimism, and irritation. These are the feelings you practiced while working on the painting, and now they are the feelings you are reminded of when you view it.

Now imagine you work on your painting, but practice feeling good along the way. You can barely make out the faint numbers, but are optimistic that you are choosing the correct colors to paint with. You realize that the bristles on the supplied brush are stiff and thick, which makes painting within the hazy lines difficult. But, you decide that if you do another Paint by Numbers, you might make a trip to your local craft store to buy a new brush. For now, you enthusiastically put paint on the canvas and believe painting out of the lines will only add to the painting. The process turns out to be much more fun and easy than you thought. You excitedly hang the painting on your wall. *Finished! Wonderful!* When having breakfast, you look at the painting and relive the feelings you practiced while painting it: feelings of optimism, and enthusiasm. These are the feelings you practiced while working on the painting and now you feel good while viewing it.

The feeling we will have upon achieving our goal will always be a match to the feeling we have while getting there. The feeling will always be a match. Practice feeling good on the journey and you will *want* to get up off that sofa and take action.

WORK BEGETS INSPIRATION

Inspiration more often comes during the work than before it, because the largest part of the job of an artist is to listen to the work. . . To pray is to listen also, to move through my own chattering to God, to that place where I can be silent and listen to what God may have to say.
Madeleine L'Engle

While living in Buck's County, Pennsylvania, my husband, elementary school-aged daughters, and I became members of the Addisville Reformed Church. With church membership comes a responsibility to donate your time to help the church operate. I was asked to help in the baby nursery, but declined. Not being a "baby person" outside of my own, I wasn't going to voluntarily expose myself to crying, drooling, pooping babies.

So, then I was asked to assist the pastor's lovely wife, Jane, for a children's Sunday school class. I gave it a shot, but quit after I was continually called "Dude" by one of the boys, and witnessed another pick his nose, and do something really disgusting with it. Oh, how I wish I could erase that mental image.

Later one day, I received a phone call from Pastor Doug Dwyer. He had attended an art show I was in, and wanted to know if I would be willing to paint a portrait of the church. Yes, yes, yes! It may sound hokey, but I thought, *Now here is a way to use my God-given talent to bring enjoyment to myself and the members of the church!*

Pastor Doug dug through the church archives and gave me all the old photos of the church he could find. (Pastor Doug, dug. That was fun to write. Doug, dug.) I wanted to add to my reference materials, so I did my own photo shoot of the beautiful, stone church that was built in 1858.

Moving around the front of the church on a sunny morning, I took several photos from many angles. Suddenly my intuition, or a God whisper, said, "Open the church doors." The interesting thing is, I had never seen the front doors open. Everyone entered the church from the parking lot through the back. I walked up to the heavy wood doors and pulled. They were locked, and didn't budge. My mind got busy convincing myself I had enough photos, and I needed to get home. Yet the voice persisted, "Open the doors."

All right, I thought. I went around to the back and entered the church. I walked down the long deserted hallway and to the front doors. They were locked from the inside as well! I searched the hallways until I found someone who had a key, and she opened the front doors for me.

I completed the painting *Sunrise Service* and donated it to the church. Many people, including Pastor Doug, commented on the open front doors. They all loved how it gave the church the feeling of being inviting and welcoming to all.

Before starting the painting, I would never have thought of opening the doors. Divine inspiration

Sunrise Service, by:
Annette Hackney Evans

came to me during the work. My point with this memory is that we should not be concerned if, before taking action, we don't have things all figured. It's our job to listen to the work after we get started. The thrilling part is the mystery of where our actions will lead us.

MASTERMIND GROUP

No single mind is complete; no one person can answer every question. But two or more minds, united behind a definite major purpose and working in harmony to achieve it, will accomplish great things.
Napoleon Hill

A way to take action, and have fun doing it, is to be part of a mastermind group. A mastermind group has two main purposes:

1   Group members brainstorm together and share resources.
2   Group members challenge each other to set goals, and then hold each accountable to accomplish them.

I was first introduced to the concept of a mastermind group in a book we discussed in Chapter 14, Napoleon Hill's *Think & Grow Rich*. It has been proven that the expression "Two heads are better than one," is true. Hill describes it like this, "No two minds ever come together without, thereby, creating a third, invisible, intangible force which may be likened to a third mind."

Whoa! We absorb and are influenced by the personality, habits and power of thought of people we associate with. Together with them, we create a third mind. Makes you want to reevaluate who you spend your time with, doesn't it?

A mastermind group can be organized, such as a group that has a weekly meeting. Or, it can be unorganized, such as bouncing ideas off of co-workers, who don't even realize they are engaging the mastermind. Keep in mind to choose positive, creative people, who want the best for you. You *don't* want to create a third mind with someone who is a negative, small thinker, and secretly feels contentment if you fail. Seriously reevaluate whom you spend your time with.

Most creative accomplishments are the product of creative alliances. Think of Marie and Pierre Curie, who together discovered radium. Think of Tenzing Norgay and Edmund Hillary, who were the first to scale Mt. Everest. Think of John Lennon and Paul McCartney, who together made The Beatles one of the most commercially successful and critically acclaimed bands in the history of popular music. When ordinary people who have a shared mission "Come Together," they can achieve extraordinary results.

I became infatuated with British interior decorator Martyn Lawrence Bullard while watching a reality TV show he stars in. Each week, while impeccably dressed, Martyn turns ordinary rooms into "delicious, decadent, and glamorous" spaces. Many of Martyn's clients are, in his words, "...amazing, incredibly talented people." As imaginative as Martyn is, he says results can be greater when he collaborates. (Read the following with an English accent and Martyn's words will sound even *more* profound!) "And actually, what really happens is I get to feed off of their talent, off of their creativity. Somehow together we kind of work and we have a creative explosion!" Martyn instinctively taps into the mastermind.

Our society likes to glorify the achievement of individuals, so it is hard for us to wrap our mind around the notion that we can improve ourselves by sharing ideas with others. But to multiply our brainpower, forming a mastermind group is exactly what we have to do. Napoleon Hill writes, "Great power can be accumulated through no other principle!"

When your mind is coordinated with one or more people, in harmony, for a definite purpose, you gain access to "Infinite Intelligence," or, God.

Your single mind is powerful.

Your single mind with God's influence is more powerful.

Your single mind, with one or more other minds, with God's influence, is most powerful!

Martyn Lawrence Bullard, by: Annette Hackney Evans

Give a Little More Than You're Asking for

To get more than we currently have, we have to give more than we are currently giving. This applies to all areas of our life. We only get out of something what we put into it. Whatever our dream or goal, we must give more than we expect to get back. Let's take a look at how this applies to three areas of our life:

Your Calling

It had long since come to my attention that people of accomplishment rarely sat back and let things happen. They went out and happened to things.
Leonardo da Vinci

If we want to grow our business, we must give our customers more than they expect from us. By exceeding their expectations, they become repeat customers and tell their friends about us.

If we want a promotion, we must give our boss more than she or he expects from us. We must take on more responsibilities or contribute more creative ideas. In short, we must earn a lot more money for the company than we are receiving in our paycheck.

Give a little more than you're asking for, and you will keep customers, gain new ones, and land that promotion.

Serving Others

Paraphrasing John F. Kennedy, "Ask not what your community can do for you, ask what you can do for your community." Whether you are hoping to get more out of your neighborhood, your church, or the park in your town square, ask yourself what action you can take to make it better. Unlike me, maybe you *are* a "baby person," and can't get enough of their fresh from heaven smell. If this is the case, volunteering in your church nursery might help you feel more connected. Inviting neighbors over for cupcakes and champagne, and developing those relationships, also might make yours feel like a tight knit neighborhood. At your local park, organize a Saturday morning park clean up, or invite a group of friends for a picnic.

When we find ourselves complaining about the lack of community in our community, it's the perfect time to turn it around, and ask ourself what we can contribute to make it better.

Family & Friends

In the song "I Just Want to Be Your Everything," Andy Gibb sings, "If you give a little more than you're asking for, your love will turn the key."

In all of our relationships, if we want to be happy, we must give a little more than we're asking for. A good relationship isn't you giving 25% and the other person 75%. It isn't even you meeting them halfway. Ideally, good relationships are both people giving 100%.

Occasionally, my daughters felt sorry for themselves for not getting invited out on a Friday night. Full disclosure...occasionally *I* feel sorry for *myself* for not getting invited out on a Friday night. The first thing I would ask them, and myself, is, "When was the last time *you* planned something. When was the last time *you* invited friends out?"

If you feel that in your relationships you are the one giving 100%, and other people are giving much less, tell them you have needs, and you need more. If they change, fantastic! If they don't, it may be time to gather new people in your life.

Put more into life than you expect to get back. Give a little more than you're asking for, and you'll be surprised at the rewards you will get back.

The next time you catch yourself complaining about something in your life, or talking about a future goal, ask yourself what actions

The artist is nothing without the gift, but the gift is nothing without the work.
Emile Zola

you have taken to improve the situation or accomplish the goal. Quit talking, get up off the sofa, and take action. Do it now. You can't take action in the past, or the future. You can only act in the *now*. Practice feeling good, expect to be inspired *after* the work has begun, and always give more than you're asking for. Create a third mind with positive, creative people who want the best for you, and for whom you want the best. Pray as though everything depends on God, but take action as though everything depends on you.

Give Up the Good for the Great

To be free, we must be willing to give up the good for the greater! We need to bless and release people, things, beliefs, actions, circumstances, and relationships from our lives that no longer reflect our current truth.

Carol A. Karpeck

Many of us are living good lives. We associate with good people, we have good things, and our days are filled with good activities. If and when we think of God, we feel that God is good.

Is all this good in our lives good enough? Have you ever observed someone else's life and thought, *Wouldn't that life be great?*

A wise art instructor once told me, "Annette, when you begin a painting, use a brush as big as a mop. Cover the canvas with paint. Then, bring the painting into focus with a smaller and smaller brush. Finally, when you get down to the last details, paint with a brush as fine as a pin."

The purpose of painting in this way, from the general to the specific, is so we don't become too attached with a portion of the painting and unwilling to paint over it. As artists, we must be willing to give up the good, a passage of the painting that we have fallen in love with, for the greater, for what is best to make the painting a success overall.

This is also true for our lives. We often hold onto people, things, and beliefs, even when they are no longer adding to the overall success of our life. This holding on not only drains a lot of our physical and emotional energy, but crowds our life so there is no room for the new. Now that we have a definite major purpose in all areas of our life, we will need to create time in our current life to support our actions. In order to create a masterpiece, we must give up some of the current good (and most if not all of the not so good) to make room for the *great*.

People

This might seem cold-hearted, but for the purposes of having a greater life, let's take inventory of the people we spend a lot of time with. Write down below 10 – 15 people that you spend most of your time with, whether it's time physically spent with them, or someone you don't see often but who occupies a large portion of your thoughts. These people could be family, friends, co-workers, neighbors, people from groups you are a member of, or even celebrities you think about a lot.

Ready, get set,…go!

1 _____ ☐

2 _____ ☐

3 _____ ☐

4 _____ ☐

5 _____ ☐

6 _____ ☐

7 _____ ☐

8 _____ ☐

9 _____ ☐

10 _____ ☐

11 _____ ☐

12 _____ ☐

13 _____ ☐

14 _____ ☐

15 _____ ☐

Next, in the box beside each name, give the person a ranking:

#1 = She or he is positive, and supportive of my dreams. Our conversations are balanced between talking and listening, and after being with her or him I feel uplifted.

#2 = She or he is a combination of #1 and #3.

#3 = She or he is negative, and not supportive of my dreams. Our conversations are unbalanced with her or him talking, and me listening. After being with her or him my energy is low.

Fill in the boxes...

Now that you've ranked the people in your life, take a look at the list. If you are serious about making your life a masterpiece, moving forward you will consciously spend more time with those #1 individuals than the #2s and #3s. By spending time with them, you will be inspired, motivated, and energized. The more room you make in your life for them, the less time you will have for the #2s and #3s. You don't have to ditch your #2s and #3s, just reduce the time you spend with them. We must make more room in our lives for those who lift us up.

In Chapter 20 we discussed the importance of a mastermind group. When two minds interact they form a third, separate mind. Look at the people on your list again. Imagine the thoughts in your

Life is too short for half-hearted connections and meaningless run-throughs.

Karen Kingsbury

Karen Kingsbury, by: Annette Hackney Evans

mind combined with the thoughts of each of these people. When your mind is mixed with theirs, is yours improved, does it stay about the same, or is it worse? In my past, there have been #3 people in my life who, because of my own insecurities, I tried to win over. I tried to earn their love. Looking back, I can honestly say, *it never worked*! What a waste of my energy. And why would I want to create a third mind with a #3 person, when hers or his would only make mine worse?

IMPORTANT MESSAGE. The #1s on your list probably didn't become positive, supportive and uplifting by accident. Most likely each worked at it, and have a support group of people who are *their* #1s. In order for them to be willing to spend more time with you, you must become a #1 person for them. Interesting how that works, isn't it?

When you spend the majority of your time with #1 people, and become "1" yourself, you will discover an interesting thing happening, you will attract more of them into your life, while the number of #2s and #3s will shrink. Make room in your life for positive people who lift you up.

THINGS

> *Life is full and overflowing with the new. But it is necessary*
> *to empty out the old to make room for the new.*
> Eileen Caddy

We know by now that being a "Material Girl" does not make us more fulfilled. Having more designer clothes, owning the latest electronic gadgets, driving a status symbol car, and living in a mansion, might bring us temporary enjoyment, but not long-term happiness.

On the other hand, having a minimal wardrobe, keeping our electric gadgets until they die, driving a Smart car, and living in a small space, doesn't necessarily bring us happiness either.

It is possible to be happy living in a mansion with the best that money can buy, or living in one room with the bare essentials. Your comfort level in between these two extremes is *individual*, it is *specific to you*.

What does contribute to our happiness is that the things in our surroundings make us feel good. As people, we are continually evolving, and our surroundings should reflect who we are today. It is necessary to empty out the old to make room for the new.

What percentage of the things in your home do you actually use, wear, or enjoy looking at? 75%? 50%? 10%? If you are like me, you've accumulated a lot of things over the years that no longer reflect who you are. Now is the time to simplify.

Sometimes we need to simplify out of necessity, such as when my family moved in 2008 from our house in Indiana to a house half the size in Orange County, California. I found it hard to part with old household items and artwork, but there would be no real room for them in the new space. Then God intervened, and sent a flood to the house we were leaving. Not a Noah's Ark scale flood, but a flood that put the basement a foot deep in water. A lot of furniture was ruined, and household items such as games, bedding, and collectables. But the most meaningful things damaged were much of my artwork I had saved since childhood.

While our neighbors, who suffered similarly with the flood, were sad and complained about their destroyed "things," I felt a slight relief. I was free from these things that I couldn't part with on my own. Chances were my childhood art would never be auctioned off at Christie's anyway! And now I had less stuff to haul 2,000 miles across the country.

Life is constantly renewing itself, and it's important to keep things circulating. We breathe in, we breathe out. We breathe in, we breathe out. We take in energy through food, we expend energy through action. We take in energy, we expend energy. We accumulate things in our life, we simplify and give things away. We accumulate, we give away.

> The ability to simplify means to eliminate the unnecessary so that the necessary may speak.
> Hans Hofmann

My rule of thumb is, any "thing" in my environment that doesn't *clearly* make me feel good, I get rid of. I once read about a famous pop star who owned an original Frida Kahlo painting. Frida Kahlo was a Mexican artist who had a difficult life and expressed this through sometimes unsettling images. The painting this pop star owned was particularly grotesque, but the star said that anyone in her home that viewed this painting and didn't like it, couldn't be her friend. Well, I guess I can't be her friend. I don't want to look at, or create, art that makes me feel bad. I want to create art that makes me, and the viewer, feel good. I want to collect art from *other* artists that makes me feel good. I can turn on the news and feel bad. Why do I want to hang a painting on my wall that does that? I believe artist Henri Matisse felt the same. "What I dream of is an art of balance, of purity and serenity devoid of troubling or depressing subject matter—a soothing, calming influence on the mind, rather like a good armchair which provides relaxation from physical fatigue."

Surrounding yourself with things that make you feel good might mean keepsakes that help you recall good times, books that deliver positive messages, or painting a room your favorite color.

Get rid of the things in your surroundings that don't bring you happiness. Make room for new things that do. Walking into your home and feeling comfortable and content completely wins over walking into a large home packed with expensive things that don't bring you joy. Let go of what was once good, and is no longer, to make room for the greater.

INVOLVEMENTS AND INTERESTS

The more attachments we have, the less room there is in our lives for new involvements and interests.
Carol A. Karpeck

When she was in fourth grade, my daughter Isabella developed a strong attachment to the color green. For three years, anything I bought for her, from clothing to room décor, had to be green. She got up every morning and put on an outfit of head-to-toe green. She mixed yellow green, lime green, Kelly green, forest green and army green, to her heart's content. In art class, Isabella only painted with shades of green. Her fifth grade art teacher informed her that the sky is not green. She was not intrigued by Isabella's preference for green; she was critical of it. Picasso's blue period was motivated by the loss of a good friend; perhaps Isabella's green period was inspired by an intense period of growth.

One Sunday evening, Isabella came to me with a non-green sweater in her hand and asked, "Mommy, can we talk?"

"Of course," I said, and motioned for her to sit down beside me. "What's up?"

"Well," she said, "I think I want to wear this sweater to school tomorrow, and I'm afraid the kids in my class will ask me why I'm not wearing green. And I don't want that attention."

My older daughter had given Isabella the hand-me-down sweater, and Isabella liked it. The problem was, it was white with orange trim. After three years, Isabella was ready to expand her identity, but she wasn't sure her classmates, who had come to accept her as "The Green Girl," would now accept her new image.

Sometimes living our lives to please other people can get us stuck in a role we have long since out grown. To turn our lives into a masterpiece, and continue evolving into the people we are meant to be, we have to be able to let go of old labels, old beliefs, old involvements and interests to make room for the new. What are you holding onto today, out of habit, or to please other people? Think of the energy and new opportunities that will open up if you let it go.

I told Isabella to wear that sweater on Monday. I told her to try it out, don't wear green for a day. The first day will be the hardest, but nothing has to be forever. She could always go back to wearing green on Tuesday.

As an adult it is often difficult to let go of an attachment, and I was concerned how a child, my ten-year-old daughter, would handle it. As soon as Isabella left for school wearing the white sweater with orange trim, I called the school psychologist and asked if she would discreetly check on Isabella that day. I received a phone call in the afternoon informing me that Isabella appeared to be laughing and having fun with classmates, just as she normally did. From that day forward, Isabella's color repertoire has expanded in her wardrobe and bedroom décor. And her landscapes usually include blue skies.

GOD

We must free ourselves to be filled by God.
Even God cannot fill what is full.
Mother Teresa

There is a common saying that we all have a God shaped hole in our hearts. It is a place in our hearts where we long to feel inner peace. If we have experienced great hurt or loss in our life, sometimes the pain from this hole is unbearable. We may go for the short cut, the easy fix, the Band-Aid. We may try to feel better through self-medication, whether it be drugs, alcohol, or food. We may try to fill this hole by staying really busy, such as being a workaholic, overly involved in our children's lives, or belonging to too many clubs and organizations. We may try to fill the hole by attempting to win love from others by achieving fame or having the finest material possessions. Or we may simply try to distract ourselves with travel and entertainment.

Often, we don't even have to try to fill this hole ourselves. Society tries to fill it for us. Our literal and cyber mailboxes are full of junk mail, mail order catalogs and newsletters. Magazines and newspapers bombard us with mostly irrelevant knowledge. Our minds are over-stimulated by radio and television going all the time. Most stores and restaurants keep this chatter going. Billboards are in the periphery of everywhere we drive. This information overload is filling us up, yet we still feel unfulfilled!

If we are brave, we will sit still, be quiet, and let ourselves feel this spiritual void. This place may be painful, but it is also the place where inner peace can be found. God is ready to fill us with inner peace, but even He cannot fill what is already full.

God is love. The only relief from the God shaped hole in our hearts is to fill our lives with love. Love God, love yourself, love the work you do, love others, and love serving others. Give up some of the chatter in your life to make room for that which is greater, and more important.

> Don't be afraid to give up the good to go for the great.
> John D. Rockefeller

To live the life of our dreams, we must be willing to give up the good for the great. We must give up some time spent with #2 and #3 people in our life in order to make more time for #1s. We must release some of the material things in our lives in order to make room for things that reflect who we are today. We must be willing to let go of attachments, involvements and interests that we may be doing to please others, in order to pursue new involvements and interests that please us. We must be willing to let go of the distractions and noise in our lives in order to be filled by God. We don't have to wait for a flood, we can release things willingly. Free yourself to be filled by God.

Expand Your Comfort Zone

Both authenticity and adventure require a point of departure, the willingness to shed what's safe and predictable in order to embrace the new—people, places, predicaments, pleasures, and passions.
Sarah Ban Breathnach

I used to think some people just didn't get nervous. I believed a performer could casually stroll on stage at the Academy Awards and, without a spike in blood pressure, tell a joke, present an award, or give an acceptance speech, in front of over three thousand people in the live audience, and forty million American viewers in their homes. I was wrong. People who are living their dreams aren't people who never get nervous, they are people who are willing to shed what's safe and predictable if it will help them reach their goals.

When I go see a live performer, or even watch one performing live on television, I look closely for signs of nervousness. I especially pay attention to hands. Do the performers' hands shake while holding the microphone, or while opening the envelope and simultaneously saying, "And the winner is…" Very often their hands *are* trembling, and this makes me feel so related to them! I don't want them to fail. I want them to succeed. But I know if they can succeed while nervous and stretching their comfort zone, then so can I.

The following diagram is a "Comfort Zone Circle." The center circle is our Comfort Zone and represents where we are today, and everything that we are comfortable doing. These would be things that are part of our everyday lives, which aren't challenging for us. It's normal to want to stay within this Comfort Zone and feel cozy and safe. But, if we are serious about accomplishing the things on our Self-Portrait Plan, and I know that you are, then staying in this inner circle is not an option. We are born wanting an exciting life, full of adventure. Everything new we want to achieve or experience is currently outside of this inner circle.

Avoiding danger is no safer in the long run than outright exposure. Life is either a daring adventure, or nothing.
Helen Keller

The second circle is the Stretch Zone circle. This middle circle consists of new activities that make us uncomfortable. These activities stretch our capabilities, and maybe even our attitudes, to carry out.

The third circle is the Panic! Zone circle. This moves from just stretching our capabilities and into one of panic, as in, "OMG, why did I agree to do this? Adrenaline is shooting through me, my heart is pounding, and I have to go to the bathroom!"

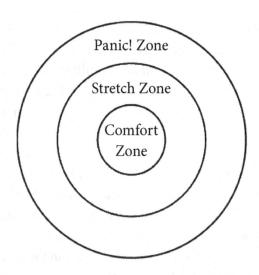

Every Thanksgiving Eve, I make traditional pumpkin pies. Stretching our Comfort Zone is like stretching pie dough. I mix the ingredients for the dough and then place the ball on my lightly floured, cool, marble countertop. (Honestly, I usually buy pre-made deep-dish piecrust. But stick with me, I like this analogy.) Next, I take a lightly floured rolling pin and roll the dough out. I make it bigger, and bigger, until it fits into the pie dish. It wasn't natural for the lump of dough to be 9" across, but with stretching, it got there. It was always the same dough, but stretching it gave the dough a new shape. You don't have to change the ingredients of who you are to reach your goals, but you do have to stretch the radius of your current Comfort Zone.

If we're not stretching, we're not growing. We can only get closer to our dreams by expanding into our Stretch Zone. Many people say you have to *step* out of your Comfort Zone. I say you have to *expand* your Comfort Zone. Your Comfort Zone will be surrounding you for the rest of your life. How large it expands or contracts is up to you.

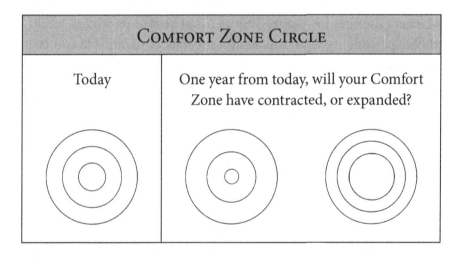

COMFORT ZONE CIRCLE

Today

One year from today, will your Comfort Zone have contracted, or expanded?

Everything in the Universe is continually contracting or expanding. The only thing constant is change. In one year will our Comfort Zone have contracted, or expanded?

I learned to drive the Los Angeles freeways at sixteen, so early on I became quite comfortable darting in and out of six lanes of traffic. Then, after living for fifteen years in states where I mostly drove on two lane highways, when I moved back to California I realized my Comfort Zone had shrunk. At first, driving on the freeways again was in my Stretch Zone, and often in my Panic! Zone. But with time and practice, I am now comfortable again. In what area of your life has your Comfort Zone expanded, contracted, and then expanded again?

Our dreams are outside of our Comfort Zone. In one year, will you have expanded, and be closer to those dreams? Or will you have contracted, and be farther away? The choice is yours. The following ideas will help us expand our Comfort Zone.

Baby Steps

Baby steps till 4 o'clock. Baby steps till 4 o'clock.
Bob in the movie *What About Bob?*

In the 1991 comedy *What About Bob?*, New York psychiatrist Dr. Leo Marvin describes his patient Bob as "…an almost-paralyzed, multiphobic personality who is in a constant state of panic." He counsels Bob to face his fears by taking "baby steps," which is also the title of the doctor's new book.

When Dr. Marvin goes on a family vacation to Lake Winnipesaukee, New Hampshire, Bob is unable to cope. Applying what he learned in the book *Baby Steps*, Bob stretches his Comfort Zone and follows Dr. Marvin to his vacation home, where the hilarity of the film continues.

Taking baby steps truly is one of the best ways to overcome our fears and stretch our Comfort Zone. Our fearful thoughts can be overwhelming. Taking baby steps allows us to stretch our Comfort Zone slowly, making it less frightening. First identify an action you are afraid to take. Second, break down your action into baby steps. With baby steps planned out, you will be able to slowly decrease your discomfort and move toward your goals.

To get into a pool of cool water, some of us like to run across the cement, push off the edge of the pool, and do a cannonball to make a huge splash, while yelling, "Geronimo!" Others like to take small, slow, baby steps down the pool stairs. Either way will work! Baby steps are the most peaceful and perhaps lasting in terms of progress.

Take a Friend

Walking with a friend in the dark
is better than walking alone in the light.
Helen Keller

Our Comfort Zone is what is familiar to us: it is well lit, and makes us feel safe. Our Stretch Zone is unfamiliar to us, and we may feel we are groping in the dark, and thus more vulnerable. Having a friend by our side may soothe our nerves and give us a sense of security.

If you are feeling uncomfortable about an action you want to take in your life, try inviting a friend along. This is probably the most popular way to stretch our Comfort Zone, especially for some of us women. After all, some women even have the reputation of enjoying going to the Ladies Room together.

John Lennon wrote, "I get by with a little help from my friends." Friends can help us move out of our Comfort Zone in every area of our lives:

Health = Studies show again and again that people who have a "diet buddy" lose more weight and keep it off longer. A diet buddy is someone who shares our weight loss and workout goals. Often, failure in a weight-loss program has less to do with the method we choose and more to do with the lack of a good support system. Teaming up is more fun, and it's been proven to get better results.

My Calling = When we follow our calling, there *will* be times we are in our Stretch Zone, and possibly our Panic! Zone. We women need to support each other as we pursue our dreams. If we need to take a class to learn a new skill, we can ask if a friend would like to enroll too. If we are nervous about a speech we will be giving, we can invite a friend to sit in the audience. Whenever possible, I like to reciprocate by cheering on my friends as they cross finish lines, by being a familiar face in the audience as they give a speech, or by attending an event when they are marketing a new product.

Serving Others = What could make us feel better than helping others while having fun with a friend by our side? Helping others is always a positive group effort.

Family & Friends = We've all been in our Comfort Zone in a relationship, and then had it end. Moving on, by ourselves, puts us in the Stretch Zone or Panic! Zone. It is comforting to have friends to talk things through with. And we sometimes need friends to help us "get back out there."

EDUCATE YOURSELF

Fears are educated into us, and can, if we wish, be educated out.
Karl Augustus Menninger

My big brother Ronny Dale (now that he's an adult, we call him R.D., or Ron) had a paper route as a kid. He rode his bike all over Orleans throwing papers on driveways. He became a reliable resource in knowing which streets housed the biggest, most vicious, *biting*, dogs. He also informed me that when anyone gets bitten by a dog, they must undergo rabies shots...in the stomach! When I was a child, I endured weekly allergy shots in the arm, and imagining getting shots in my stomach sounded more painful than getting bitten by a dog!

Anytime I rode my hot-pink bicycle around town, I was paranoid. *Is this the street he said that mean dog lives on? Or is it that one? And what about the dog who roams from neighborhood to neighborhood?* My imagination went wild. I saw myself getting chased by a barking dog with foam flying from his mouth. I would pedal more quickly, but in my mind the dog was too fast and would clamp his teeth around my ankle. I imagined screaming, my bike wobbling, then crashing. The pain would be intense and the dog would continue biting my arms and face as I writhed in agony on the hot, black asphalt. The next thing I knew, I would be in a doctor's office, and more painful than the bike crash or the dog bites, I would be getting rabies shots in my stomach! So, as you can see, it was hard to enjoy my bike ride to Grandma Frances' with all of this going through my mind.

My fear of dogs changed nine years ago when we got our dog Fritz. I read books on training dogs, and even hired a dog trainer to come to our home. But the best education I got was watching the *Dog Whisperer* Cesar Milan, in his show on the *National Geographic* channel. After absorbing his teaching on how dogs think, I am happy to say I am no longer fearful of all dogs, and have become a decent pack leader.

Do you have a fear that someone passed down to you? A fear of dogs? A fear of flying? A fear of math? Your Comfort Zone might be protecting you from *imaginary* dangers, things that actually aren't as scary as you think. Do some research by reading books, looking things up online, and asking others how they overcame their fear. Getting good information will lessen your fear and nervousness, and educate the fear right out of you.

ENTERTAIN THE UNCOMFORTABLE

Venturing out of your comfort zone may be dangerous, yet you do it anyway because our ability to grow is directly proportional to an ability to entertain the uncomfortable.
Twyla Tharp

Twyla Tharp is a dancer / choreographer who has choreographed 129 dances, twelve television specials, six Hollywood movies, four full-length ballets, four Broadway shows and two figure skating routines. She currently lives in New York City, but originally she was a fellow Hoosier! Tharp is a true artist, and a person who creates something from nothing. Every time she begins a new project, she stretches her Comfort Zone and entertains the uncomfortable. Tharp acknowledges that her work sometimes feels dangerous. And to create great art, she *will* feel uncomfortable. Yet, she does it anyway because that's how she knows she can grow and explore.

Taking baby steps, having a friend by our side, and educating ourselves away from fear, are ways to stretch our Comfort Zone as easily as possible. At the same time, we have to realize that there just *will* be moments we are uncomfortable. I have heard a weight-loss guru say that to lose weight we sometimes have to be comfortable having a hungry feeling. And a world-class athlete has said when racing long distance he can win any "suffer fest." Whether we are creating art, losing weight, or competing in sports, success will come when we are willing to give up always being comfortable.

Remember, whatever our goal, other people were uncomfortable getting there too. If we are not entertaining the uncomfortable, then we are not growing, and not stretching our Comfort Zone; and goals are naturally out of our Comfort Zone, otherwise we wouldn't have them.

Trust in God

The fear of human opinion disables you:
trusting in God protects you from that.
Proverbs 29:25

It's normal to be concerned about, and to even be afraid of, what other people think about us. In cavewoman times, a healthy sense of fear instilled by leaders regarding how to act in the community likely saved many lives, in terms of learning about wild animals and aggressive weather patterns. It wouldn't surprise me if there were some forever-lost historic rules that included chastisement if they weren't followed, like, "we will all consider anyone who runs out of the cave into the thunderstorm a complete fool and not worthy of respect." Such social rules we fear to break may have also enabled strong social ties, if people were afraid to separate from their groups—fearing they wouldn't survive on their own. Many places in the world have groups of people who know from experience that having a good relationship with your village neighbors can ensure survival, and they fear breaking from these groups because of that.

Part of what happens, though, in these protective groups, is that we fear disapproval—in other words, in a very secure, tight group of people, we tend to fear being different or leaving, if we want to keep the good feelings and support of the group. Yet, though we may be in some ways "hard-wired" to fear negative human opinions, let's look at the big picture. In the USA today, you will not be sent off to a deserted island if you act socially awkward at a party. And you won't be stoned if you don't deliver a flawless speech at a posh function.

Remember, whatever we are thinking is going out as a prayer. When we are trying something new and stretch our Comfort Zone to do it, are we thinking, *I'm going to make a fool out of myself in front of everyone!* Or are we praying, *God, I'm nervous, but I know that with your help I'll get through this.*

At the Sorbonne in Paris, France, 1910, Theodore Roosevelt delivered the speech *Citizen In A Republic*. The following is an excerpt from that speech.

THE MAN IN THE ARENA

It is not the critic who counts; not the man who points out how the strong man stumbles, or where the doer of deeds could have done them better. The credit belongs to the man who is actually in the arena, whose face is marred by dust and sweat and blood; who strives valiantly; who errs, who comes short again and again, because there is no effort without error and shortcoming; but who does actually strive to do the deeds; who knows great enthusiasms, the great devotions; who spends himself in a worthy cause; who at the best knows in the end the triumph of high achievement, and who at the worst, if he fails, at least fails while daring greatly, so that his place shall never be with those cold and timid souls who neither know victory nor defeat.

It is hard to fail, but it is worse never to have tried to succeed.

Theodore Roosevelt

Theodore Roosevelt, by: John Singer Sargent

Stretch your Comfort Zone by taking the focus off of your fear of critics. Know that when we get in the arena and try, we *will* sometimes fail. Even if human opinion is not good, the consequences will likely not be that bad. Instead, focus on the image in your mind of things going well, and trust that God will, eventually, make that happen for you. We must have the courage to stretch beyond our fear of failure if we will ever know the feeling of success.

Let's do a little exercise. Stand up and stretch you hands to the ceiling…just kidding. This isn't a physical exercise; it's a mental one. Refer to your 25 Coming Attractions list. Choose something off of your list that if you had to perform *today*, would send you straight into a Panic! Zone.

Now, let's go through the 5 steps we just covered to see how we can make stretching our Comfort Zone easier. I'll go first.

PANIC! ZONE GOAL:

In five years, do a live portrait painting demonstration at the Portrait Society of America Conference.

1 BABY STEPS
   a. Paint five days a week.
   b. Do portrait painting demonstrations for local, smaller audiences.

2 TAKE A FRIEND
   a. Ask friends to model for me so I can build my confidence painting from live models.

3 EDUCATE YOURSELF
   a. Sign up for a workshop from a portrait painter who has demonstrated at the PSA Conference.
   b. Plan on attending future conferences and carefully observe the artists who give demonstrations.

4 ENTERTAIN THE UNCOMFORTABLE
   a. Be aware of, and emotionally accept, bouts of nervousness.
   b. Recognize all the other demonstrators had a "first time" too.
   c. Focus on enjoying the experience, not the outcome of the painting, as I make it.

5 TRUST IN GOD
   a. Tell God my worries that people in the audience won't think I'm good enough.
   b. Remember God gave me a desire to teach, and teaching is a positive activity that helps people.
   c. Pray to God to ease my concerns and allow me to express my skills patiently and joyously in front of others to help them learn too.

Get the idea? Okay, your turn. Take one thing from your 25 Coming Attractions list that is currently in your Panic! Zone. What steps can you take to accomplish your goal?

PANIC! ZONE GOAL:

_____

1 BABY STEPS

_____

_____

_____

2 TAKE A FRIEND

_____

_____

_____

3   EDUCATE YOURSELF

_____

_____

_____

4   ENTERTAIN THE UNCOMFORTABLE

_____

_____

_____

5   TRUST IN GOD

_____

_____

_____

See, you've got this! I've heard it said that at the end of our lives, our biggest regrets are not the things we did, but the things that we didn't do. Get in the arena and take action. Be courageous. Stretch your Comfort Zone. Every time you do, it will feel more and more comfortable. How else will we know what we are capable of becoming if we don't stretch and see?

Focused Persistence

Nothing in this world can take the place of persistence. Talent will not; nothing is more common than unsuccessful people with talent. Genius will not; unrewarded genius is almost a proverb. Education will not; the world is full of educated failures. Persistence and determination alone are omnipotent.
Calvin Coolidge

From the record below, can you guess who this person is?

At 22 years old he...	failed in business.
At 23 years old he...	ran for legislature and was defeated.
At 24 years old he...	again failed in business.
At 25 years old he...	was elected to legislature.
At 26 years old his...	sweetheart died.
At 27 years old he...	had a nervous breakdown.
At 29 years old he...	was defeated for speaker.
At 31 years old he...	was defeated for elector.
At 34 years old he...	was defeated for congress.
At 37 years old he...	was elected to congress.
At 39 years old he...	was defeated for congress.
At 46 years old he...	was defeated for senate.
At 47 years old he...	was defeated for vice president.
At 49 years old he...	was defeated for senate.
At 51 years old he...	was elected President of the U.S.A.

This is the record of...

Abraham Lincoln, by: William Willard

Abraham Lincoln! Abraham Lincoln is consistently ranked as one of, if not *the*, top American President of all time. Besides his presidential accomplishments, he is a role model for focused, persistent action in following his dreams. He wrote, "Always bear in mind that your own resolution to succeed is more important than any other." We can learn from his "never give up" attitude.

Odds are our name won't go down in the annals of American History like Abraham Lincoln's. Yet we can still make a name for ourselves by taking consistent action towards our dreams. An author named Kathryn is a star example.

On September 11, 2001, Kathryn was living in Manhattan and working in magazine publishing and marketing. After the terrorist attack on the Twin Towers of the World Trade Center, she was unable to contact family living in her home state of Mississippi. In those early days after the tragic attack, waiting for the phone connections to come back online, Kathryn experienced a severe moment of homesickness, and started to write a novel in a soothing, comforting voice she felt exemplified the tone of her childhood in the South, never intending it to be published.

As she adjusted to life in NYC post 9/11, she continued with the book, enjoying and still finding comfort in her memories of a loved place and its people. After a year and a half of writing, she completed the book. Her next step was to find a literary agent, so she sent off her manuscript.

Six weeks later she received her first rejection letter stating, "Story did not sustain my interest." Was she discouraged? No, she was thrilled! An agent had read her novel! Right away, she began to edit her draft.

A few months later she sent it to fifteen more agents...and got fifteen more rejections.

One and a half years later, she had received 25 more rejection letters. The fortieth one said, "There is no market for this kind of tiring writing." Although this rejection did make her cry, she remained persistent.

She made more revisions and received five more rejections. And during this set of revisions, she also had a baby! Yet, she still moved forward on her book.

She made more revisions and received fifteen more rejections.

After five years of writing, and rewriting, and three and a half years of being rejected by sixty literary agents, submission number 61 was accepted by an agent! Three weeks later, the book was sold to a publisher!

Who is the author with this record? Kathryn Stockett. What is the title of the book she wrote? *The Help.*

The Help was released in February, 2009 and spent over 100 weeks on *The New York Times* Best Seller list. It has sold more than 5 million copies.

The Help film adaptation was released in August of 2011 and was nominated for Best Picture at the 2012 Academy Awards. The movie has earned a worldwide total of over $200 million, and continues to grow.

> When it is obvious that the goals cannot be reached, don't adjust the goals, adjust the action steps.
> Confucius

Kathryn Stockett calls herself stubborn. I say she was persistent. What if she had given up after her second rejection? Her thirtieth, or even her sixtieth? When have we given up after just one rejection? God sees a need on this earth and gives us a dream to fulfill it. Kathryn trusted her dream and consistently acted. Sure, she had talent, sure she had an education, but it took persistence to manifest her dream.

While pursuing our dreams, persistence is omnipotent. To be unstoppable, we also have to stay focused on the same goal. Author and speaker Seth Godin says, "Persistence isn't using the same tactics over and over. That's just annoying. Persistence is having the same goal over and over." Kathryn Stockett's goal was to find a literary agent who would find a publisher to publish her novel. For three and a half years, this goal never changed, but her tactics did. The novel she sent to the first literary agent was not the same as the novel she sent to the 61st. With each rejection, she went back to editing to "…make the story tenser, more riveting, better." She had no hard feelings towards the literary agents who rejected her novel, she wanted to send them thank you cards for encouraging her to make it better.

PROCRASTINATION

A bad habit that sometimes gets in our way (and by *our*, I mean *my*) of taking persistent action is procrastination. Procrastination isn't just lying around doing nothing. Well, it could be. But it really refers to the act of replacing higher-priority actions with tasks of lower-priority.

Robert Genn, the artist I mentioned in Chapter 20, who took a vow to "understate and over-prove," has a "Twice-Weekly Letter" to online subscribers. He receives letters from artists, many of whom tell him they want to paint, but they keep getting distracted. In other words, they procrastinate. Below is a sampling of excuses people gave him for why they aren't painting.

REASONS WHY I WON'T PAINT TODAY

"I am unable to paint because a neighbor is using some sort of Weed Eater or Leaf Blower."
"I ran out of yellow ochre (paint)."
"I saw ants in the studio."
"I was too hot."
"I was too cold."
"Our Jack Russell, 'Jack Russell' had to go to the vet."
"This day next week my sister-in-law is coming."
"My brother is moving out."
"I had to help Dad with his walk-in bath."
"I couldn't find my sketches from last year."
"My brushes are in too poor shape."
"My Pontiac worried me; it needs replacing."

Oh, how I can relate to many of those excuses. I've chosen to write more than paint these days, as I focus on this book, but in either art, I can be seriously tempted to procrastinate.

REASONS WHY I WON'T WRITE TODAY

"Camille is home from college for spring break."
"Because of day-light savings time change, I feel too groggy this
morning to concentrate."
"My book club meets in two days, and I still have 149 pages to read."
"Dennis just sent me the first 45 pages of his screen play and would
like for me to read it and make comments…today."
"It's been so long since I painted and I really miss it. Maybe I'll start
a painting today!"

Do you have a goal you have delayed acting on? If so, think
of some of the excuses you've been giving yourself for not getting
started. Better yet, if you write them down, you just might see that
the excuses holding you back may not be insurmountable. The way
to reach our goals is with focused, persistent, action.

10 TACTICS TO QUIT PROCRASTINATING

1   Work on High Priority Actions in the Morning
    The best time to work on high priority actions is first thing in the
    morning. Get started before thinking of a good reason not to.
    Don't check e-mail or social network sites first. If you do, other
    people's wants, needs, and thoughts will steal your time and take
    up mental space.

2   Set a Timer
    Whatever you are working on, whether it is a report, a speech, or
    just cleaning the house, set a timer. Use an egg timer or the timer
    on your phone. Any task is easier when we have a definite start-
    time and a definite end-time, especially if it is a task that is hard
    for us to begin. If I set a timer for 60 minutes and say "I'm going
    to write for this hour," it's less stress for me than just "sitting down
    to write." I write for my 60 minutes and then, when the hour is
    up, I feel very accomplished. If I couldn't find the right words, I

say, "Well, that was 60 minutes of making an effort. I'll do it again tomorrow." It makes us more productive when we know time is scheduled—it makes fitting everything in possible.

3   Progress – Not Perfection
Many times we don't get started because we want to do a "perfect" job. If we are a portrait painter, we want them to be as good as John Singer Sargent's...on our first try! We have to *get over it!* Sargent (1856-1925), who painted the commanding portrait of Theodore Roosevelt in Chapter 22, is considered the "leading portrait painter of his generation." Yet even he wrote, "Mine is the horny hand of toil." I translate that to mean, "My hands are hardened and calloused by the many hours I spend on my art." Yes, he was born with talent, but it was his persistent progress, towards an illusive perfection, that made him a master artist. Whatever your work, the key to making progress is to get something down, anything, even if it's not what you want it to be, and then revise, edit, consider. Have patience to both express yourself freely to explore your creativity, and then revise and edit with a keen eye for what you want your goal to be.

4   If You Did Know How to Do It, How Would You Do It?
We sometimes procrastinate because we don't know where to begin. We don't know how to refinish the chest-of-drawers or setup our wireless printer. A great question to ask ourselves is, "If I did know how to do it, how would I do it?" It may seem like a silly question, but by asking our brain to imagine how we'd solve the problem, we are more likely to trigger thoughts that come up with solutions, such as finding how-to videos on the Internet or asking a knowledgeable friend for help.

5   Imagine the Task Completed
When we have a task to do that we think is unpleasant, we procrastinate. Sometimes we just don't feel like doing what we know we need to do. To chip away at this feeling and find the

determination and excitement to begin any task, from unpleasant to fun, first, think of how good you will feel *after* the task is done, with all that work behind you.

Next, ask yourself, "How can I make this unpleasant task more enjoyable?" If you need to return a lot of phone calls, imagine how good it will feel as you check that task off your to-do list. To enjoy the process, perhaps make the calls while taking a walk.

If you need to sit at your desk for hours, imagine how good you will feel after having completed your high priority tasks. Maybe you would enjoy the process more if you placed a vase of fresh cut flowers nearby to enjoy.

If you don't enjoy going to the grocery store, imagine how good it will feel to have food in your refrigerator and pantry. Then, while shopping, open a bag of your favorite snack to savor to make the task more pleasurable.

6   Take Breaks

Nowadays, we are so busy, it's hard to sit still and concentrate. Yet after we settle down, sit still, and concentrate, it's hard for us to get up! For every hour that you set your timer to get work done, for the last five to ten minutes, get up and move around. Sitting still causes our blood to pump slower and slower, making us tired, and not think as quickly. Getting up to stretch and walk around gets the blood pumping again and boosts creative thoughts.

7   Have a Motivational Buddy

Having another person to be accountable to is a great way to stop procrastinating. You're less likely to procrastinate exercising if you're meeting a friend at the gym. If you know you will be sharing your weekly progress on Monday with your Mastermind Group, you'll be more likely to take action on your high priority items because you want to share something you feel good about.

8   Track Your Progress
This has been the best tool for me to curb my procrastination. Whatever it is you want to make progress on, track it. When we track something, it increases. Make a spreadsheet, and track your exercise program, track how far you're getting on your big project, and track your net worth. At the end of the day, you will get a thrill seeing how you are moving closer to your dreams.

9   Change Your Current Goal
This book clearly focuses on goal-setting as a way to find persistent happiness. Sometimes, though, our goals are big and they take a long while to accomplish. Before you bog yourself down with negative feelings from procrastination and lack of confidence because you have a big goal to accomplish, change your current goal to something more short-term and accessible. Short-term goals build to long-term goals; they are part of the progress process for our emotional, physical and material well-being. And all goal completion, of any size, makes you feel good.

10 If Everyday Looked Like Today…
Ask yourself, "If I spend ten minutes working on my dream today, how long will it take me to reach it?" How about one hour? Three hours? If everyday looked like today, will you reach your goal in one year, five years, or *never* years? Procrastinating today may seem harmless enough, but build up days of procrastination, one on top of the other, and that creates a life of unfulfilled dreams. Quit procrastinating and start producing.

Don't let procrastination become a habit. To get closer to the life we want, we have to take focused, persistent, action. When we do, we send a clear message that says, "Honey, there's no way I am settling for less than the life of my dreams!" What you accomplish…*just might change the world!*

STEP #5

ALLOW THE MASTERPIECE

*Everything comes to us that belongs to us
if we create the capacity to receive it.*
Rabindranath Tagore

*Be true to yourself, help others, make each
day your masterpiece, make friendship a
fine art, drink deeply from good books—
especially the Bible, build shelter against
a rainy day, give thanks for your blessings
and pray for guidance every day.*
John Wooden

Work for God

When a poor person dies of hunger, it has not happened because God did not take care of him or her. It has happened because neither you nor I wanted to give that person what he or she needed. We have refused to be instruments of love in the hands of God...
Mother Teresa

In 1982, Bob Macauley founded AmeriCares, a relief organization that distributes medicine and medical supplies to the world's poor in times of disaster. In his work, he crossed paths with Mother Teresa. He wrote about one such meeting in *Guideposts*, a spiritual magazine that offers "true stories by ordinary people who share their experiences about extraordinary events in their lives."

In the story Macauley tells, he and Mother Teresa had visited several orphanages in Guatemala, and were now on a flight headed to Mexico City. When the flight attendant brought their lunches, Mother Teresa asked, "Excuse me. How much does this meal cost?"

The flight attendant had probably never been asked this question before. She shrugged, and replied, "I don't know. About one dollar in U.S. currency."

"If I give it back to you," Mother said, "would you give me that dollar to give to the poor?"

The flight attendant went to the front of the plane to ask the pilot. Upon returning, she said, "Yes, Mother. You may have the money for the poor."

*We all have the duty
to serve God where we
are called to do so.*

Mother Teresa

Mother Teresa, by: Annette Hackney Evans

"Here you are," Mother Teresa said, and handed the flight attendant the tray. Soon, one by one, everyone on the flight handed back their lunches. Macauley stood up and counted. Mother Teresa had just raised $129 for the poor.

To Macauley's surprise, she wasn't finished. When the plane landed, she asked for the *lunches*. After working this out with the airline officials, she next asked for a truck to cart them!

A few minutes later, Macauley was riding beside Mother Teresa, who drove the truck without any problem, though she was so short, she had to peer between the steering wheel and the dashboard during the whole thirty-minute drive to a poor Mexican neighborhood. When she pulled up to the cardboard shanties, kids and parents gathered around the truck. Mother Teresa got out and handed out the 129 meals. When finished, she got into the truck and drove back to the airport.

Bob Macauley passed away in 2010, and I am grateful he shared this story about Mother Teresa before he died. His story of her is yet another example of how this small woman was clearly an instrument of love in the hands of God. She worked tirelessly for God to feed the poor.

God wants to express Himself, and He does this through *people*. He looks for people who are the most receptive, and will take the greatest positive action. One of those people was Mother Teresa, and He wants another of those people to be you. We are not asked to quit our job so that we may work for God. We can work for God through whatever job we have. For instance, Marianne Williamson is a spiritual teacher, author, and speaker. She says that back in her waitressing days, she often acted as a spiritual teacher to her customers! We are called to make the world better through whatever job or charitable work we do.

You have always known that you were supposed to do something important with your life. God has been calling you for a very long time. Pause for a moment... Do you feel it? Have you been receptive to God calling in the past? If not, that's okay, God was fine with that. He just moved on to the next person who *was* ready. It's your turn now. It's your turn to say, "Okay, I'm ready. God, now I'm ready for You to use me to do Your work."

USE ME

> *God is looking for people to use, and if you can get*
> *usable, He will wear you out. The most dangerous*
> *prayer you can pray is this: 'Use me.'*
> Rick Warren

Are you a brave person? Is "God, use me," a prayer you are willing to pray? If so, get a good night's sleep, because you are about to get busy!

We don't have to be "really religious" to communicate with and be used by God. We just have to be open to the idea that He exists. Even if you have doubts, try to let go of resistant thoughts, and allow the communication to grow.

Throughout your day, listen for God's voice to guide you. Have you ever been in a meeting where everyone is talking at once? Then, the leader of the group speaks up with an authority that makes everyone quiet down and pay attention? That's what God's voice will sound like in your mind. Your mind chatters on and on, and then a voice will come in that is calmer, louder, and holds more authority. God's voice may guide you in small ways, and in large ways; if you pay attention, you will hear Him.

Last week, I was shopping for a sympathy card at Target. A photo on a card from the humor section caught my eye. The image was of a woman with cold cream all over her face and her hair in rollers. Smiling to myself, I plucked up the card and it made me think of my friend Bernadine, who now lives three thousand miles away. *She would get a kick out of this card*, I thought. *But if I buy it, I'll have to write her a note, address it, find a stamp and mail it. I don't need more on my To Do List!* Then the voice said, "Buy the card and send it to Bernadine. It will make her feel good to know you're thinking of her." I listened, and took action. In this small way, God was using me to let Bernadine know she is loved.

The most difficult time for me to listen to this voice is when I am having a disagreement with someone. A few times in the past, I've been in the middle of a "heated discussion" with one of my daughters and during it, I'd hear the voice say, "What you are arguing about is unimportant. Overall, she is a fantastic girl, and making a good case for her defense. Say what you need to say, smile, then drop it." Oh…how I want to prove that I'm right, but oh…how it's usually not important to do so and doesn't end up making me feel good. I *try* to listen to that voice in my mind, and take action accordingly, and in many of those discussions, I've succeeded. I just had to listen to the voice inside me.

I am fortunate to live fifteen minutes away from Saddleback Church in Lake Forest, CA, where Rick Warren is the senior pastor. He makes himself usable to God, and boy, does God use him to do a lot of good work. He founded Saddleback, which is currently the eighth largest church in the United States. He is the author of many books, one of them being *The Purpose Driven Church: Every Church Is Big in God's Eyes*, which inspired a series of conferences on Christian ministry and evangelism. Warren is best known for his follow-up book, *The Purpose Driven Life: What on Earth Am I Here For?*, that has sold over 30 million copies, making Warren a *New York Times* bestselling author. Yet, it's not the size of the church and number of books sold that make Pastor Rick successful; it's the amount of people whose lives he has touched in a positive way.

God may use you today to brighten a friend's day, to see "the big picture" while in the middle of an argument, or make the world better like Pastor Rick, by following your calling. The most dynamic and successful prayer you can pray is, "Use me."

GOD QUALIFIED YOU

God doesn't call the qualified; He qualifies the called.
Reverend Michael Beckwith

You might be thinking, "Who am I, to work for God? I wasn't blessed with extraordinary talents. I don't have connections, or a big influence. Why would God want to use me?" I'm so glad you asked.

When we hire people to work for us, we usually choose people who have proven to be successful in their fields. We will hire employees for our company based on their resume of education and work experience. We hire a housecleaner who is reliable and does a good job, based on a friend's recommendation. We will choose a realtor based on how many houses she has previously sold. God, however, doesn't hire us based on our past successes.

When we apply to work for God, He doesn't care about our education, work experience, or references. He doesn't care if in our past we were reliable or had a good sales record. He only cares that we have a willingness to listen to His guidance, and the faith and courage to act on it. This is all we need to be qualified for the job.

An African-American proverb says, "God makes three requests of his children: Do the best you can, where you are, with what you have, now." It's so easy to watch TV and see wealthy people doing good deeds on a big scale. It's tempting to sit back and think, *Well, I don't have the talents they do. I don't live in a geographically convenient location. I don't have their money, connections, or fame, so what difference can I make?* God knows this. He knows our circumstances, and still wants to use us. He wants YOU to carry out His plans. Do the best you are capable of, wherever you are physically or mentally, with your resources, right now!

Our job is to be willing to listen to God and take action. His job is to rearrange circumstances so that we may do this successfully. With God as the boss, all things are possible.

WHAT'S IN IT FOR ME?

*Whoever renders service to many puts himself in
line for Greatness—great wealth, great return, great
satisfaction, great reputation, and great joy.*
Jim Rohn

Working for God sounds like a lot of work, right? It's human nature to ask, "My God, what's in it for me?" The answer is, *a lot!*

People often judge us based on our homes, our cars, and even the vacations we take. People may reward us based on how beautiful they think we are, if we have a "good personality," or our profit margin. Obviously, God doesn't care about these things.

Moses was given the Ten Commandments on Mt. Sinai. Interestingly, these commandments are a list of ten things that we *shalt not* do. Approximately 1,400 years later, Jesus added an Eleventh Commandment, and it is something that we *shalt* do:

A new commandment I give unto you, that you love one another.
Jesus, John 13:34

I don't believe that God judges or rewards us at all. I believe that when we use the gifts we were born with, and use them in a way to serve and love others, God will use all of His great power to help us. **When we work for God, God works for us.** (Whoa…writing that made me cry—I feel so certain about it.)

Sharing our gifts brings us joy. Serving and loving others brings us joy. And sharing our gifts and serving *many* others, brings us *great* joy. A life of joy. That's what's in it for you.

Work for God. Like Mother Teresa, dedicate yourself to be of maximum service to God and those around you. Feeding the hungry was just another day at the office for her. Ask God to use you through *your* calling, and then remain responsive to His guidance. God is the greatest employer we will ever have. What other boss will love us, want the best for us, and everyone around us? There is no better feeling than believing the work we are doing is making the world better.

25

Master Receiver

*The Universe is moving through everyone and
every circumstance to give to you.*
Rhonda Byrne

I wish I liked football. Really, I do. My sisters Teri and Sandy do. My brothers R.D. and Dennis do too. Recently, Dennis explained to me what the job of a football receiver is. Apparently, a receiver's principal role is to catch passes from the quarterback. He will do everything in his power to catch that ball.

Not long ago, I had an epiphany. I realized, at times, I was a poor receiver. Not in football, I've never played the game, not even Powder Puff football for women. I realized I was a poor receiver in life. When blessings came dropping out of the sky with my name on them, I didn't always do everything in my power to catch them. All that changed, though, over the course of a week.

MONDAY

Rhonda Byrne, author of the book *The Secret*, sends out a periodic e-mail to her subscribers. On this day she wrote:

Here is a checklist to make sure you have your receiving channels open: Do you receive compliments well? Do you receive unexpected gifts easily? Do you accept help when it is offered? Do you accept your meal being paid for by a friend?

These are little things, but they will help you know if you are open to receiving. Remember, the Universe is moving through everyone and every circumstance to give to you.

I reread the e-mail again…and then again. I couldn't believe it. According to my answers to the questions, my receiving channels were closed. I was a poor receiver! I had been asking God for a lot at that point, more than during any other time in my life. Could it be that God was trying to give to me, and I wasn't open to receiving what He was sending my way?

I thought back to my childhood in Indiana, and I remembered a day riding in the backseat of our station wagon. Mommy and I were dropping off Grandma Frances after a lovely afternoon of lunch and shopping. As Grandma was getting out of the car, my mom tried to slip money in her purse.

Pushing her hand away, Grandma said, "Now Jeanie, you put that money back in your purse. You don't owe me that!"

Pushing back, Mommy said, "Mother, I owe you this and I want you to take it."

Grandma said, "No you don't, now take this back!"

This went back and forth like a Ping-Pong match and at one point I offered to help by suggesting, "I'll take the money!"

Mommy did not find humor in this.

Thinking back, I can't remember who won the argument. To them, the winner was the one who got away *without* the money. One thing was clear, Grandma Frances' receiving channels were closed, Mommy's receiving channels were closed, and now in my adult life, as a learned habit, *my* receiving channels were closed. It had been passed down from generation to generation. I decided to break the cycle. If I was asking God for blessings, then I better be sure to have my receiving channels open.

TUESDAY

At seven o'clock in the morning, I acted as Toastmaster at my weekly Toastmasters Club. That meant it was my responsibility to host the meeting for approximately twenty people at our local community center, and set the tone for high energy and fun.

After the meeting, two of the club members, Patrick and Chris, approached me to compliment me on my "Toasting" skills. They said it was the most enjoyable meeting they had attended in awhile.

Did I have my receiving channels open? Did I simply say, "Thank you," and take in the blessings? Not a chance. I found every reason not to accept their good words. "Oh, thanks," I replied, "But I really stumbled over some words while reading the passage from the book I brought in. And I really should have let the Table Topics Master call on at least one more person because we ended up having extra time at the end of the meeting. And..." blah, blah, blah.

I packed up my things, walked out of the building, then realized, *Oh, no. I did it again. I deflected their compliments!* The good news was at least now I was aware of it, and vowed to do better at my next opportunity.

THURSDAY

At 6:30 pm I was hosting Wine Club...no, I'm sorry, ahem, we call ourselves Book Club...at my house for sixteen wonderful women. My fellow Toastmaster Louise was scheduled to give a speech about the relationship of this month's book *The Help* (one of the rare months we actually read a book) and her childhood in South Africa. The other women in Book Club often cook full, sit-down dinners when it is their turn to host. I thought for this gathering, appetizers would be sufficient so as not to distract from Louise's speech, and it would cut down on the amount of work for me. Even with saving time on cooking, it took me all day to straighten up my house, sweep away dust bunnies, grocery shop and prepare the food. At 6:00 pm, I set up the food and beverage tables with the items on the menu.

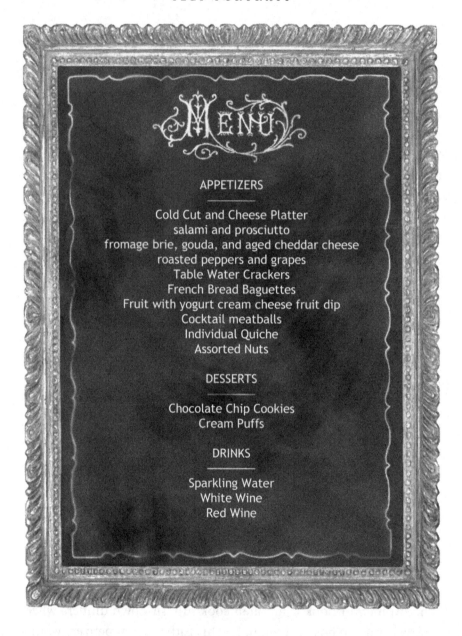

MENU

APPETIZERS

Cold Cut and Cheese Platter
salami and prosciutto
fromage brie, gouda, and aged cheddar cheese
roasted peppers and grapes
Table Water Crackers
French Bread Baguettes
Fruit with yogurt cream cheese fruit dip
Cocktail meatballs
Individual Quiche
Assorted Nuts

DESSERTS

Chocolate Chip Cookies
Cream Puffs

DRINKS

Sparkling Water
White Wine
Red Wine

My friends started arriving and as usual, we began congregating in the kitchen. Music was playing, candles were flickering, wine was flowing, and ladies were laughing and sharing stories about their lives from the past month.

On the outside, it looked like I was having a good time, but on the inside I was feeling insecure. I shared with you the menu, not to make you hungry, but so you could see, there was a lot of food. Yet, I still felt I hadn't done enough. *I didn't prepare enough food! My friends are going to be disappointed. They're probably wondering when I am going to put out the MAIN course!*

"Annette, the food is delicious," said Tricia. "Where did you buy this cheese?" She seemed sincere.

Cindy said, "Oh, I like these cocktail meatballs."

"What a great idea to just do appetizers!" said Gaye. "I'm going to do that next time." I hoped she *would* do appetizers next time. I didn't want to be the only one to lower the bar.

Even though their compliments were heartfelt, I so badly wanted to tell them that the next time I hosted, I would do better! But I didn't. Instead, I took a deep breath, left aside my concerns, and remembered to practice receiving. With all my might, I graciously said, "Thank you." I was beginning to receive compliments better.

SATURDAY

My brother Dennis, newly single, bought a beautiful home in Temecula, CA. He asked me over to give him some womanly decorating advice. We went shopping for accessories and then out to dinner at Noodles of the World.

My twelve-year-old nephew, named Trust, joined us and we enjoyed conversation over our bowl of noodles and Boba Smoothies. (If you've never tried boba balls, they are little black tapioca balls that sit in the bottom of the drink. Extra big straws are used to draw up the tapioca with the drink, so you drink and chew simultaneously. But...I digress...)

While drinking and chewing, I told Dennis all about the e-mail I received on Monday, about how it's good to keep our receiving channels open. I told him about the compliments I deflected from fellow Toastmasters on Tuesday, but received from my Book Club friends on Thursday. I also said, "Because I'm on this new receiving program, don't offer to pay for dinner unless you mean it, because

I'll accept!" He *did* offer, and even though I had just made him spend $157 on decorative pillows, I ACCEPTED—very graciously, of course, but accept I did!

After finishing our dinner, with a mischievous look on his face, Trust said, "Now we're going out for dessert, and I'm going to *receive* my ice-cream being paid for by Aunt Annette!" How are kids so good at this stuff?

MONDAY

Soon it was Monday again, just one week after I read the "open your receiving channels" e-mail, and committed myself to being a better receiver. I took my daughter Isabella to her tennis lesson, and afterward we had lunch at a Chinese fast food restaurant. Crossing the parking lot to our car, something on the ground caught my eye. I looked down, saw that it was a folded bill, and I quickly snatched it up. Unfolding it I was shocked at what I saw…a one hundred dollar bill! So many thoughts flooded my mind!

OMG! I just found $100!

I'm glad I saw it before Isabella!

Is there a hidden camera around watching me take it?

I don't want to ask anyone if they lost it…I want to keep it. But, I always try to do the right thing, and that doesn't feel right.

"Isabella," I whispered, still walking, "I just found money on the road." Sure enough, she told me I better start asking around to see if anyone lost it.

Well, I wasn't going to wave a $100 bill over my head and say, "Hey, did anyone lose this?" Was she crazy? Who raised her, anyway? I decided on a compromise. I would ask the four firemen who had been walking in front of us if it was theirs.

I approached the fire truck parked just past our car, and asked, "Did any of you happen to drop money on the road back there?" They all checked their pockets. I have to admit I was happy when they all responded in the negative.

We drove past the spot I found the money and neither Isabella nor I saw anyone frantically searching for the money, so I headed home. It was mine. The money was mine!

Later I called Dennis and said, "This receiving thing really works. I found $100!" And that's when he told me about receivers in football. They are among the fastest and most agile players on the field, and television highlight-reel favorites. Just then, I imagined God as our quarterback, throwing blessing after blessing to us. It is not our job to decide if we *want* to catch it or not. Like a football receiver, it is our job to do everything in our power to receive.

If you, my dear reader, are the person who lost a $100 bill in the parking lot in Rancho Santa Margarita, California, I would like for you to know your money went to good use.

1   Finding the money was my inspiration for a humorous speech I gave at my Toastmasters club, titled *Master Receiver,* on which this chapter is based. Near the end of the speech, I pulled the bill out of my pocket to show the audience the rewards of keeping our receiving channels open. Many people since then have told me that listening to the speech actually *has* helped them become better receivers.

2   After giving my speech at the Toastmasters meeting, some friends and I went to a local coffee shop. Driving home, I felt in my pocket and found that the money was gone! Now *I* had lost it. Driving back to the coffee shop, I was aware that I really had no right to the money, yet I had been asked to give the same speech to a larger audience in one week, and I didn't have a $100 bill to replace it. I walked in and searched the corner where I had been sitting. No money. I went to the counter and inquired about it, and the employee said, "Yes, I found it!" and she gave me back the money. I was so grateful, and impressed with her goodness, that now an honest, coffee shop employee is $20 richer.

3   Once I had given my speech for the second time, and no longer needed the money as a prop, I couldn't bring myself to spend it. So, I gave the money to my favorite charity, the *National Alopecia Areata Foundation.* NAAF's mission is to support research to find a cure or acceptable treatment for alopecia areata, support those with the disease, and educate the public about alopecia areata.

A Barrier to Receiving

If you say you're worthy, you are.
If you say you're not worthy, you're not.
T. Harv Eker

God is continuously giving, or attempting to give to us through people and circumstances. The biggest barrier to us receiving these gifts is feeling unworthy. No matter what people have said about you in your past, *you* are the only person who gets to decide if you are worthy or unworthy.

In Chapter 10, "Have a Happy Childhood," I told the story about Chloe and her feelings of unworthiness because of an abusive father. I would bet Chloe isn't good at accepting compliments. We are all born as a precious baby, with equal worthiness to have an abundant life. **Believe you are worthy, because you *are.***

Feeling unworthy is a limiting belief. Some people might actually prefer to feel unworthy, than worthy. But why? Why would someone prefer to adopt a belief that would hold her or him back in life? Well, it can give people a good excuse to snuggle into their Comfort Zone and not stretch. When they start feeling the fear of stretching, and doing something more with their lives, it may feel less scary to say, "Oh, I'm not worthy anyway, so I'll stay where I am." This feeling of unworthiness enables them to rationalize themselves as "off the hook" —they don't have to spend the energy it takes to create the life they really desire because they aren't worth it to themselves, or anyone else.

Make a decision right now to believe that you *are* as worthy as anyone else ever born. Why? Because you are! If you have done things in your past that you are not proud of, keep them in the past. It's time to create a new history. And in this new history, Your Highness, you are definitely worthy!

How to Be a Good Receiver

Now you know how important it is to be a good receiver. When you are, money might literally fall at your feet! So how do we become a good receiver? How do we go about keeping our receiving channels open, every day? Here are three ways to strengthen our receiving muscles:

#1 Give to Yourself

To form a new habit requires repetition of a new behavior. We can become better receivers by pampering ourselves. Whether you feel worthy or not, spoil yourself. My friend Alexis said she always feels good with, "a balloon bobbing in my home or a little posy at my bedside." You might prefer soaking in a bubble bath. Or, go to the restaurant in the fanciest hotel in your city and simply order a glass of champagne. While there, be sure to check your lipstick in the mirror and tell yourself how *dazzling* you are. Pampering yourself doesn't have to be expensive or time-consuming; a small treat can instantly give us the feeling of being "gifted."

#2 Be Grateful When You Receive

The only thing required of you when receiving is to simply say a sincere, "Thank you." It makes others feel good when they give to you and you're a good receiver. If someone gives to you, and you either won't receive, or don't seem appreciative, she or he will quit giving. If people give to you, and you receive and say, "Thank you!" and seem to genuinely appreciate it, they will want to give you more and more.

When God gives to you, and you receive and say, "Thank you!" and genuinely appreciate it, He wants to give you more, and more, and more!

#3 Receive Abundantly to Give Abundantly

I like to think of myself as a giver. It makes me feel good to give. I love finding the perfect gift for special people in my life and watch their faces light up as they receive it. I love being helpful to others when they could use a little help. I love celebrating milestones and accomplishments that my loved ones have in their life to confirm who they are and what they do has value.

On the other hand, it stretches my Comfort Zone to feel comfortable receiving gifts, accepting help, and being a guest of honor. I even feel uncomfortable asking to be fairly compensated for my work. American Christian Evangelist Billy Graham said, "God has given us two hands, one to receive with and the other to give with." It's a perfect cycle, receive, then give. Breathe in, breathe out. It is a natural flow. If I don't receive, I have nothing to give. I must be open to receive abundantly, in order to be able to *give* abundantly.

Prayer of a Master Receiver

Dear God,

I ask You for the best of everything this world has to offer. I realize I sometimes resist compliments, gifts, offers of help, and fair payment for my work. I now see these things as gifts from You, as answers to my prayers. You are moving through everyone and every circumstance to give to me.

I desire to give to others in a big way, and in order to do this I must receive. I will receive with one hand so that I have something to give with the other.

When I graciously receive small things, I demonstrate my ability to receive big things. I practice receiving by treating myself well and being enthusiastically grateful when I receive.

Everything comes to me that I ask for when my receiving channels are open. I am a master receiver!

Amen

I may have inherited a habit of crossing my arms and resisting blessings coming to me, but I am breaking the cycle. I am opening my arms wide to catch any and all blessings coming my way. I am a master receiver! I hope you will become one too. Everything God has for you will be yours if you keep your receiving channels open.

The day I was writing this chapter, Isabella and I went back to the Chinese fast food restaurant for lunch. No, I didn't find another $100 bill, but I did get a very interesting fortune in my fortune cookie:

Coincidence?

Change Your Mind

It is not the strongest of the species that survive,
nor the most intelligent,
but the one most responsive to change.
Charles Darwin

We realize that housework is never done. As soon as we clean, the house gets dirty again. We know as soon as we finish one big project at work, there will be another one that is equally as important. We know as soon as we buy the leopard print dress we've had our eye on, we will want red pumps to wear with it (I'm still looking for those shoes.) Let's face it, we are never going to get it all done, or have everything we desire. And…we're not supposed to! We are created to continuously focus on new goals; set a goal, reach it, set a new goal, reach it.

We've heard the saying, "It is a woman's prerogative to change her mind." It is not only our right to change our mind, but we ought to be continuously changing our mind. Our world is constantly changing, and if we want to enjoy the ride, we must change too. Our mind must be flexible and open to change regarding physical potential, beliefs, and goals.

To survive and thrive, we don't have to be the strongest or most intelligent, we only have to keep our minds open to change.

GROW OR DECAY

*Biologically, there is no such thing as retirement, or
even aging. There is only growth or decay, and your
body looks to you to choose between them.*
Henry S. Lodge, MD

In the book *Younger Next Year,* authors Chris Crowley and Henry
Lodge, MD, clearly make the point that when we are in our forties
and fifties, our bodies switch into a "default to decay" mode. If our
brain doesn't send our body signals to grow, meaning "stay young,"
decay will win, meaning "we will get old." Chris and Henry (who
throughout their book are referred to by their given names) claim
that 70% of people experiencing premature aging and early death
have conditions caused by their lifestyle choices. This is good news!
We *can* slow, and reverse, the aging process. The secret to staying
young, to being younger next year, is to change the signals we give to
our body. Are we signaling our body to grow or to decay?

GROW We signal our bodies to grow when:	DECAY We signal our bodies to decay when:
We exercise *daily.* This is the best signal to grow.	We are sedentary. Inactivity is the biggest decay signal.
We eat well. We have reasonable nutrition.	We eat unhealthy food and drink too much alcohol.
We care about someone (this could even be a pet) and have emotional commitments.	We withdraw from social contact and are lonely.
We care about something and are engaged in our life.	We are apathetic, indifferent, bored, show a lack of interest.
We get plenty of sleep.	We don't get enough sleep.

Has your body been getting signals to grow…or decay? If your mind has been sending it signals to grow, then your body can literally be younger next year. If the signals have been to physically decay, besides your physical health suffering, you could suffer low-grade depression as well.

Chris and Henry write, "The physical messages you send by being consciously and steadily active, and the emotional messages you send by being engaged in the great hunt of life, can override the default message. With relatively little effort, you can mimic a younger woman in her prime—exercising, interacting, making love – and your body will go along." You *will* evolve. In one year, do you want your body to have decayed and aged, or to have grown younger? Your body is looking for you to choose between the two.

CHANGE BEFORE YOU HAVE TO

Everything is changing. Things are either getting better or worse, growing or decaying, moving forward or going backward. Nothing stays the same. Staying where you currently are, by the laws of nature, is not an option. We *are* going to change, and it is best to change positively, on our terms.

"Change before you have to," says Jack Welch, former Chairman and CEO of General Electric from 1981-2001. "An organization's ability to learn, and translate that learning into action rapidly, is the ultimate competitive edge." Organizations have to change in order to survive. Unfortunately, Borders Books, a once-viable competitor of Barnes & Noble, is an example of not translating learning into action rapidly, and it led to their extinction.

In 1971, Borders began as an 800-square foot used bookstore called Borders Book Shop in Ann Arbor, MI. At its peak in 2003, Borders had more than 1,200 stores around the country. Although the company clearly had strengths that led to its expansion, they developed weaknesses that led to their ultimate failure.

Times and conditions change so rapidly that we must keep our aim constantly focused on the future.

Walt Disney

Walt Disney, by: Casey Childs

In the 1990s, a large portion of floor space in a Borders Bookstore was used for CD sales. At this time, customers were buying iPods and phasing out of buying CD's. By the time Borders began reducing their music inventory, they had been paying for expensive retail space they didn't need and couldn't afford. They didn't phase out their CD stock early enough, essentially because they didn't allow for change in their business plan.

In the late 1990's, their competitor, Barnes & Noble, began selling books online and officially launched its own website in 1997. It was not until 2001 that Borders struck a deal with web retailer *Amazon. com* to sell its products online. That relationship lasted until 2008, when Borders finally launched its own website. Borders lagged behind their competition by more than a decade. They didn't change before they had to.

Barnes & Noble pioneered the idea of a big retail bookstore being a community center. They made an agreement with coffeehouse giant Starbucks, and opened the first in-store Starbucks café in 1993. In 2004, Borders signed a deal with Starbucks Corp. to run Seattle's Best Coffee café operations in its stores. Again, this came a decade after Barnes & Noble. They didn't change before they had to.

> *If you don't like change, you're going to like irrelevance even less.*
> General Eric Shinseki

In 2007, Amazon introduced their e-book device Kindle. In 2009, Barnes & Noble launched its e-bookstore and their e-reader Nook. In 2010, Borders launched an e-bookstore and started selling e-readers. Yet again, they didn't change before they had to.

In 2011, Borders announced plans to liquidate all of their stores, and approximately 10,700 people lost their jobs. All because the company didn't change before they had to.

One year from now, in every area of your life, there will be change. Your health, your career, and your relationships will have changed for the better or worse in subtle ways, or big ways. Are you going to be a person who tries putting out the fire once negative change has happened? Or will you avoid the fires, and change before you have to?

Fear of the unknown keeps us from changing. There's nothing wrong with being afraid, we can't eliminate it, and we can't be fearless all of the time. But we can acknowledge it, feel it, and take action *anyway*. **We can face our fear of the unknown and initiate positive change, or we will face the known experience of circumstances getting worse.**

REINVENT YOURSELF

> *My new motto is:*
> *When you're through changing, you're through.*
> Martha Stewart

Martha Stewart is a career woman who exemplifies someone who is never through changing. Whether or not you respect her business practices, she has a gift for reinventing herself. Here's a brief list of the titles she's held in her life…so far:

Model – Martha began modeling in her late teens and continued through her early twenties.

Stockbroker – When her modeling career fizzled out, she reinvented herself into a stockbroker. At 24, the same year she had her only child, she became a Wall Street stockbroker. Although she had financial success the first few years, by the summer of 1973, the stock market was tanking and her commission income dwindled. This reality, combined with the fact that several of her friends lost money as a result of following her financial advice, prompted Martha to quit her job.

Home Renovator – Two years previously, Martha purchased an abandoned six-room farmhouse in Westport, Connecticut. At 35, Martha reinvented herself via refurbishing her home, Turkey Hill.

Caterer - She started a catering business out of her "lower level suite," a.k.a. the basement.

Author - A mere six years later, her first book was published, *Entertaining*. It featured beautiful glossy photos of many of her catering jobs, along with images of the renovations she made to Turkey Hill. Her career as a domestic diva burst into bloom from there.

Publisher of Martha Stewart Living Magazine – In 1990, Martha developed her own magazine and became editor-in-chief.

Television Personality – In 1993, she began a weekly television show based on her magazine.

Martha Stewart Living Omnimedia – In 1997, with a business partner, Martha purchased an assortment of her television, print, and merchandising projects and consolidated them into Martha Stewart Living Omnimedia. She also started a catalog business and a floral business.

Billionaire - On October 19, 1999, Martha Stewart Living Omnimedia went public on the New York Stock Exchange. By the end of trading, Stewart was a billionaire on paper. In fact, she became the first female, self-made billionaire in the USA.

However, a "not so good thing" happened in 2004.

Convicted Felon – At the age of 63, Martha was convicted of lying to investigators about a stock sale. She served five months in federal prison followed by five months of home detention.

If Martha had been through changing after going to prison, her name would have been forever tarnished. Not Martha, she got out her tarnish remover, buffed up her image, and started changing once again.

Master of Reinvention – Martha's 2005 comeback campaign was successful and she developed many new projects: craft items for a large discount department store, a line of paper-based crafts for a creative consumers products company, a line of housewares for a mid-range/upscale department store, a line of ready-made home furnishings for a discount store, furniture for a furniture manufacturer, floor coverings for a company that makes a system of carpet squares, an interior paint line for a mid-range department store, wall color for a home improvement store, new books, a radio show, and new television shows. And she's created some unusual products: frozen and fresh food with a membership-only warehouse club, a wine brand with a winery, and, drum roll please, a line of houses with her name on them, built by a home building company!

Martha Stewart is now a true household name that has shown again and again her career choices are never through, because she is never through changing. We probably won't have to reinvent ourselves as many times as Martha to move forward in our life. But surely, we can pull a few new personas out of our freshly pressed sleeve.

Life is an ongoing, never-ending adventure. We set a goal, reach it, set a new goal, reach it. Keep moving forward, and reinventing yourself.

Life should not be a journey to the grave with the intention of arriving safely in a pretty and well preserved body, but rather to skid in broadside in a cloud of smoke, thoroughly used up, totally worn out, and loudly proclaiming "Wow! What a Ride!"
Hunter S. Thompson

Whether you think change is something to fear or an exciting adventure…change exists; it happens to all of us. Have a mind that is eager for change. You are an always unfolding, eternally evolving being. Use yourself up, wear yourself out, so in the end you can proclaim, "What a ride!"

We are In God, God is In Us

Remember God is in you as the ocean is in the wave. There is no possible way in which the wave can be separated from the ocean, and there is no way in which you can be separated from God. Because you are the activity of God in manifestation, there is no place in all the world where you can get closer to God than where you are right now.
Eric Butterworth

The highest revelation is that God is in every man.
Ralph Waldo Emerson

The sermon was titled "Membership: Part Four—The Connection Experience." *Perfect,* I thought, *this is the message I need to hear. Sell me on why I should become a member of this church.*

It was 2005, the summer my husband, daughters and I, moved from Pennsylvania back to Indiana. After we moved out of the apartments, and got settled into our new home, I set about finding a church that would be a good fit for our young family. It's sometimes difficult to find a new church home when you move, and I've looked for a new one four times in fifteen years. On this particular Sunday, I was sitting in the pew of a mega church. The preacher talked about connecting with God and the importance of baptism. I'm paraphrasing, but what I understood him to say is, "When a person gets baptized, the Holy Spirit comes down and enters his or her body. This presence of Spirit doesn't create change in the physical body, but a change in his or her thinking. The only people who have the Holy Spirit inside them are baptized Christians. The Holy Spirit is what connects us to God."

What?! I thought. I wanted to jump up from my pew, turn and face the 1,321 people in the congregation and shout, "I object!" Instead, my objections exploded internally within me:

"I object that God is separate from the Holy Spirit. God *is* Spirit!"

"I object that the Holy Spirit is what connects us to God. God is in us, and we are in God. God is present everywhere! There is no place that God isn't!"

"I object that God's spirit is only inside Christians. God is in every woman and man, and all living things. Everyone has God within!"

I believe God is a nonmaterial force, around us, and in us. It is up to us to find God within, and to listen to, trust, and manifest His glory in the world.

NONMATERIAL FORCE

In the book *Discover the Power Within*, Eric Butterworth helps us see the Divine within ourselves as a resource of limitless abundance. The following passage from his book is fascinating:

> In a film entitled *The Development of the Chick*, we see the egg in the process of incubation. We see a strange pulsation commence in the yolk. It is the beating of the heart before there is any heart to beat. And then before our eyes we see the embryo form and a heart take shape and take up the beat that came first. This is an evidence that even more significant than the physical egg is the nonmaterial force that is the pattern from which the chick and the whole chicken develops.

This is incredible! There is a measurable heartbeat of the chick before there is even a heart to beat! It is truly a miracle. What is this nonmaterial force? What is this energy that is assisting and sustaining the life of a chicken?

This energy is God.

God is a nonmaterial force, the energy in all things. God is the nonmaterial force that is the pattern from which the chicken develops, and that from which *we* develop too. This nonmaterial force is in all people, regardless of their religion.

In describing Jesus' unique concept of God, Eric Butterworth writes, "To him, God was not an object but a Presence dwelling in us, a force around us, and a Principle by which we live." God is a Presence that dwells in all people, whether they are "good" or "bad." When we are injured, such as getting a cut, the Presence dwelling within us, heals it. It doesn't matter if we are "good" or "bad" to ourselves or others. So too, God's force surrounds all people, not just those we may deem "worthy." God's force around us, in the form of air and gravity, is available to all people, all the time. Thus, God is assisting in, and sustaining the life of all of us, equally, all the time!

There Is No Place That God Isn't

> *That deep emotional conviction of the presence of a superior reasoning power, which is revealed in the incomprehensible universe, forms my idea of God.*
> Albert Einstein

What does God look like? Close your eyes, and visualize how you imagine God. What does He look like to you? To some people God is a "He" and has human form. Maybe He has a beard, appears to be in his seventies, and sits on a throne someplace, up high, 24/7.

Michelangelo's "portrait of God" is an elderly male in human form, with a beard and white robe. However, some researchers suggest that in this famous painting Michelangelo embedded an outline of the human brain. When we look at the outline surrounding God, a silhouette of the brain is, indeed, visible. In an article in the May, 2010 issue of *Neurosurgery, official journal of the Congress of Neurological Surgeons,* medical illustrator Ian Suk, BSc, BMC, and neurosurgeon Rafael Tamargo, MD, of The Johns Hopkins School of Medicine, Baltimore write that Michelangelo, "cleverly enhanced his depiction of God...with concealed images of the brain, and in this way celebrated not only the glory of God but also that of His most magnificent creation."

Creation of Adam, by: Michelangelo, 1511-1512
Sistine Chapel ceiling, Vatican City, Rome, Italy

In another church, in another state, I beheld what I believe to be a glimpse of God. Back in Pennsylvania, at Addisville Reformed Church, around the time I was painting the church portrait, Pastor Doug Dwyer was preaching an inspiring sermon. Although Pastor Doug delivers inspirational sermons every week, this Sunday morning God didn't speak to me through the message, but through a stained glass window in the church.

This particular morning, I felt happy. My husband and I had transferred our memberships from our childhood churches, and I felt good surrounded by our new church family. Our girls were in Sunday school and getting the same religious education I'm grateful my mom made sure I received as a child.

I'm a visual person, and while listening to the sermon, I gazed at the row of stained glass windows on the south-facing wall. Warm sunlight was pushing through the green, blue, and gold stained glass, and I could make out a silhouette of a tree outside the window. A gentle wind was blowing, and fall leaves were drifting to the ground, slowly swaying, back and forth, back and forth.

That's when I felt it. In my chest, in my heart, I felt a *knowing* that

I was observing God. The sunlight, the vibrant colors in the glass, the silhouette of the tree, and the wind made visible by falling leaves. My world stood still as I became the audience to the beautiful scene God was orchestrating. It was breathtaking.

God speaks to different people in different ways, and being a visual person, I "hear" best through sight. No one else in the congregation seemed to notice God's presence by the window, yet it is, to date, the most religious experience I've had in church. I don't remember Pastor Doug's words from that day, but he surely set the mood for me to open my heart and mind to feel God's presence inside us and around us.

Theologian Mary Daly said, "Why indeed must 'God' be a noun? Why not a verb...the most active and dynamic of all?" I saw the actions of God through my limited human vision when I watched the tree through the colors of the window. My mind can't fully fathom all the ways God is showing Himself that I *can't* see. The air we breathe is made up of Nitrogen, Oxygen, Argon, Carbon Dioxide, and tiny percentages of other gases in varying amounts, all of which together are invisible to the naked eye. I can see a beautifully clear mid-day's *blue* sky because of how sunlight refracts through clean air. Yet, right in front of me, I can't see the air. At human eye-level, air is invisible. But I know it's still there; I'm breathing. God is present, acting with us, in this way too. He invisibly infuses us with love, energy, and life force. He is in us and all around us. He is present in our inner world and outer world, filling the Universe. There is no place that God isn't.

FIND GOD WITHIN

We are inherently a part of God/Goddess/Source. Jesus said
that the kingdom of heaven is within, and we can make
this spiritual connection through our inner guidance.
We need go no further than ourselves.
Christiane Northrup, M.D.

In relationships, I'm sure you would agree that our lives feel smooth when they are good, and rocky when they are bad. When we are in a good romantic relationship, we experience relationship "goodies," such as feeling love, joy, excitement, satisfaction, adoration, appreciation, and fun. Similarly, when we find God within and make the spiritual connection, a burden is lifted from us and an empty space in our hearts and our lives is gone. We enjoy relationship goodies of forgiveness, acceptance, and peace. The relationship we have with our Creator has the biggest impact on our happiness, more than any other!

You might be thinking, *Find God within? Then make a connection? Does that mean I will have to be good all the time? I don't want a parental figure with me all the time saying, "Don't do this. How could you do that? What were you thinking?" This inner voice doesn't sound fun. It sounds stressful!* In reality, there are many perks to being one with God, and they are not stressful at all.

When we find God within, and listen to our inner guidance, our relationships will improve. We will also enjoy more energy and better health. We will acquire a more optimistic attitude about the future, knowing that we fill a valuable purpose on earth. We pursue our calling, and it brings joy to ourselves and others. We develop a strong faith that God is guiding our footsteps in all areas of our life, and know that we are on the right path for us.

I believe in God, but not as one thing, not as an old man in the sky. I believe that what people call God is something in all of us.

John Lennon

For God to guide our footsteps, we must hear what He is telling us, and then act on it. How do we do this? Mother Teresa said, "We need to find God, and he cannot be found in noise and restlessness. God is the friend of silence. See how nature— trees, flowers, grass—grows in silence; see the stars, the moon and the sun, how they move in silence." Mother Teresa's words remind us that to hear God clearly, we must be silent, as the trees, flowers and grass. Prayer and meditation are ways we can link with God, and these acts require us to be still and quiet.

When prayer or meditation become habits, we are more in tune with our inner voice. Yet, how can we be sure that this inner voice is the voice of God? We can ask ourselves, "Is what I feel I am being led to do, in the best interest for me, and everyone involved?" If the answer is yes, it is God you are hearing. The voice of God will always nudge us toward doing the right thing. God's desire is to make the world better, through us.

Listening and taking action is wonderful, and another way to benefit from what we hear is to co-create and manifest things in our lives. God is the "thinking stuff" from which everything is created. This thinking stuff is in us and all around us; it fills the Universe. When we think, the thing we imagine manifests. We can form our thoughts, and through meditation and prayer, we can cause what we think about to be created. We can become spiritually connected with God through our inner guidance. To do this, we don't need to look outside ourself, but within.

Manifest the Glory of God Within You

In our culture, we are constantly reminded how small we are. If our problems seem large, well-meaning loved ones might remind us how insignificant we are in the scheme of things. As the band Kansas sang in 1974, "Dust in the wind. All we are is dust in the wind...just a drop of water in an endless sea." Wouldn't it be more helpful, however, to remember how BIG we are? That there has never been, and will never be, anyone just like us? And we were born to manifest the glory of God that is within us? We're not insignificant and small, we are significant and huge! Even if we feel small in size, we are made up of the same nonmaterial substance of that which is huge!

Imagine you are in space. You are floating in blackness... peacefully...looking all around you. The vast darkness goes on forever and ever. There is no edge, no boundary. My mind cannot even conceive the limitlessness of this. Eric Butterworth says, "What we have called 'space' is really a presence, for there is one continuous, unified, intelligent, and inexhaustible potential that here and there precipitates itself as that which we call matter." What is this presence that is space?

We ask ourselves, who am I to be brilliant, gorgeous, talented, fabulous? But actually, who are you NOT to be? You are a child of God. Your playing small does not serve the world. There is nothing enlightened about shrinking so that other people won't feel insecure around you. You were born to manifest the glory of God that is within you.

Marianne Williamson

Marianne Williamson, by: Annette Hackney Evans

To understand the big outer space, let's look first at something smaller, something that is *slightly* easier to wrap our minds around: our solar system. We can see the sun, and it's big. Really, really, big. In distribution of mass in the solar system, the sun takes up 99.85%. Next we have planets, comets, satellites, minor planets, meteoroids, and interplanetary medium. How does this remaining .15% of mass do its choreographed dance around the sun?

To look out at this kind of creation out here and not believe in God is to me impossible,… it just strengthens my faith. I wish there were words to describe what it's like.
John Glenn

Now our focus is on, and we are floating above, planet Earth. The earth, sometimes called the Big Blue Marble, science estimates to be approximately 4.5 billion years old. If we look down on the earth, we see land, water, white swirling clouds, and a moon in orbit around it. We know gravity keeps the water from falling out of the deep land crevices. And gravity keeps the moon from drifting off. But what is the force that is gravity?

Now let's really focus in…on you. There you are, reading a book, breathing in air, and pumping blood throughout your body. How is this possible?

This presence that is space, this choreographer of the solar system, this force that is gravity, and energy that keeps you alive, is all God. We are physically very small in comparison to the planets, the seas and clouds, but operating under the same power as things that are very, very big. We're not supposed to play small. We are supposed to manifest the glory of God that is within us!

God gave each of us a variety of talents and wisdom. If any of us feel we are lacking talents and wisdom, we are not; we are only lacking a belief that they are there.

Meister Eckhart said, "Let God be God in you." We unconsciously let God be God in us, in many ways. We don't think about our heart pumping or our lungs taking in oxygen. We don't think about how our body heals itself when we get hurt. And the biggest miracle of all, as women, we don't think about how our bodies create a baby from a fertilized egg—our bodies just know how to do it. We let God be God. So why can't we *consciously* let God be God within us? He does a pretty good job with everything else! If we consciously allow our awareness of Him to exist, we can feel the huge wonderment that is our life!

Whether you're an artist, a writer, a mother, a doctor, or an astronaut, it's time to manifest the glory of God that is within you. You were born to be brilliant, gorgeous, talented and fabulous!

THE VITRUVIAN WOMAN

I could prove God statistically. Take a look at the human body alone—the chance that all the functions of an individual would just happen is a statistically monstrosity.
George Gallup
Inventor of the Gallup poll, a statistical method of
survey sampling for measuring public opinion.

Marcus Vitruvius Pollio, who lived before the Christian era (BCE), approximately between 80-70 to just after 15 BCE, was a Roman author, architect, and engineer. He wrote *De Architectura: The Planning of Temples,* in which he explains that to design a structurally sound and elegant temple, it is necessary to have symmetry and proportion, similar to that of a well-proportioned human body. He observed that Nature planned the human body so that:

The body is eight heads tall.
The foot is a sixth of the height of the body.
If a person lies on her back, with hands and feet spread out, and the center of a circle is placed on her naval, her fingers and toes will touch the circumference of the circle around her.
The naval is the exact center of the body.
A square is found within the figure in the same way as a circle.

337

If we measure from the sole of the foot to the top of the head, and apply the measure to the outstretched hands, the breadth is equal to the height.

The human foot is a masterpiece of engineering and a work of art.
Leonardo da Vinci

Self-Portrait, by: Leonardo da Vinci

Around 1490, with inspiration from Vitruvius' text, Leonardo da Vinci drew a male human body with these proportions in his sketchbook. This finely balanced human body within a circle and a square is his famous sketch, *The Vitruvian Man.*

Without a woman, there would be no man, so for you I have painted the Vitruvian man's equal counterpart, *The Vitruvian Woman.*

The human body is a masterpiece. The odds that this work of art just *happened*, is a statistical impossibility. Our actual bodies are further proof that we are the greatest creation, of the great Creator.

A Gallup poll in 2011 asked Americans the question, "Do you believe in God?" 7% said no, 1% had no opinion, and a remarkable 92% said yes. Can this many people, along with some of the greatest minds in recorded history, be wrong?

God is not someone up in heaven, deeming us as worthy or unworthy. God is a non-material force, a presence, a superior reasoning power. God is Spirit, present everywhere, the energy behind, in, and through all things, visible and invisible. There is no place in the world where you can get closer to God than where you are right now.

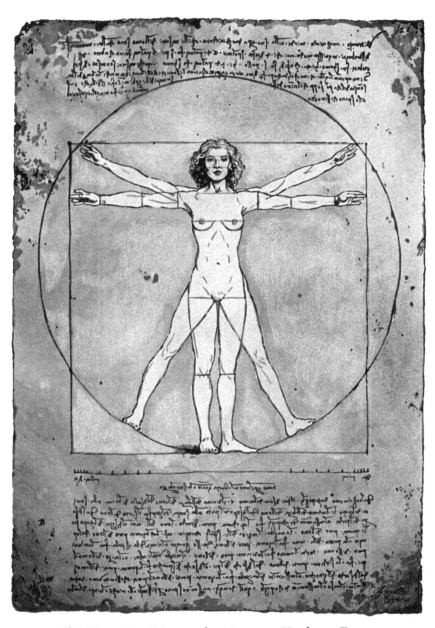

The Vitruvian Woman, by: Annette Hackney Evans

FINISHING
TOUCHES

*Nobody can go back
and start a new beginning,
but anyone can start today
and make a new ending.*
Maria Robinson

Answering Common Life Questions

*Winners have the ability to step back from the canvas of
their lives like an artist gaining perspective. They make
their lives a work of art—an individual masterpiece.*
Denis Waitley

Have you ever noticed that most artists stand while they paint? The main reason for this is that it takes less effort to step back from the canvas to gain perspective on their painting. Newton's first law of motion says that an object at rest stays at rest, and an object in motion stays in motion. If an artist is sitting while painting, she or he may not make the effort to get up, stand back, and gain perspective as often. Therefore, hours could be spent painting an image that may later need to be re-painted. If the artist is already standing, it is more natural to regularly stand back several feet every so often to check her progress. From a distance, mistakes, or areas to improve, are much more apparent to the eye.

Many of us get so busy in our daily lives, and so focused on the details, that we forget to stand back to see the whole of what we are creating. We let habit and routine run our schedule. To make our life a work of art, every so often, we must stand back several "emotional" feet to gain perspective.

In the introduction of this book, "Letter to an Artist," I posed five common life questions that most women ask themselves at some point in their lives. Those questions again are:

"How can I feel happy more often?"

"When will I get the appreciation I deserve for all I do?"

"I put everyone else first. When is it my turn to come first?"

"My big dreams haven't come true. Is it too late for me?"

And the mother of all questions...

"Does my life even matter?"

When we can positively answer these questions, those answers give us a feeling of peace and sense of purpose that we may have never experienced before. So! Mentally get up, stand back several "emotional or mental" feet from your daily self, and take a long, honest, earnest look at your life. This perspective will help you to see how to answer those questions, and the tools in this book will help you manifest those answers into your life, allowing you to become your own masterpiece.

How can I feel happy more often?

Author and motivational speaker Dr. Wayne W. Dyer held an orange in the palm of his hand. As he began tossing the orange up and down, he posed a question to his audience. "If I were to squeeze this orange," he asked, "what would come out? Do you think apple juice would come out? No?" He then answered his own question, "Of course, orange juice would come out. Whatever is inside, must be what comes out."

When an orange is squeezed, orange juice comes out. This is a metaphor for a question we can ask ourselves. When we get "squeezed" by daily life, what inside of us comes out? For example, if you are squeezed by someone's criticism, what comes out of you—how do you respond? If someone cuts in front of you in a long line, or steals the parking space you have been waiting for, what is your reaction? Do you get angry or vengeful? Or do you remain content, and happy? Whatever is inside must be what comes out.

We are human beings, and we have been shaped by our families and our cultures; not all of this shaping has been positive and loving—most of us have a variety of experiences. So, reacting in a loving way in all situations is nearly impossible. Even if we want to, it's hard to control what comes out during an adrenaline rush, because some negative reactions are common to every person's experience when something really bugs us—when we get squeezed in a negative way. We *can*, however, practice feeling joy daily. When being happy becomes a habit, it is just less likely that anger will come out when we are squeezed.

To feel happy more often, all we need to do is feel happier, right now. If you are in a bad mood, look back at THE ART OF HAPPINESS SCALE, and decide to practice being happy. Assess, Request, and be Thankful. Say to yourself, "Right now, the most important thing is for me to feel good." Next say, "I want to find a reason to feel good." Notice that your mind always comes up with a reason. The mind is awesome at doing that, if you give it a chance.

If we catch ourselves dwelling on negative events from our past, we can feel better by shifting our thoughts to a happier memory, or focusing on the good happening in the current moment. And if we catch ourselves imagining something negative that might happen in the future, we can change that image to one of visualizing everything working out perfectly. Feeling happy in the current moment is, moment by moment, creating a happy life.

> *Happiness cannot be traveled to, owned, earned, worn or consumed. Happiness is the spiritual experience of living every minute with love, grace and gratitude.*
> Denis Waitley

Another simple way to be happier is to help other people feel happier. Every day, no matter who you are with or where you are, you can spread happiness to others. Smile, and give sincere compliments. Try to make everyone's day a little better because her or his path crossed yours. We were born to lift each other up. It makes us feel good. First make yourself happy, then help make others happy. This will bring *you* more and more happiness, and others as well!

Studies show that strong friendships help you live longer, improve your immune system, and cut the risk of depression. Friendships are worth the time and effort because they make us happier. At the end of their lives, many people realize the benefits of staying in touch with old friends. Put in the time and effort that friendships deserve.

Being filled with happiness doesn't mean that when someone squeezes you, you become a doormat and let her or him get away with it. We can be calmly assertive, state our needs, and keep our happiness in tact. Practice being happy, and you will be happy more often.

When will I get the appreciation I deserve for all I do?

Stand back, and look at your relationships. Are you being appreciated? Is the care you are giving others being reciprocated? During one of my Book Club gatherings, I told my friend Shelly that I didn't feel appreciated by some of the people in my life. She replied, "Annette, go around the table and ask everyone here…I *know* they don't feel appreciated by some of the people in their life either." She had an excellent point. Yet, it's good to remember that just because it's a common experience of many to feel under-appreciated by some, that commonality does not make the experience okay. As women, most of us were taught to take care of and please others. There's nothing wrong with that, but when we feel unappreciated, when we feel that no one is taking care of and trying to please us, we run out of anything to give. We need to learn to increase the people in our lives who do appreciate us.

It's not ironic that those of us who believe we are worthy of appreciation usually get it. When I notice I don't feel appreciated, it hurts. Yet when I get really honest with myself, I sometimes don't appreciate myself. For example, I at times have undervalued the job I did as a stay-at-home mom. In not valuing what I did, I taught others not to appreciate me. We can begin feeling appreciated when we give it to ourselves and simultaneously show appreciation towards others.

Appreciating yourself works just like having the feeling of happiness. First you give it to yourself, then give it to others, and then good feelings of thanks and joy abound in you and around you. Like attracts like. Appreciate yourself by saying out loud, "Hey, I did a really good job!" or "It was really nice of me to do that." Admire yourself for all you do. When you do that, you can welcome others appreciating you, and return that feeling with gusto, rather than a feeling of giving too much.

Give away appreciation by telling others you are grateful for all the little things they do. Appreciate your daughter for feeding the dogs without being told. Appreciate your significant other for giving you a back rub, appreciate your friend for calling you "just because." By appreciating others, we get the benefit of feeling that feeling, and therefore we attract more appreciation into our lives.

Think back to the imaginary Masterpiece Gallery with the 5 Rooms: It really does help to imagine we *already* have the feeling that we want. It doesn't matter if it's real yet—if we imagine it, it will become real.

So tell me again, how did it feel on your recent milestone birthday, when all those close, personal friends shared the day with you? And, what did your family think of that vacation you took them on last summer just to show how much you appreciate them? I'm also dying to know, how did it feel appearing on the cover of *TIME* Magazine, with the caption "Most Appreciated Woman Alive?" I bet those feelings are all fantastic, because you are a fantastic person!

I put everyone else first. When is it my turn to come first?

My friend Bradley is vice president and second generation at his family run business, which employs over 200 people. A few years ago, when the economy took a turn for the worse, he worked non-stop trying to retain the company's current sales so no employees would be laid-off. He took it so personally that when a few people eventually had to be let go, he literally had a nervous breakdown. One afternoon during lunch he told me, "One thing I learned from that experience is no one else is ever going to tell me to not work so hard, to take a few days off, and not worry so much about everyone else. That's something *I* have to give myself permission to do."

Bradley put his employees well-being first, at the expense of his physical and mental health. Many women do this everyday while taking care of children, spouses, parents, and careers. Many of us are brought up to put others needs first, and to please others, without giving much thought to what pleases us. Yet, the reality is, we are of no good to anyone when we are physically and emotionally worn out, carrying the weight of the world alone on our shoulders.

Putting ourselves first means worrying less about other people and taking better care of ourselves. Our turn is now! Take some of the love and care you spend on other people and invest it in yourself. Cook your favorite meal for yourself. Do something fun this weekend that *you* want to do. Take a few days off.

The most caring thing you can do for yourself of all is...pursue your calling. You know what your dreams are, and now you have your Self-Portrait Notebook to remind you daily. And God knows the fastest way for you to reach your dreams. Start living the life that you want, *today*. Do your part by visualizing and taking baby steps each day. Some of us might say, "I'm too busy taking care of others to pursue my big dreams." I say, don't let others be your excuse to stay safe in your Comfort Zone. Plus, "others" don't want that burden! It *is* scary not knowing if we will succeed or fail, but it is a bigger risk to get to the end of our lives unhappy that we never put ourselves first. You may need to let others do a little more for themselves so that you have more time to do a little more for yourself. Everyone will grow positively from doing so.

It is also time to have equality in your relationships. Make sure your needs are being met. Do you freely express your feelings? Do you say things such as, "You hurt my feelings," or "I would like for you to listen to me," or "I need to be held right now"? Start including those kinds of phrases in your conversations when you need to express yourself. You don't have to yell to be heard. Calm and earnest statements *will* be heard by people who really care about you. And those who don't hear you—that tells you more about them than it does about you. Don't deny your feelings to keep peace with others. Suppressing resentment may lead to physical illness. Don't do that to yourself.

Being honest about how we feel may require us to stretch our

Comfort Zone. It may make us feel vulnerable to tell someone she or he has hurt us, and it may make us feel vulnerable to tell people we love them. If you feel God nudging you to call someone to mend a disagreement, do it. If you feel God nudge you to tell someone you love her or him, do it. You may not get another chance to create peace and joy between yourself and a loved one.

Worry a little less about others, and take a little better care of yourself. Follow your calling. Make sure there is equality in your relationships, and have the courage to express your feelings. Now is the time for you to come first in a positive, pro-active way.

My big dreams haven't come true. Is it too late for me?

If you believe your dreams have passed you by and it is too late for you, then I'm sorry to tell you, it *is*—you've made a self-fulfilling prophecy. But, if you believe you can start today and make a new ending, then I'm happy to tell you, *you can!* Looking back to where you started from, you're way ahead of schedule!

Now is the time to gather up the courage to live a life true to yourself. You are done living the life others expect of you. Time is ticking, Baby! Don't let your dreams go unfulfilled.

> *Great works and great people meet nothing strong enough to oppose their destiny.*
> Cecilia Beaux

Are you putting limitations on yourself (a.k.a., excuses)? "I'm too old," or "I'm too young," or "I *might* be able to accomplish this, but *definitely* not that." Has anyone said to you, "Who do you think you are?" or "You don't have the education to do that"? The truth is, *what you believe yourself to be, you are.* When you believe you can reach your dreams, you will have the courage to imagine and take action towards those dreams. Believing is what sets everything in motion.

First comes the belief, and then comes the dream. You have to believe that dreams are possible, and then make a dream for yourself. Just remember, unclear dreams produce unclear results. Be crystal clear. One way to get clear is to notice what you *don't* want. What you

349

don't like in your current reality often gives birth to your dream of a better life. Line up your dreams with your God-given talents.

Next comes the action. Look at your Self-Portrait Notebook daily. In your mind, live more in the world you are creating than your current reality. Our past thoughts and actions brought us to our current reality, and our new thoughts and actions will take us to the life of our dreams. Be content in your present, but focus on your dreams. Let God figure out how to fill in the gap.

You don't know what you are capable of until you try. There is no such thing as failure if you get back up, learn, and try another way. Nothing takes the place of persistence.

Right now, imagine yourself in the future, and everything you have dreamed of for your life has manifested. You believed, envisioned, took Divine action, and now all your dreams are a reality. You did it! You're living in the place, doing the things, and are surrounded by the people that you love, and who reciprocate that love. Not only did everything in your Self-Portrait Notebook come true, but you also had a lot of happy surprises God threw in just for fun. Look around, and enjoy it all. See…it was never too late for your dreams to come true!

Does my life even matter?

Of course your life matters! You wouldn't be here if it didn't! You're breathing, aren't you? Then you're supposed to be here. You are a part of the Divine, and you are here to do your part.

An insight into the absolute unity of the Human Existence with the divine is certainly the profoundest knowledge that man can attain.
Johann Gottlieb Fichte

You and God are the only two who know your reason for being. Listen for God's voice and amend your path accordingly. Your feelings guide you to your calling. Make your thoughts, feelings, and actions that of joy. You have a job that only you can do. If it stops being joyful, amend your path until it is.

What if your thoughts were actually God speaking to you? I'm not talking about your negative ones; we have to take ownership of those. But what if your loving, optimistic, and happy thoughts were all God, God, and God? When you listen to the thoughts of God, and act on them, your life serves a big purpose and matters greatly.

A part of our purpose is serving others. Humans are community beings and we function best when we function together, in service to each other. When I think of serving others, I immediately visualize working at a soup kitchen. That's serving, but so is *any* contribution we make. We can serve others by listening when someone needs to be heard. We can serve others by helping when someone needs help. We can serve others through our career or our calling. Dale Carnegie said, "The world is full of people who are grabbing and self-seeking. So the rare individual who unselfishly tries to serve others has an enormous advantage. He has little competition."

Your life matters. Fill your life with joy. Daydream, laugh with friends, snuggle with a pet, smell flowers and apply turquoise nail polish! The more happiness we feel today, the more happiness we create in our future.

Let your self-portrait masterpiece always continue. While painting our lives, we must focus on our goals—it is this desire that summons life to thrive through us. Having a dream and acting on that dream is more important than having the dream come true. Life is not the achievement of the dream, but the journey to the dream. Make your journey a joyous one. Remember most importantly on your way to making your life a masterpiece, that you, my Beloved, *already are one.* See it and you will flourish.

Sometime during your journey, you may feel like giving up on your dream, or a relationship, or *yourself.* This just means that while you anticipated joy in reaching your destination, the journey to that place stopped being fun. It didn't produce the joy you were hoping for. That's okay. It may not mean you need to change or adjust your goal. It may just mean you need to adjust your action steps. Keep adjusting until you feel the joy again.

My friend Margie Brown, whom I met in Toastmasters, lives her life this way. She is 85 years old, and "God ain't through with her yet."

Margie still gives speeches, enters speech contests, and is the founder of a senior women's exercise group at our local community center. At last year's Toastmasters Christmas party, while mingling with other partygoers, she asked around if anyone was in a book club she could join!

Margie was recently hospitalized and I went to visit her. After making a lap around the corridors with her walker and physical therapist, she got back to her bed and informed me, "Annette, I have you scheduled to give a speech to my senior women's exercise group next Wednesday." I couldn't believe it. She was in the hospital, with no planned release date, and she was scheduling speakers for her women's group?! How could I say no?

People who are living long, happy lives, are those who continue to envision and manifest, envision and manifest. This is what draws Life Source through us. It doesn't matter what we are manifesting, it only matters that it is positive and sparks our enthusiasm. We must be the leading lady in our own life. Even at 85, Margie is not a co-star in anyone else's life, she is the star of *her* life!

I used to think I could be happy (and lovable) if my surroundings were perfect, if I had more money, and *if* my hair grew back. I pray that someday there will be a cure for alopecia, but I won't put my happiness on hold until "someday" arrives. My journey has taught me this: **To increase your happiness, simply increase your grateful and loving thoughts.** Within these pages I've chosen to be vulnerable, and bold, letting the world see me "just as I am." I hope I inspired *you* to love yourself more, imperfections and all. I want to someday be remembered as the woman who used her God-given gifts, shared them with others, and made the world a little bit better.

Consciously create your life. The brush is in your hand and the work of art you are creating is whatever you choose yourself to be, at any given moment in your life. You are extraordinarily unique, a "one in *7 billion!*" Make it your intent to feel good, believe you are deserving, envision your future, take Divine action and allow the masterpiece. Make your self-portrait a reflection of your authentic self. It's God's gift to you that you can, in joyous wonder, love and appreciation, continually master the art of you. Your life…is your masterpiece.

Just as I Am (Self-Portrait), by: Annette Hackney Evans

The Portrait Sitting

The reason some portraits don't look true to life is that some people make no effort to resemble their pictures.
Salvador Dali

Some people make no effort to resemble their pictures... Ha! This is the quote on my coffee mug and it makes me smile every morning. Gotta love the eccentric Salvador Dali.

I take the last drink of my coffee and sit the mug on the kitchen counter. I've been waiting for this day for over a month. It's the day I finally get to meet *you*! You're coming to my studio this morning so I can begin painting your portrait. It's so wonderful that a loved one (is it yourself?) is giving this gift to you—an image of yourself which you and your family can cherish. It just shows me how special you must be.

I like to learn a little bit about my sitter before the session, and from what I've learned so far, you are a kind, generous person, with a wide circle of friends. You also like to read, and enjoy learning new things.

Looking out the kitchen window, I see the fog is thick, masking the Saddleback Mountains. You're due to arrive in ten minutes, at 9 o'clock. I head to my studio and put a log in the fireplace and light it. It will burn for approximately three hours, the length of your portrait sitting. Now it's time to squeeze the juicy oil paints onto my much-loved and well-used wood palette:

355

Permalba White

Cadmium Yellow Light

Raw Sienna

Cadmium Red Light

Grumbacher Red – I love having this happy hue on my palette.
Red is my favorite color.

Alizarin Crimson

Burnt Sienna

Burnt Umber

Cerulean Blue

French Ultramarine Blue – I also adore anything with French in
the name.

Sap Green

No Black – If the Impressionists didn't need it, neither do I.

So! Painting medium – check. Mineral spirits – check. Stained 30" x 24" canvas – check. I put on music just as the doorbell rings.

My Bichon Frises, whom you are about to meet, start barking excitedly, and with their tails wagging, bound to the door. They think you are coming just to play with them. Following close behind, I quickly give them a treat to divert their attention so you don't get overwhelmed by their exuberance as you enter.

Swinging open the door, I extend my right arm and say, "Hi, I'm Annette. It's so nice to meet you."

"Oh, hi!" you say enthusiastically as you make friendly direct eye contact and shake my hand. "It's so nice to finally meet you, too! I've heard wonderful things about you." Your gaze drifts to the floor and you say, "Oh, your dogs are adorable! What are their names?"

I like you. I like you already. Is it because you seem to like *me*? And my dogs? Well, that helps…but you have this open smile. You look like someone who has never had a bad day in her life. I know, of course, that you have. You are a human being, after all. But you have this wonderful, relaxed feeling about you. I match it with my own, and it feels we are sharing the bonds of sisterhood.

"His name is Fritz, with the blue collar. And she's Hazel, with the pink one. My Grandma Hackney's name was Hazel, and she also had white, fluffy, hair. Let me take your sweater and purse," I say, guiding you into the now comfortably warm studio.

Ten minutes later, I'm helping you up onto the model stand and you sink down into the wood trimmed, velvet chair. Deciding on a background, I drape a few different backdrops behind you, a light color one first, and then a medium color. Yes, the medium color looks best. Fritz and Hazel have already cuddled up side by side on the daybed, playing the role of your admiring fans.

Standing behind my easel, I study you before beginning. Artists are supposed to spend more time looking at the subject they are painting than at the canvas. I realize while observing you that your beauty is special, better than a cover girl's. There is something in your eyes that convey kindness. And something in your smile…it's subtle, but I feel your smile says *joy*.

With a large brush, I begin sketching in the major proportions of your head and shoulders on the canvas. I make your head approximately life size, a good rule for a portrait. I leave room above your head, and plenty below.

I enjoy talking with my subjects, and continue our conversation in a general, easy way. "It's really foggy outside today, isn't it?"

"The weather is wonderful…moody. It's the best day ever," you say.

I see what you see. We're taking life as it is, and seeing the beauty in it together. I smile and nod, in total agreement with your appreciation of the moment.

"Do you have plans for the weekend?" I ask.

"Yes," you say, "Let me see... Friday night I'm doing volunteer work with a few of my neighbors. We always have a great time. Saturday morning it's the usual chores and errands, but in the afternoon I'm going out with friends to see the new Meryl Streep movie." You turn your head, looking directly at me, and say jovially, "*Love* her!" Then you turn your head back to the three-quarter pose, respecting the job you've asked me to do for you.

I smile and continue painting as I say, "I know, she's the best. I wasn't aware that movie is out already." Now, I've got the shape of your head down. I begin to sketch in your facial features: eyes, nose, and mouth.

"Oh, yeah," you reply, doing very well at keeping your calm, comfortable pose, "I've been looking forward to it for months." You continue, "So, let's see. On Sunday, I'm not exactly sure of my plans. I may go on a hike, but I might just sleep in and then see what I feel like doing."

"Wow," I say, "You sure do pack in a lot."

"Well, I love my weekends. They go by so fast! Before I know it, it's Sunday night, and I'm getting organized for the coming week," you explain. "What are you doing this weekend?"

"Um...well..." I say. It is sometimes difficult for me to talk and paint at the same time. Language is controlled by the left side of the brain, and painting is controlled by the right. I pause to think and then say, "Friday night there is a church outing planned, and Saturday I'm going canoeing with my daughters. I'm so excited that they'll both be home." I begin now sketching in your neck and shoulders and I notice the beautiful necklace you are wearing. I'll paint that in later, along with other finishing touches. "Do you like your job?" I ask.

"I *love* my job," you respond. "I'm one of the lucky ones, like you, who get to do what they love."

You're right, I *do* love this. I'm now massing in the big shapes of the composition on my canvas so I pause, squint to block out small details and get the big images, then begin painting again.

My timer goes off when 30 minutes are up. You hop down and

walk around the easel to see my progress. "Oh! I like it! Wow, it's really starting to look like me."

"I'm so glad you like it," I say. I know from experience that when a client likes their portrait, it has as much to do with their self-esteem as it does my painting ability.

For the next two hours I paint, you pose, we chat, and you take much-needed breaks to stretch. I establish the overall effect of light, shape and pose. I also begin refining the painting and maintain a greater degree of detail in your facial features.

Our conversation is lively and interesting. You say something that intrigues me and I just can't get it out of my mind. When I asked you how you stay so positive, so happy, you say, "Well I know this is going to sound corny, but my life is rich in love."

Yes, it is a little corny, I think, *in the best way. Your life is rich in love. I like that. It's not about your bank account. Your life is rich in loving others and being loved.*

Soon, way too soon it seems because we're having such a nice time together, three hours are up. The burning log is now just glowing the color of cadmium red light. I take photographs of you in pose before you go, and will use them as my painting reference material to continue work during the week. I'm pleased with your portrait so far, and know it is only going to get better.

"I'll have your portrait done and ready for you to pick up in two weeks," I say.

While I hand you your sweater and purse, you respond, "I can't wait to see it finished!"

We plan to meet at the same time, day, and place in two weeks. I walk you to the door and extend my hand to say goodbye. You open you arms wide and give me a hug instead.

"Have a good weekend," I shout, as you stroll down the walkway. Fritz and Hazel bark a happy farewell to you.

As I work on your portrait over the next two weeks, I realize I'm enjoying spending time with you. Even though it's just an image of you, I like your company. You seem familiar, like family.

I'm passionate about the painting process. The back and forth pushing and pulling with paint to make you appear three-dimensional on a two-dimensional surface. The darker shadows along the right side of your face make the well-lit left side come forward. Artist Everett Raymond Kinstler likens painting to playing the piano. He says that a pianist plays piano mostly off the middle, and then adds the low notes and high notes. So should a painter paint mostly in the middle values, and then add darks and highlights.

I add the highlights to your hair where the light is falling across the upper-left side of your head. I add the glint on the beautiful pendant you are wearing; the piece was a special gift, you explained, as you shared fond memories with me. And now for the highlight in your eyes; the *highest* high note. The sparkle. With paint on the very tip of my brush, I touch it to the canvas. First one eye, and then the other. Voila, you seem to come to life! It is as if you are looking back at me, and you are there, a clear masterpiece of a person with whom I got to spend a lovely afternoon.

Standing back, ten feet away, I admire you. I have satisfactorily captured your outer beauty, and I believe that a viewer will more importantly *feel* your inner magnificence shine through.

I sign the painting in the lower right corner in my signature red, and move your finished portrait from the easel to the mantle above the fireplace to dry. I believe you will like the finished piece. And I feel, thanks to your willingness to sit for me, that I truly am enjoying my journey to becoming a master artist, just as you are enjoying the journey of becoming the master of things you love in your life.

I am so glad I had the privilege of spending time with you. I am so happy that our paths crossed. You, my friend, are an original work of art, a true masterpiece.

Framework

You don't have to be a genius or a visionary or even a college graduate to be successful. You just need a framework and a dream.
Michael Dell

STEP #1: FEEL GOOD

Think Good Thoughts

Take thoughts *off* autopilot and choose to think good thoughts.

Thinking positive thoughts, a majority of the time,
is the only way to feel good a majority of the time.

All thoughts are prayers, a "request" for more of what you are thinking about. Those thoughts, whether positive or negative, create your mood, and draw in related material things and circumstances.

The Art of Happiness

Move up THE ART OF HAPPINESS SCALE
Assess the mood you are in, and allow yourself to feel it.
Request of God and yourself to think better thoughts.
Be **T**hankful because only with gratitude, can there be joy.

With proactive thinking you may flow up THE ART
OF HAPPINESS SCALE 1 or 2 levels at a time. Once
at the top of the SCALE, resolve to keep happy.

10 WAYS TO STAY AT THE TOP OF THE SCALE

1 Be Consciously Thankful	6 LOL!
2 Move That Body	7 Love a Pet
3 Get Outdoors	8 Listen to Music
4 Play	9 Read Inspirational Books
5 Associate with Positive People	10 Get Enough Sleep

A Grateful Mind

Grateful thoughts are closely connected to the mind of God.

Focus on the goodness in life to create better relationships and
more financial abundance. Feeling love and gratitude also defends,
sharpens, calms, strengthens and heals your physical body.

Be grateful for any and everything beyond food to sustain, basic
clothing and shelter to protect, and necessary medical attention.

Love the Body You're With

Remember your reality is better than a celebrity's image.
Talk to yourself as you would someone you love.
Nurture your body.
Appreciate all the functions your body performs each day.
Wear clothes that compliment your figure.
Maintain good grooming.
The only opinions that matter are yours, those who love you, and your doctor.
Be happy! Being happy and having an internal, spiritual beauty, makes you externally beautiful.

Lovely on the Inside

Change childhood labels that are not serving you.
Repeat positive affirmations daily.
Focus on your successes.
Compare yourself to where you've been.
Focus on others.
Take action towards success.

To Be Loved...Love

Be a "There you are!" person.
Treat everyone with politeness.
See the Divine in others.
Don't judge, or you will feel judged.
Be a good listener:
     give your full attention

resist the impulse to "chime in"
face the one speaking and make eye contact
try to see things from her or his perspective
ask about her or his interests
empathize
don't give advice unless asked
don't criticize, judge, or *share* what the person says
Bless those who are finding abundance.
Maintain inner peace despite difficult people:
    pray for the difficult person
    see their good qualities, the amount we love an imperfect person
        is the amount we believe others can love imperfect us
    choose to practice the *opposite* of their behavior
    shift your focus to the wonderful people around you

To Be Loved...Be Lovable

Open your heart to receive love. You may be vulnerable to hurt, but it's the only way to allow in a lot of love.
Find good in yourself by first finding it in others.
Forgive. *You* deserve to be free from emotional pain. Forgiving improves physical health and allows space in our heart to love.
If needed, get help. We are difficult to love when wounded from past hurts. Talk with a professional therapist to gain insights, learn coping skills and to have compassion for yourself.
Don't complain.
Walk away from negative people. They draw the positive mental attitude out of you and drain your energy. Surround yourself with happy people to improve your own chance of being happy.
Don't take things personally. Someone's approval of us depends on her or his belief system. Don't spend energy defending your choices, spend it on people and things that are important to *you.*

STEP #2: BELIEVE YOU ARE DESERVING

Believe You Deserve Your Masterpiece

Believe you are as worthy as anyone ever born.
Believe you are worthy of receiving love.
Believe you deserve to be treated with dignity and respect.
Believe you are here for a purpose.
Believe you deserve for your voice to be heard.
Believe when you base the majority of your thoughts, words, and actions in believing, your dreams will become your reality.

Have a Happy Childhood

Fulfill the dreams of your youth by giving yourself today the things you wish you had received in childhood.

Family - Surround yourself with a "family" of people who support and want the best for you.

Pets - Contemplate having the pet you longed for as a child.

Material Things - Consider owning things you desired as a child.

Travel - Travel to the destination that has been calling your name.

Occupation - Fit your childhood passion into your life in any quantity that you can.

Extracurricular Activities:

Sports - Participate in sports.

The Arts - Whether observing or participating, enjoy the arts!

Volunteer - Choose a cause that may have meaning to you from childhood. You'll heal your soul while benefiting the community.

Play - Play stimulates creativity and brings enthusiasm to life.

Happy Birthday to You!

You deserve to have a truly *happy* birthday!
Fill your day with self-love, and you'll have the capacity
to appreciate the caring gestures of loved ones.

STEP #3: ENVISION YOUR FUTURE

Tell Me What You Want

Allow yourself to want what you really, really want without
concern for how you will get it. Write it down and say it aloud.

Find Your Calling

Remember the activities that brought you joy as a child.
Listen to your inner voice. Answer these questions:
    Where do I feel most like me?
    What activities give me energy?
    What is my heart telling me?
Serve others. Find a way to use your gifts to serve others.
Look forward to your past. You are thrown a party at the Masterpiece
    Gallery to receive a lifetime achievement award.
    The Health Room – In the photos on the wall what are the physical
    activities you have enjoyed throughout the years?

The Legacy Room – In the photos on the wall what are you doing in your life's work?

The Philanthropy Room – In the photos on the wall who are the people whose lives have benefited because of you?

The Material Things Room – In the photos on the wall what are the material things that have brought you pleasure?

The Family & Friends Room – In the photos on the wall who are the people who you have loved and who have loved you?

Your Definite Purpose 14

Definiteness of purpose is the starting point of all achievement.

WE ARE GIVEN 2 ENVELOPES AT BIRTH

One envelope contains the *Riches* you may enjoy if you take control of your mind and direct it to your clear purpose.	One envelope contains *Penalties* you must pay if you don't take control of your mind and direct it.
1 Good heath	1 Ill health
2 Peace of mind	2 Frustration, discouragement
3 Labors of love	3 Indecision and doubt
4 Faith and confidence	4 Fear and worry
5 Hope, positivity, earnestness	5 Envy, angst, hatred
6 Material riches you choose	6 Poverty, lack, want

Your definite purpose is your major desire in life, right now.
It is your life's work

Imagine

Use your imagination to create images in your mind that
make you feel good, that make you excited to be alive.
Imagination is the preview of life's coming attractions.

Imagination is more important than knowledge. Don't limit
your dreams because of limited knowledge. Knowledge
comes *after* we begin pursuing our dreams, not before.

We must carry the picture of the life we want to live in
our mind before we can live it. We cannot give birth
to anything that we haven't first conceived of.

Your Self-Portrait Reference Materials

Reference Material #1: Self-Portrait Plan
> Supply your subconscious mind with a clear purpose to
> move towards in the 5 areas of your life: health, your calling,
> serving others, material things, family & friends. Next, decide
> what action you are willing to take to manifest these main,
> definite purposes.

Reference Material #2: Coming Attractions and Highlight Reel
> List 25 good things that are going to happen in your life and
> 25 good things that have already happened.

Reference Material #3: Self-Portrait Notebook
> Create your notebook and look at it daily. Our subconscious
> mind cannot tell the difference between reality and what
> we imagine, so let your mind work to make these imagined
> images a reality.

17 Focus

Be a vibrational match to your goal. When we are consciously grateful, joyous and enthusiastic, a dominant amount of the time, we will become a vibrational match to the things we desire.

Focus not on success, but on significance. Lean your ladder against a wall that has significance for you and enjoy the climb.

Move towards your definite purposes by focusing on them daily.
1 Review your Self-Portrait Notebook at least 5-10 minutes a day.
2 Focus with faith that God will respond to your request.
3 Focus with Gratitude that your desires are being granted.

STEP #4: TAKE DIVINE ACTION

Close the Gap Between Where You Are and Where You Will Be

The quickest route from point A (where you are now) to point B (the Definite Purposes on your Self-Portrait Plan) is:

B	→	T	→	F	→	A	=	R
e		h		e		c		e
l		o		e		t		s
i		u		l		i		u
e		g		i		o		l
f		h		n		n		t
s		t		g		s		s
		s		s				

If we **believe** we can accomplish our dream, if we have **thoughts** and **feelings** that our dream has already come true, and take **action** by emulating people getting the results we desire, we *will* see positive **results**.

A Powerful Prayer

Dear God,
Spoil me with blessings!
I desire a bigger life.
Please be with me when it feels like my calling is too big.
I will listen for your voice to guide my thoughts, words and actions.
Keep temptation away from me.
Help me forgive myself for my mistakes and shortcomings and help
    me forgive those who have harmed me.
Thank You for responding to my needs.
I now feel the joy I will feel when my requests are fulfilled.
                            Amen

Take Action!

Quit *talking* about taking action and begin *taking* action.

Practice feeling good. The feeling you have upon achieving your goal is a match to the feeling you have while getting there.

Work begets inspiration.

Join a mastermind group. Two minds coming together form a 3rd mind, which increases creative accomplishments.

Give more than you're asking for in work and relationships. To get more than you currently have, you have to give more than you are currently giving.

Give Up the Good for the Great

People - Give up some time spent with #2 and #3 people in your life in order to make more time for #1 people.

Things - Release some of the material things in your life in order to make room for things that reflect who you are today.

Involvements and Interests - Let go of attachments, involvements and interests that you do to please others, in order to pursue new involvements and interests that please you.

God - Be willing to let go of the distractions and noise in your life in order to be filled by God.

Expand Your Comfort Zone

The only constant is change.
In one year will your Comfort Zone have contracted or expanded?

Baby Steps – Taking baby steps allows you to slowly decrease your discomfort and move toward your goals.

Take a Friend - Having a friend by your side may soothe nerves and give you a sense of security.

Educate Yourself - Your Comfort Zone may be protecting you from *imaginary* dangers. Getting good information will lessen your anxiety and educate the fear out of you.

Entertain the Uncomfortable - Your ability to grow is in direct proportion to your ability to be uncomfortable.

Trust in God – Fear of criticism disables you but trusting in God will protect you from that.

Focused Persistence

23

Accomplishing a dream takes focused, persistent, action.

10 TACTICS TO QUIT PROCRASTINATING

1   Work on high priority actions in the morning.
2   Set a timer.
3   Strive for progress, not perfection.
4   Ask yourself, "If I did know how to do it, how would I do it?"
5   Imagine the task completed.
6   Take breaks.
7   Have a motivational buddy.
8   Track your progress.
9   Break up a large goal into smaller short-term goals.
10 Ask yourself, "If everyday looked like today, how long would it take me to reach my goal?"

STEP #5: ALLOW THE MASTERPIECE

Work for God

24

Serve God where you are called to do so. God expresses Himself through people. He looks for people who are the most receptive, and will take the greatest positive action.

Throughout your day, listen for God's voice to guide you. Say, "I'm ready for you to *use me* to do your work."

God qualified you to work for Him. Your upbringing, education, and work experience do not matter. He only cares that you have a willingness to listen to His guidance, and the faith and courage to act on it.

What's in it for you? When you work for God, God works for you. Sharing your gifts and serving others brings you joy.

Master Receiver

God is moving through everyone and every circumstance to give to you. Keep your receiving channels open.

The biggest barrier to receiving is feeling unworthy. Make the decision to believe you are as worthy as anyone ever born.

HOW TO BE A GOOD RECEIVER

1 Give to yourself.
2 Be grateful when you receive.
3 Receive abundantly to be able to give abundantly.

Change Your Mind

You don't need to be the strongest or most intelligent to thrive, but the most responsive to change.

Signal your body to grow younger by exercising daily, eating well, caring about someone and something, and getting plenty of sleep.

Change before you have to.
One year from now your health, your career, and your relationships will have changed for the better or worse.

Reinvent yourself.
When you are through changing, you are through.

We are In God, God is In Us

27

God is a nonmaterial force
that is the energy in all things and all people.

God is the "thinking stuff" from which everything is
created. This thinking stuff is in us and all around us,
filling the Universe. There is no place that God isn't. When
thinking, you cause what you think about to be created.

Manifest the glory of God within you.
You were born to be brilliant, gorgeous, talented and fabulous!

The human body is a masterpiece. The odds that this work of
art just *happened* is a statistical impossibility. Your body is
proof that you are the greatest creation, of the great Creator.

PORTRAIT, SUBJECT, & ARTISTS' INFORMATION

Letter to an Artist

Portrait: *Portrait of the Artist at His Easel* (Self-Portrait), 1660, Oil on canvas, 43½ x 35½", Musée du Louvre, Paris, France

Subject & Artist: Rembrandt Harmenszoon van Rijn (1606-1669) was a Dutch painter and etcher. He is generally considered one of the greatest painters and printmakers in European art and the most important in Dutch history.

Portrait: *Self-Portrait*, 1800, Oil on canvas, 31 x 26¾", State Hermitage Museum, St. Petersburg, Russia

Subject & Artist: Elisabeth Vigée-Lebrun, also known as Madame Lebrun (1755-1842) was a French painter, who over a six-year period painted more than 30 portraits of Marie Antoinette and her family. She is recognized as the most important female painter of the 18th century.

Chapter 1

Portrait: *Grandma Frances,* 2013, Pencil on paper, 11 x 8"

Subject: Golda Frances Riester Lawyer (1916-2003) was a beloved stay-at-home mother of 5 children and earned extra money taking in washing and ironing. She was a talented artist and seamstress.

Artist: Annette Hackney Evans (1964-present)

Chapter 3

Portrait: *Helen Keller,* Charcoal on paper, 14 x 8½"

Subject: Helen Keller (1880-1968) was deafened and blinded by a childhood disease. Overcoming her disabilities, she became one of the 20th century's leading humanitarians, as well as co-founder of the American Civil Liberties Union (ACLU).

Artist: Casey Childs (1974-present) is a fine artist based in Pleasant Grove, Utah. His book, *Influential Figures: A Fine Art Drawing Series,* contains 25 charcoal portrait drawings along with biographies of prominent individuals in our recent history.

Chapter 4

Portrait: *Sarah Ban Breathnach,* 2013, Pencil on paper, 20 x 14"

Subject: Sarah Ban Breathnach is the author of 12 books including the two *New York Times* bestselling titles *Simple Abundance* and *Something More.* She currently resides in California.

Artist: Annette Hackney Evans

Chapter 5

Portrait: *Diana Vreeland,* 1989, Artwork ©Richard Ely, Crayon, ink and gouache on paper, 12½ x 9½", National Portrait Gallery, Smithsonian Institute, Washington D.C., Photo Credit: National Portrait Gallery, Smithsonian Institution / Art Resource, NY

Subject: Diana Vreeland (1903-1989) was an influential figure in American fashion during the 20th century. She worked as an editor for *Harper's Bazaar* and *Vogue* and as a special consultant at the Costume Institute of the Metropolitan Museum of Art.

Artist: Richard Ely (1928-2009) was a fine artist, fashion illustrator. Based in Manhattan, Mr. Ely taught Fashion Illustration at the New York City Fashion Institute of Technology in their School of Art and Design.

Chapter 6

Portrait: *Ivanka Trump*, 2013, Pencil on paper, 8 x 8"
Subject: Ivanka Trump (1981-present) is a businesswoman, writer, heiress, and former model.
Artist: Annette Hackney Evans

Chapter 7

Portrait: *Susie Lawyer Briggs*, 2013, Pencil on paper, 12 x 9"
Subject: Susie Lawyer Briggs, M.S., CMHC (1969-present) is a therapist practicing in Layton, Utah.
Artist: Annette Hackney Evans

Chapter 8

Portrait: *Brené Brown*, 2013, Pencil on paper, 12 x 9"
Subject: Brené Brown, Ph.D. LMSW (1965-present) is a scholar, author, public speaker, and a research professor at the University of Houston Graduate College of Social Work. Her 2010 TEDx Houston talk on the power of vulnerability is one of the most watched talks on TED.com.
Artist: Annette Hackney Evans

Chapter 9

Portrait: *Self-Portrait*, 1984/2005, Oil on canvas (5 panels), 73 x 22½" overall, ©David Hockney, Collection the David Hockney Foundation, Photo Credit: Richard Schmidt
Subject & Artist: David Hockney (1937-present) is an English painter, draughtsman, printmaker, stage designer and photographer. Known for his photo collages and paintings of Los Angeles swimming pools, he is considered one of the most influential British artists of the 20th century.

Chapter 10

Portrait: *Self-Portrait with a Palette,* 1906, Oil on canvas, 15½ x
11¹³/₁₆", Philadelphia Museum of Art, Philadelphia, Pennsylvania

Subject & Artist: Pablo Picasso (1881-1973) was a Spanish painter,
sculptor, printmaker, ceramicist, and stage designer who spent
most of his adult life in France. He was the co-creator of Cubism,
and one of the most influential artists of the 20th century.

Portrait: *Self-Portrait with Shirley Temple,* 1936, Oil on canvas

Subject: Shirley Temple Black (1928-present) is perhaps the most
famous child star of all time. She received a special Oscar, starred
in films such as *Bright Eyes* and *Heidi,* and as an adult became an
ambassador to Ghana and Czechoslovakia.

Artist: Sir John Lavery (1856-1941) was an Irish painter best known
for his portraits.

Chapter 11

Portrait: *Theodor Geisel* (Dr. Seuss), Artwork ©1982 Everett Raymond
Kinstler, Oil on canvas, 44 x 44" Collection: Hood Museum,
Dartmouth College, Hanover, New Hampshire

Subject: Theodor Geisel (1904-1991) was a writer, poet, and cartoonist.
He is most widely known as the author of 60 children's books
including *The Cat in the Hat* and *Green Eggs and Ham.* At the
time of his death 200 million copies of his books were in print
around the world. Sales continue to climb with an estimated 300
million more in print since 1991.

Artist: Everett Raymond Kinstler (1926-present) is an artist, author,
and beloved teacher. One of the nation's foremost portrait
painters, Mr. Kinstler has painted over 50 cabinet officers, more
than any artist in the country's history. Seven Presidents have
posed for him, and his portraits of Ford and Reagan are the
official White House portraits. The National Portrait Gallery,
Washington, D.C., has acquired 75 of his original works for its
permanent collection.

Chapter 12

Portrait: *Coco Chanel*, 2013, Pencil on paper, 12½ x 8¼"

Subject: Gabrielle "Coco" Chanel (1883-1971) was a French fashion designer and founder of the Chanel brand, creating timeless designs that are still popular today. She is the only fashion designer to appear on *Time* magazine's list of the 100 most influential people of the 20th century.

Artist: Annette Hackney Evans

Chapter 13

Portrait: *Portrait of J. K. Rowling*, 2005, Oil on board construction with coloured pencil on paper, $38^1/_4$ x $28^3/_8$", National Portrait Gallery, London, England

Subject: Joanne "Jo" Rowling, pen name J. K. Rowling (1965-present) is a British novelist. She is best known as the author of the Harry Potter fantasy series, one of the most popular book and film franchises in history.

Artist: Stuart Pearson Wright (1975-present) is an award-winning English artist best known for his irreverent and detailed figurative portraits. The National Portrait Gallery, London, has 31 of his original works in their collection.

Chapter 14

Portrait: *Napoleon Hill*, 2013, Charcoal and pencil on paper, 12 x 9"

Subject: Napoleon Hill (1883-1970) was a motivational author widely considered to be one of the great writers on success. He is best known for his 1937 book *Think and Grow Rich*, which has sold over 70 million copies worldwide.

Artist: Annette Hackney Evans

Chapter 15

Portrait: *Albert Einstein*, 1921, Drawing and wash, Academie des Sciences, Paris, France, Photo Credit: Erich Lessing / Art Resource, NY

Subject: Albert Einstein (1879-1955) was a German-born (later nationalized Swiss and American) theoretical physicist, most known for developing the theory of relativity. Named by *Time* magazine as the #1 most influential person of the 20th century.

Artist: Max Wulfart (1876-1955) was a German portrait painter. Above Wulfart's signature, Einstein wrote: "Gut gemalt in kurzer Frist – das Modell zufrieden ist" (Well painted in a short time – the model is pleased).

Chapter 16

Portrait: *Mark Twain*, 1935, Oil on canvas, 48 x 36", National Portrait Gallery, Smithsonian Institution, Washington D.C., Photo Credit: National Portrait Gallery, Smithsonian Institution / Art Resource, NY

Subject: Samuel L. Clemens, pen name Mark Twain, (1835-1910) was a riverboat pilot, journalist, lecturer, entrepreneur, inventor, and best known for his classic American novels *The Adventures of Tom Sawyer* and *The Adventures of Huckleberry Finn*.

Artist: Frank Edwin Larson (1895-1991) was a portrait and landscape painter.

Chapter 17

Portrait: *Oprah Winfrey*, Oil on linen, 72 x 50"

Subject: Oprah Gail Winfrey (1954-present) is an actress, philanthropist, publisher, and producer. For 25 seasons, 1986-2011, she hosted *The Oprah Winfrey Show*, the highest-rated talk show in American television history.

Artist: Simmie Knox (1935-present) is a portrait artist and has painted sports figures, entertainment celebrities, educators, religious leaders, military officers and prominent politicians. He is best known for his official White House portrait of former United States President Bill Clinton and First Lady Hillary Rodham Clinton.

Chapter 18

Portrait: *Portrait of the Artist* (Self-Portrait), 1878, Gouache on paper, $23^5/_8$ x $16^{13}/_{16}$", Metropolitan Museum of Art, New York City.

Subject & Artist: Mary Stevenson Cassatt (1844-1926) was an American painter and printmaker who lived much of her adult life in France. She was one of the leading artists in the Impressionist movement of the later part of the 1800s.

Portrait: *Self-Portrait*, 2011, Oil on canvas, 52 x 36", Nashville, Tennessee

Subject & Artist: Michael Shane Neal (1968-present) is a fine artist and teacher based in Nashville, Tennessee. He has created official portraits for the United States Capitol and over 400 works of art depicting various public figures.

Chapter 19

Portrait: *Jesus Christ*, 1980, Oil on canvas, 70 x 54", Fifth Avenue Presbyterian Church, New York City, New York

Subject: Jesus, also referred to as Jesus of Nazareth, (7-2 BC to 30–33 AD) is the founder and central figure of Christianity, one of the world's most influential religions. His teachings and life are recorded in the Bible's New Testament and emulated by Christians all over the world.

Artist: John Howard Sanden (1935-present) is a portrait artist, teacher, and author of four books on portraiture. He has completed more than five hundred portraits of prominent figures in American public, professional and business life. Mr. Sanden painted the official White House portraits of President George W. Bush and First Lady Laura Bush.

Chapter 20

Portrait: *Martyn Lawrence Bullard*, 2013, Oil on canvas, 20" x 16"

Subject: Martyn Lawrence Bullard is a British multi-award-winning Los Angeles based interior designer and television personality. He is consistently named one of the world's top 100 interior designers by *Architectural Digest*.

Artist: Annette Hackney Evans

Chapter 21

Portrait: *Karen Kingsbury*, 2013, Oil on canvas, 20 x 16"

Subject: Karen Kingsbury (1963-present) is a Christian inspirational novelist. There are more than 25 million copies of her award-winning books in print. She is also a public speaker, reaching more than 100,000 women annually through various national events. Karen lives and works outside of Nashville, Tennessee.

Artist: Annette Hackney Evans

Chapter 22

Portrait: *Theodore Roosevelt*, 1903, Oil on canvas, 58 x 40", the White House, Washington, D.C.

Subject: Theodore "Teddy" Roosevelt (1858-1919) was a New York Governor who became the 26th U.S. President. He is remembered for his foreign policy, corporate reforms and ecological preservation. A popular toy named after Roosevelt is the "teddy" bear.

Artist: John Singer Sargent (1856-1925) was an Italian-born American painter whose portraits of the wealthy and privileged provide an enduring image of Edwardian-age society.

Chapter 23

Portrait: *Abraham Lincoln*, 1864, Oil on canvas, National Portrait Gallery, Smithsonian Institution, Washington, D.C.

Subject: Abraham Lincoln (1809-1865) was the 16th President of the United States. He preserved the Union during the U.S. Civil War and brought about the emancipation of slaves.

Artist: William Willard (1819-1904) was a portrait painter and art instructor based in Boston, Massachusetts. He based the portrait on a photograph taken by Anthony Berger in 1964. This version appears on the copper penny, first minted in 1909.

Chapter 24

Portrait: *Mother Teresa*, 2013, Pencil on paper, 12 x 9"

Subject: The Blessed Teresa of Calcutta, commonly known as Mother Teresa, (1910-1997) was an Albanian born, Indian Roman Catholic Religious Sister. She was the founder of the Order of the Missionaries of Charity, a Roman Catholic congregation of women dedicated to helping the poor.

Artist: Annette Hackney Evans

Chapter 26

Portrait: *Walt Disney*, Charcoal on paper, 14 x 8½"

Subject: Walter Elias Disney (1901-1966) was a motion-picture and television producer and showman, famous as a pioneer of cartoon films and as the creator of Disneyland. During his lifetime he received 4 honorary Academy Awards and won 22, giving him more Oscars than any other individual in history.

Artist: Casey Childs (see information under Chapter 3)

Chapter 27

Portrait: *Marianne Williamson*, 2013, Pencil on paper, 11½ x 7¾"

Subject: Marianne Williamson (1952-present) is a spiritual teacher, author and lecturer. She has published ten books, six on the *New York Times* #1 Best Seller list, including the spiritual guide *A Return to Love*.

Artist: Annette Hackney Evans

Chapter 28

Portrait: *Just as I Am* (Self-Portrait), 2013, Charcoal on paper, 17 x 13"

Subject & Artist: Annette Hackney Evans

ACKNOWLEDGEMENTS

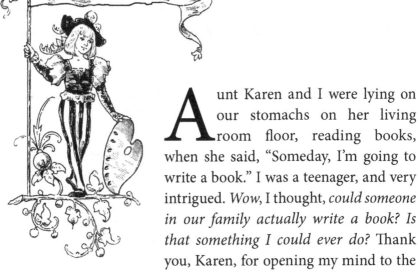

Aunt Karen and I were lying on our stomachs on her living room floor, reading books, when she said, "Someday, I'm going to write a book." I was a teenager, and very intrigued. *Wow*, I thought, *could someone in our family actually write a book? Is that something I could ever do?* Thank you, Karen, for opening my mind to the possibility of being an author.

Thank you, Jonathan Evans, for supporting me through this process. It would have been impossible to complete this book without your help.

Thank you to my brother, Dennis Hackney. Your emotional support over the past 2 years has been invaluable. Thank you for proof reading my book and being as concerned about comma placement as I am. Actions speak louder than words, and you consistently showed up and helped.

Thank you Louise Hyland and Seth Sherwood, my *Writers Group*. Sitting around our dining room tables, evaluating each other's work, was a highlight of my week. Discussing my book out loud, and being taken seriously, helped me believe my dream could become a reality.

Thank you, Alexis Pavenick, editor extraordinaire. I felt we understood each other with our first e-mails. I was moved when you wrote, "You asked God for a fair, friendly, reasonably priced editor, and I asked for extra money to get my website finally up and also go on a truly 'find myself again' vacation for my birthday this year! Clearly, everything you suggest in your book works. (: " God couldn't have sent me a better editor than you.

Thank you to all those whose quotes I have used throughout the book. Your words have brought understanding, comfort and inspiration to me in the past, and will continue to do so in the future.

Thank you to the present-day artists who so graciously allowed me to include their artwork in the book: Casey Childs, David Hockney, Everett Raymond Kinstler, Stuart Pearson Wright, Simmie Knox, Michael Shane Neal, and John Howard Sanden. Your generosity in sharing your time and talent inspires artists like me, and you make the world a more beautiful place.

Thank you to the National Alopecia Areata Foundation. When I was diagnosed with alopecia at 16, I didn't know anyone who had the disease and felt like I was all alone. One year later, in 1981, the NAAF was founded. Since then you have helped people feel less isolated. Thank you for supporting research and educating the public.

Thank you to the family and friends who took the time to proof read parts of this book and to the many who upon greeting me asked, "How's the book coming?" Your interest and support motivated me to complete it.